HOW TO SUCCEED IN EMPLOYEE DEVELOPMENT

Latest titles in the McGraw-Hill Training Series

Details of these and other titles in the series are available from:

The Product Manager, Professional Books, McGraw-Hill Publishing Company,
Shoppenhangers Road, Maidenhead, Berkshire SL6 2QL, United Kingdom
Tel: 01628 23432 Fax: 01628 770224

How to Succeed in Employee Development

Moving from vision to results

SECOND EDITION

Ed Moorby

The McGraw-Hill Companies

London · New York · St Louis · San Francisco · Auckland
Bogotá · Caracas · Lisbon · Madrid · Mexico · Milan
Montreal · New Delhi · Panama · Paris · San Juan · São Paulo
Singapore · Sydney · Tokyo · Toronto

Published by
McGraw-Hill Publishing Company
Shoppenhangers Road, Maidenhead, Berkshire SL6 2QL, England
Telephone: 01628 23432
Fax: 01628 770224

British Library Cataloguing in Publication Data
Moorby, Ed
    How to succeed in employee development : moving from vision
to results.—2nd ed.—(McGraw-Hill training series)
    1. Employees—Training of 2. Personnel management
    I. Title
    658.3'124

    ISBN 0-07-709151-5

Library of Congress Cataloging-in-publication Data
Moorby, Ed (Edward)
    How to succeed in employee development: moving from vision to
results / Ed Moorby.—2nd ed.
        p.   cm.—(The McGraw-Hill training series)
    Includes bibliographical references and index.
    ISBN 0-07-709151-5 (pbk. : alk. paper)
    1. Personnel management—Handbooks, manuals, etc. 2. Employees—
Training of—Handbooks, manuals, etc. 3. Career development—
Handbooks, manuals, etc.   I. Title.   II. Series.
HF5549.M59   1996
658.3'124—dc20   96-12284
                                                                CIP

McGraw-Hill
\ Division of The *McGraw·Hill* Companies

12345 CUP 99876

Typeset by BookEns Limited, Royston, Herts.
and printed and bound in Great Britain at the University Press, Cambridge

Printed on permanent paper in compliance with ISO Standard 9706.

To Clare, Gina and Edward
in the fond hope that they will never stop developing

Contents

Series preface

Training and development are now firmly centre stage in most organizations, if not all. Nothing unusual in that—for some organizations. They have always seen training and development as part of the heart of their businesses—but more and more must see it that same way.

The demographic trends through the 1990s will inject into the marketplace severe competition for good people who will need good training. Young people without conventional qualifications, skilled workers in redundant crafts, people out of work, women wishing to return to work—all will require excellent training to fit them to meet the job demands of the 1990s and beyond.

But excellent training does not spring from what we have done well in the past. T&D specialists are in a new ball game. 'Maintenance' training—training to keep up skill levels to do what we have always done—will be less in demand. Rather, organization, work and market change training are now much more important and will remain so for some time. Changing organizations and people is no easy task, requiring special skills and expertise which, sadly, many T&D specialists do not possess.

To work as a 'change' specialist requires us to get to centre stage—to the heart of the company's business. This means we have to ask about future goals and strategies, and even be involved in their development, at least as far as T&D policies are concerned.

This demands excellent communication skills, political expertise, negotiating ability, diagnostic skills—indeed, all the skills a good internal consultant requires.

The implications for T&D specialists are considerable. It is not enough merely to be skilled in the basics of training, we must also begin to act like business people and to think in business terms and talk the language of business. We must be able to resource training not just from within but by using the vast array of external resources. We must be able to manage our activities as well as any other manager. We must share in the creation and communication of the company's vision. We must never let the goals of the company out of our sight.

In short, we may have to grow and change with the business. It will be hard. We shall have to demonstrate not only relevance but also value for money and achievement of results. We shall be our own boss, as accountable for results as any other line manager, and we shall have to deal with fewer internal resources.

The challenge is on, as many T&D specialists have demonstrated to me over the past few years. We need to be capable of meeting that challenge. This is why McGraw-Hill Book Company Europe have planned and launched this major new training series—to help us meet that challenge.

The series covers all aspects of T&D and provides the knowledge base from which we can develop plans to meet the challenge. They are practical books for the professional person. They are a starting point for planning our journey into the twenty-first century.

Use them well. Don't just read them. Highlight key ideas, thoughts, action pointers or whatever, and have a go at doing something with them. Through experimentation we evolve; through stagnation we die.

I know that all the authors in the McGraw-Hill Training Series would want me to wish you good luck. Have a great journey into the twenty-first century.

ROGER BENNETT
Series Editor

About the series editor

Roger Bennett has over 20 years' experience in training, management education, research and consulting. He has long been involved with trainer training and trainer effectiveness. He has carried out research into trainer effectiveness, and conducted workshops, seminars, and conferences on the subject around the world. He has written extensively on the subject including the book *Improving Trainer Effectiveness*, Gower. His work has taken him all over the world and has involved directors of companies as well as managers and trainers.

Dr Bennett has worked in engineering, several business schools (including the International Management Centre, where he launched the UK's first masters degree in T&D), and has been a board director of two companies. He is the editor of the *Journal of European Industrial Training* and was series editor of the ITD's *Get In There* workbook and video package for the managers of training departments. He now runs his own business called The Management Development Consultancy.

About the author

Ed Moorby has over 25 years' experience in the development of people. He has worked with senior management in many top organizations and has himself held several senior employee development posts. His wide-ranging experience includes work in the motor industry, air transport, the engineering industry, and banking and finance, in addition to a substantial period in the public sector with industrial training boards.

A qualified chartered engineer, he obtained both a BSc (Econ) and an MPhil degree while working as a manager.

Committed to the professional growth of both practitioners and students of employee development, Ed Moorby took up the appointment as Chief Examiner in Employee Development for the IPM (now IPD) in 1992. He works as an international consultant in employee development and is actively involved in research into how the brain functions and its contribution to managerial excellence.

Preface

This book sets out to capture the realities of employee development. It is based on personal experience gained from being closely involved in major change activities such as the revitalization of the Prudential Corporation.

It is designed to serve as something of an antidote to detailed analytical and uninvolved descriptions of training and development. It will have served a purpose if it conveys just a little of the emotion, joy, frustration and pressure which the development of people can generate.

I was prompted to write by my friend Art Miller of People Management Inc. who encouraged me to step into the void from a life cocooned by predictable routines. For this I would like to thank him. Thanks also are due to Reg Revans who helped to keep my belief in action alive through some of the difficult times.

Working with professionals, particularly at Ford Motor Company, Prudential Corporation, TSB England & Wales and in the airline industry, taught me a great deal—some of which is reflected in what follows.

This second edition has been completely revised to reflect the many changes that have occurred in recent years. In particular, a chapter has been added on project management to incorporate in more detail this important aspect of dealing with change. Prompted by a very constructive review of the first edition by Alan Mumford, chapters on learning, motivation and self-development have been added to capture the important perspective of Individual Development. The book has also been reorganized to accommodate this new material.

Finally, I would like to thank my wife Jean who produced the first draft from my far from easy to read handwriting. Throughout the process she added encouragement and excitement.

This book has one essential purpose. It is to help you to develop and grow.

Ed Moorby

PART ONE

The organizational perspectives

1 The practicalities: living in the real world

We win because we get the ideas out of the heads of everybody. You lose because you waste your most valuable resource: your people.

Konosuke Matsushita,
Founder and President,
Matsushita Electric

This book sets out to describe how to succeed in managing employee development. It seeks to capture the joys and tribulations, challenges and frustrations, to describe the skills and gifts required and to explore and identify the ingredients for success. It will be wide-ranging. Tomorrow's professional manager or developer will need substantial competencies in areas ranging from computer-based training (CBT) through learning design to budget variance analysis.

One of the more important changes over the last decade has been the increasing need to integrate human resource development into the strategy of the organization. This brings with it the need to cope with many conflicts. Huge communication chasms have to be bridged among the many increasingly specialized individuals involved. Complexity has to be understood and dealt with. Many contemporary organizations are competing in a world of new concepts, ideas and service. The effective use of the human resource can and does have a really significant impact on the bottom line, as successful organizations have demonstrated.

Human resource development in its broadest sense stretches from pre-kindergarten school to learning to cope with old age. From the cradle to the grave is perhaps the most apt description. From a national view-point it includes education in all its forms, various government schemes, television and radio, the print media and countless other activities. It is a central issue in government policy on employment and the management of the economy. Without skills, firms, regions and countries cannot compete globally.

More specifically, the following chapters address the *why, what, who, how, when* and *where* of employee development. They will seek to encompass the needs of large, medium and small organizations, the public and private sector perspective, and the needs and rights of individuals to generate knowledge and skill for themselves. It will be assumed that the 'function' may be carried out by either a full-time or part-time individual who is responsible formally for employee development. The real thrust of the function is demonstrated by the quotation from Konosuke Matsushita at the start of this chapter. Employee development must be managed by all managers and directors in an enterprise since it will often be the most cost-effective way to obtain a competitive edge—whether in selling life insurance or replacing heart valves.

Whether you, the reader, are a full-time employee development practitioner, a manager interested in getting the most from the talents of those with whom you work or a student searching to understand the function, you will find some challenging and practical views in these pages. They will only be worth anything if you yourself then do something with them.

The scope of human resource development

Human resource development (HRD) or human resource management are recent terms, used primarily in the West and particularly in the United States and Western Europe. A North American multinational might have a vice-president (human resource development), a French organization a directeur de la formation and an Hungarian institute a director, National Pedagogical Institute. Understanding the language used is becoming increasingly important in the field of management and HRD. Not only the meaning of words but even translation between different languages becomes crucial as individuals struggle to develop human resources in Eastern Europe, China, the Far East, and much of the Third World. Economic success will be closely bound up with the ability to understand HRD. For this reason, the scope of HRD and how it is interpreted in what follows demands some explanation.

In broad terms, the human resource development function can be regarded as encompassing what is often described as training and development, the field of motivation or reward that is usually functionally organized as compensation and benefits, job description and job evaluation, management and/or career development (which covers high-flyer and graduate schemes) and the whole question of career management, recruitment and assessment. Assessment would include assessment centres, psychometric testing, performance appraisal and specialized motivational selection approaches such as Selection Research Inc. (SRI) and the approaches of Art Miller (SIMA). More recently, considerable attention has been paid to performance management systems (PMS) which are approaches designed to assess the level of implementation of aspects of the management process and performance against predetermined standards. In the UK a good deal of energy is being put by the Training Agency into identifying the

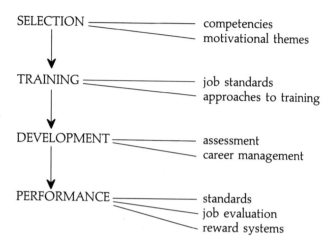

Figure 1.1 *The scope of employee development*

competencies required for jobs and by the National Council for Vocational Qualifications (NCVQ) into the development of standards. It might help clarification of the total scope of employee development to consider it diagrammatically, as in Figure 1.1.

At the organization level, there are other aspects that need to be included for completeness. These are change management, project management and organization development.

In the rapidly changing world of today's organizations, project management or ad hoc task groups are being increasingly used and this change in how resources are managed has significant implications for the HRD function. Project Management is considered fully in Chapter 6. Some organizations also seek to work on HRD by taking an organization development perspective and a few succeed.

In the chapters that follow, the emphasis will be on the 'employee development' aspect of the HRD function. Clearly, issues such as selection and reward systems cannot be ignored but for more detailed or specialist knowledge the reader is referred to the recommended reading throughout this book. Thus the central questions being addressed are:

What development is required?
How can it be provided?
Who should be responsible?
When is development available?
Where is it available?

Before considering the question of respective accountabilities of the line and staff managers for employee development, it will be worthwhile to examine briefly the role of the personnel function and some emerging views on the place of the HRD function within an organization.

Traditionally, employee development has reported within the personnel/HRD function to a personnel director. A good deal of personnel work in the 1970s was about conflict, job evaluation, redundancy and negotiating with trade unions. The attributes required included guile, aggression and conflict management. The thrust was towards wage-cost reductions, 'win/lose' management and either/or thinking, wasting our most valuable resource in strikes, strife and poor productivity. What is required in the 1990s is the anticipation of skill needs, effective delivery systems to create skills, and maximization of the identification and development of ability focused on achieving required standards. The thrust needs to be on using everyone's talents, seeing people as a competitive-edge form of investment, and 'win/win' management where the whole organization can benefit from good personnel management. Both the organization and the individual can then gain from human resource development. The creation of human resources able to act positively is one of the most profound challenges facing management in the West. Perhaps the directors of the HRD function should be relocated either to report directly to the chief executive or to a wealth-creating function.

Line and staff responsibilities

One of the basic challenges of managing employee development is to create a specialist function that is able and good enough to develop and deliver wide-scale improvements in skills across the organization. At the same time the function needs to gain line management commitment and action. Taking some simplified assumptions, the average employee might receive 2–5 days formal training and development in a year. This is at most 2 per cent of the time spent at work. It is no exaggeration to say that the line manager probably influences as much as 95 per cent of development at work after the full-time education phase.

Success in managing wide-scale development requires that this line management resource be harnessed. The use of relatively recent methods such as open learning, distance learning, mentoring, coaching and action learning can do much to achieve this. In fact, the medieval model of master and apprentice had much to commend it. The challenge is to ensure in organizations the high-volume transfer of skill and standards from the 'master' to the learner, whether in the context of a restaurant manager passing on flair and skill in managing a busy restaurant or the skill transfer by a driving instructor to a learner driver.

The knowledge of what is needed and the experience to judge whether training and development works often resides with the line manager. It may not be well articulated. The employee development manager has the responsibility to know how to identify in dialogue what is required and to have a mastery of the approaches available to meet the needs. Competence in the development of strategy and the achievement of implementation are the two key strands.

In developing strategy, the employee development manager needs to integrate closely with line colleagues. The task of identifying developments in the outside world and matching the skills that the organization already has with what will be required is demanding. For example, many banks are seeking to become strategically more sales and retail oriented. The identification of sales ability and the development of sales skills are areas where the great majority of bank managers do not have a history of experience or competence. Thus a strong collaboration between practitioners of banking and those experienced in identifying and developing new selling skills is required.

The role of the employee development manager can be interpreted in many ways. Aspects may include:

- Identifying development needs
- Agreeing corporate development strategy
- Obtaining finance and controlling budget
- Hiring competent development staff
- Designing learning and development programmes
- Evaluating achievements

Most of these steps require collaboration with the line manager on whose behalf, it could be argued, the development is taking place.

Some practical dilemmas

Many management tasks involve conflicts, priorities, vested interests and different viewpoints; HRD management is no exception. One way of illustrating the practical dilemmas is to identify the alternatives and to chart where you believe your organization currently stands. Some of the more commonly experienced issues are listed below. Consider how your organization usually acts on each issue and indicated in Figure 1.2 overleaf.

One of the essential abilities required of the employee development manager, if the long-term aim is continual influence on growth and development, is to assess where the organization is, how fast it might move and in what direction. The more radical approach of pushing the organization in a direction determined by the employee development manager takes a much higher risk. It can succeed gloriously, or . . .

The issues implied in the chart will be explored in more detail, since they touch on basic value conflicts that can and often do have a major impact on whether the function is managed successfully. The issues are introduced as polar opposites though in fact quite subtle differences in view can cause major difficulties.

Individual and organization needs

One view of employee development is that it should be focused essentially on organization needs. It is identified, organized and paid for by the organization. The purpose of development is seen as specific to the organization. It is designed to add value and to help the

	Typical of my organization	Occasionally acts this way	Rarely acts this way
• Individuals have the right to determine their own development needs			
• The organization prescribes development activities			
• HRD budget is set against needs identified			
• HRD budget is the first to be cut			
• Decisions on operational questions are referred to head office			
• Decisions are taken at point of sale/ service/ manufacture			
• Central policy determines local employee development activity			
• Development is determined by local needs			
• Initiative by line management is encouraged			
• Local line management is seen as disruptive by top executives			
• Managers are rewarded for using opportunistic approaches			
• Style is concerned primarily with facts and measurement			

Figure 1.2 *Personal analysis of common HRD issues*

organization achieve its aims and objectives. Thus the organization, in the form of senior management, determines how much funding will be available, what providers will be used and what issues development will address. Parts 1 and 2 address this view.

An alternative view is that individuals have the right to achieve their own potential. This viewpoint encourages open access to learning, puts choice with the individual and may use grants, subsidies or bursaries to pay for development. Part 3 addresses this in some detail in Chapters 11 and 12. Performance appraisal systems often provide the interface between the organization and the individual. What is provided internally and policy on the use of external facilities are determined by the organization. However, individual needs are discussed with the appraiser and can influence what development is actually provided. This freedom of influence over choice in a situation of limited supply often means long waiting lists for widely spread or popular development experiences.

One telling illustration of the tension between individual need, organizational need and funding is the support of MBA programmes. The organization, which may easily have to incur a cost of £50 000 per individual sponsored, will wish to ensure it gets good quality development and that it retains the individual. Employees who are keen to progress will seek a high degree of financial support together with assurances of fast-track progression. Some form of compromise is usually arrived at where the support is in the form of a loan that is repaid or written off after an agreed period of time spent in continued employment with the sponsor.

A very practical benefit to the organization of development which is strongly individual-oriented is that the recipients will often dedicate their own time to the process and may also contribute to the cost. The employee development manager has to balance the emphasis on policy between commercial considerations, motivational gains and retention of staff.

Control and chaos

Issues concerning control and change and ways of achieving maximum performance from individuals have created enormous interest in the literature. The Russian word 'glasnost' was used to describe the fierce political debate over 'freedom' in the former USSR. It is interesting to reflect that the world's most powerful economies—the United States, Japan, West Germany—all operate a democratic system in which the voters elect the political executive every four or five years. No bureaucratically controlled political system has been commercially successful in competitive markets. Also, the successful economies have operated in a system of exchange rates, interest rates and inflation, which have been almost unpredictable in the three-year time cycle and frequently chaotic on a day-to-day basis.

The relevance of these broad trends is far-reaching. They inform the marketing decisions of major oil companies and influence the growth of a particular country's approach to education. It is no accident that open learning began to flourish in the 1980s. These great paradoxes have very practical day-to-day effects. Authors such as Tom Peters and Richard Pascale have pointed out the need for flexibility and the way in which true 'learning organizations' will have to ease control and encourage confidence and competence at the point of sale or service. The concept of the creation of learning organizations is one that major research studies have predicted as the most likely to achieve success in the twenty-first century. In essence, the successful learning organization will:

- adapt to its environment;
- identify and understand the competencies it will require—in quality and quantity;
- provide a variety of flexible learning strategies;
- operate a culture where mentoring and coaching flourish;
- ensure the creation of continuous constructive feedback;
- give financial and career recognition for individual growth and achievement.

Such an organization will be one in which

$$learning \geqslant change$$

If learning is not greater than or equal to change, the organization will become out of date and uncompetitive. Eventually, like the dinosaur, it will become extinct.

It is also worth mentioning briefly here that control has a political and psychological dimension. In his book *Images of Organisation*, Gareth Morgan has a chapter titled 'Organisations as Psychic Prisons'. In it he describes how many managers act out their own neuroses in organizations for a whole host of reasons, ranging from Freudian repressed sexuality to Jungian views on repressed opposites of rationality. A manager who fears ambiguity may expend an inordinate amount of energy on planning and objective setting. This, after all, will eliminate the uncertainties of the future, at least in that manager's own mind. This, and other needs to control, e.g. the need to dominate and surround oneself with subservient subordinates are in direct conflict with the responsive essentially 'honest' organization. Managing the HRD function requires an ability to recognize and understand these issues at the appropriate level.

Hierarchical organizations with relatively static markets and technology were, until recently, able largely to ignore these complexities. Human resource development was about a menu of one-week courses that started on Sunday night and involved long days packed with activity. However, competition and change have turned a bright spotlight on reality and managers' assumptions and the 'games' they play are coming increasingly under the microscope. The HRD manager stands at the intersection of the drive for efficiency and profit, the legacy of Taylorism and the hard fact that an airline crew 10 000 miles away in Beijing will have to make its own decisions if anything unexpected happens. Getting people of varying abilities to give of their best for the organization is what Matsushita was talking about when he said 'We win because we get the ideas out of the heads of everybody'. Unlike Taylorism, he understands that everybody has ideas. That is the challenge facing the human resource development manager.

Short term *v* There is a Chinese proverb that freely translated says: Give a man a fish
long term and you feed him for a day; teach a man to fish and you feed him for life. This is the essence of the debate about 'short-termism'. It is of course driven by the need to show annual results for shareholders and the need to be aware of the analysts' continuous monitoring of these results.

Investment in human resource development is often a long-term commitment. Initial education for professions such as accountancy, actuarial work and engineering or for technicians such as systems analysts is usually long and costly. It is also portable in the sense that the newly qualified individual is usually at liberty to find alternative employment—and often does. Career development can also be quite costly and the high-flyer may be very demanding over provision of the right remuneration and motivational package. The demand for HRD usually considerably exceeds the supply in terms of what the organization is prepared to spend. There is fairly intense competition for short-term and medium-term funding among HRD, sales and marketing and management services, where the last two are able to produce what are on the surface more concrete cost justifications.

Considerable effort and debate has gone into the question of evaluation, which can be described as a means of identifying short-term return on assets employed. This is covered in Part 4. More often it is to do with an individual's immediate reactions. Less attention seems to be given, sometimes, to the return on investment (ROI) on the accountants we employ.

The sensible response is to identify the cost side of the equation as accurately as possible over a planning time frame. This can then be monitored so that expenditure can be controlled and reviewed. The benefits will be in several areas:

- Equipping new employees to operate within the employer's business, e.g. by providing product knowledge and sales skills to new salespeople.
- Enabling employees to understand and use new or different procedures and practices, e.g. a new automated teller machine.

- Focusing employees' attention on specific skill requirements, such as customer service or product quality.
- Preparing people for new roles, e.g. run an on appointment course for newly appointed managers.
- Helping people to overcome problems by working with their colleagues, e.g. in an action learning set.
- Broadening of individuals with potential, e.g. four-week senior management course.
- Launching company-wide initiatives, such as target setting for salespeople or a performance appraisal scheme.
- Preparing people for redundancy and retirement.
- Helping to introduce change, e.g. workshops on the new role for area directors.
- Providing education and training for key occupations or professions, e.g. engineering graduate training or professional accounting training or membership of a professional institution such as the Institute of Bankers.

Clearly the benefit side of the equation contains a mixture of short-term and longer-term contributions and some that may be quite indirect. The fact that you are seen as providing the best actuarial training in Europe could mean that, in twenty-five years, you have the choice between three excellent contenders of known track record for a job that in 2015 might be paying £500 000 per annum and which, done well, could increase the organization's profit by at least 10 per cent. That might be as much as £250 million per annum by then. Or product knowledge may give the new salesperson just that little extra ability to sell one more product a week. Simply watching an experienced salesperson asking the customer 'Is there anything else?' each time a sale is agreed could improve the sales of a trainee newly shown the skills of prospecting and identifying needs. The balance between short and long term and whether you can actually measure cause and effect in employee development are vexed issues, where ignorance often leads to simplistic and plausible solutions. Wisdom is more about understanding the direction of development that the business requires and about sensitive approaches to employing various strategic responses from the development armoury.

Back to basics

It is worth considering what are in essence the basics of employee development.

- All development occurs in the brain which will then use either thinking or motor skills to store and classify information or to do something.
- The input will be either existing knowledge or observation of the environment.
- The brain will either store the knowledge or use it. Use implies skill

and there is a feedback cycle whereby knowledge of results modifies action.

- All employee development involves either transmitting known knowledge or encouraging connections in the brain to derive new skills. Reg Revan's learning equation

$$L = P + Q$$

where
L = Learning
P = Programmed (or packaged pre-digested) knowledge
Q = Questioning insights (or using the brain and ideas in action to change behaviour)

expresses this notion elegantly and powerfully.

- Individuals may or may not wish to develop. Development may involve negative feedback as they learn. Positive feedback that appeals to an individual's core motivations in life can considerably accelerate learning. It is perhaps not fanciful to express this as

$$L = (P + Q) \times M$$

where M is the motivational drive of the individual. For example, a person who is motivated to serve or help others is going to learn much more quickly in the area of customer service than someone who is motivated to dominate or overwhelm others.

- The great majority of formal training and development activities can be seen as substitutes for reading and motivation. Page-turning CBT programmes, notes dictated at evening class, and lectures conveying well-documented knowledge that is given in a handout at the end of the lecture are all examples.

- Conveying knowledge and skill effectively over distances is a major challenge. As a rule of thumb, as much as one-third of the cost of conventional course-based training can be spent on board and hotel accommodation.

- Observation and imitation is the other main way of taking in knowledge, and it is often said that we learn as much at the bar as in the classroom as we observe and listen to accounts of experiences.

- Actually doing things and creating a feedback loop is the final key element. For example, you can read about bravery and listen to the experience of others, but you will not find out if you can act bravely (i.e. be brave) until you have to do something in a threatening situation.

- When we move from the individual to interaction in groups, the area of social behaviour and skills comes into play.

- In a commercial environment, these basics will need to be achieved cost effectively. Competition introduces choice between alternatives.

Thus, no matter how sophisticated or detailed descriptions of employee development become, the process is essentially about:

- acquiring knowledge by reading, listening or observation and to a limited extent by touch and smell;
- taking action and developing skills;
- doing this by receiving feedback;
- copying observed or described behaviour, using role models;
- making this development your own and responding to personal motivation;
- adapting learning through social interaction;
- developing cost-effective alternatives.

Whether we are addressing a two-year-old learning from mother how to speak a language or eat food, or a senior manager attending a one-year course, the fundamental process revolves around learning programmed knowledge and questioning. Both individuals will need to take action and receive feedback. Rates of progress will vary. Motivation to learn will be one factor as will skill in learning techniques.

To achieve success in employee development a fundamental grasp of basics, as with any activity, is essential.

Staying focused

Most success stories have, as an essential ingredient, a high degree of focus on specific outcomes and the expenditure of significant quantities of skilled energy to achieve the outcomes—which for some reason are important to the individual. In the day-to-day world of organizations there is a multitude of deflectors designed to take employee development strategies away from success. Later chapters describe such issues as the need to control, politics, competition for funds, and pressure in the short term. The outside environment, technology and changing customer demands push organizations towards chaos. Bureaucracy provides ways of pretending it is not happening and that everything is measurable, predictable and risk-free. Perhaps the three or four crucial themes to keep in mind are a commitment to development and growth, and to achieving excellence in human beings, the routine measurement of progress and relevance to the business, and the interpersonal skills to deal with the significant political pressures described in Chapter 3.

Summary

The main points this chapter has covered are:

- The *why, what, who, how, when* and *where* of employee development.
- The full-time employee development executive will need a wide range of skills to succeed.
- Everybody is responsible for the development of at least themselves and often of others.
- Human resource development, of which employee development is an

integral part, incorporates recruitment, selection, compensation and benefits, performance management, motivation, training and development, assessment, appraisal, career development and management, redundancy and retirement, and industrial relations, discipline, wage bargaining, salary/payroll and communications and health care.

- The role of specialist staff and line management and supervision in achieving successful employee development.
- How to assess where your organization currently stands on the question of employee development.
- Is it possible to reconcile individual development needs and what the organization judges it can afford and needs to provide to meet its strategic aims?
- The paradox of how bureaucracies need to control and standardize products and services in the interest of economy, while also providing services tailored to individual customer needs at the point of sale. The conflict between control and chaos, risk aversion and risk, that is inherent in the learning process.
- Reconciling short-term return on investment and shareholder dividend pressures with the longer-term investment needed for employee development and career management. Some practical aspects of controlling costs and liberating benefits.
- The basic components of development and learning. The relationship between programmed or packaged learning, questioning and action, negative feedback and motivated themes.
- The need to stay focused on the basic requirements for successful development and learning in an environment of political manoeuvring and personal needs. Whose ego counts?

Recommended reading

Miller, Art and Mattson, R.T., 1989 *The Truth about You*, Ten Speed Press, California.
Morgan, G., 1986 *Images of Organisation*, Sage Publications Inc.
Pascale, R. and Athos, A., 1982 *The Art of Japanese Management*, Penguin.
Revans, Professor R., 1983 *ABC of Action Learning*, Chartwell-Bratt.

2 An employee development director's week

Most of this book concentrates on how to identify what has to be done to develop employees and how to implement this successfully. Before considering such aspects as the politics involved and the preparation of strategic plans, this chapter gives a glimpse of some activities the employee development director of a large organization might undertake. All the activities described were real and could just happen in the same week. The chapter seeks to capture the flavour of what it is like to do the job, and the activities were selected from a rich and varied range. Later in the book, when the organization of the function is considered, some of the activities typically carried out by training managers, training officers, internal consultants, CBT analysts and training administrators will be described. This is what the week looked like.

Sunday

The opportunity for a late start to the day. No train to catch and a chance to read the Sunday newspaper. After a light breakfast, get the map out to see just where 'somewhere near Oxford' the Operation Raleigh selection exercise is taking place. My wife Jean joins me, as we try to do things together in our leisure time. The visit to the exercise is partly to weigh up the professionalism of Operation Raleigh staff (very impressive), partly to see some of the bank's young staff in the outdoor development environment and partly to show solidarity with my own staff, who have given up their weekend to supervise our staff. We take the opportunity to visit Henley on the way back and have refreshments by the River Thames.

Sit down in the evening to read papers for the personnel director's Monday morning management meeting. Highlight items relevant to employee development and issues for clarification or opposition with colleagues while watching television.

Monday

Alarm rings at 6.45. Coffee, toast and an eight-minute drive to reach the station by 7.26a.m. That train will get to Marylebone by 8.04a.m.

Assuming the tube is running, I will be at the bank in good time for the 9a.m. personnel director's meeting.

The meeting usually lasts 2–3 hours and is attended by the human resources specialists—group personnel director in the chair, with the group personnel manager, compensation and benefits manager, UK, retail personnel director, property services personnel director and the northern and southern regional personnel managers together with the industrial relations manager and the employee development director. The agenda usually concentrates on such topics as decentralization and bargaining procedures, the implementation of the redundancy programme and progress in building the new management training centre. The group personnel director briefs everyone on the most recent executive board meeting and the operational personnel people outline developments in their areas. You need to keep an eye on the minutes and action dates.

At noon I often see one of the consultants or professionals who is working with us. Today Reg Revans and my management development manager are joining me for a working lunch to discuss how our wide-scale action learning programme is progressing and what role we will take in two action learning sets for divisional managers that we are organizing. As always, Reg is good value—right to the point, practical and positive.

We finish at 3p.m. and then, after half an hour answering correspondence and responding to messages with my secretary, I am joined by my retail training manager and college director. We spend an hour analysing our budget performance for the half-year and deciding how we will approach the employee development executive meeting on Friday. I take the opportunity to walk the patch, get a feel for what is happening in the London training centre, and then walk over to see the retail sales director at about 5.30 p.m. This is the best time to see him, I have learned. Spend about an hour discussing the potential of his area retail directors and the succession situation for the next year or two.

Get home about 8p.m. and watch some television. Use the train journey to read mainly professional articles or the press coverage of our organization's annual results.

Tuesday

9a.m. meeting with general manager (insurance group) to agree design of change management programme for 160 managers. Agree aims and outcomes required, produce outline design and suggest tutors and consultants for four-day event. Get agreement to initiate an action learning element in the programme and commitment to fund a 'Putting People First' element from Time Manager International.

Next, interview candidates for senior development consultants' vacancies with head office training manager, starting at 10.30a.m. Original applicants have been screened by the staff in the unit using an assessment centre approach and we are looking to fill two vacancies from the four candidates. Use working lunch to check out the suitability of three already interviewed and for update on progress in head office development. Agree to offer one post and continue interviewing until 3p.m.

Deal with post and messages and then visit CBT centre at 3.30p.m. to work through our first programme on insurance. Impressed with the programme and spend half an hour with programmers and CBT manager to get a feel for the pace and quality of development. Walk back through department and talk with senior consultant about design problems on a project management seminar she is developing.

Prepare myself for visit to training college in Midlands and speak on phone to college director to check all is ready for chief executive's visit to the college next day. Read various papers relating to discussions with the two departmental heads at the college on the train home.

Wednesday

Leave at 7.15a.m. and drive myself to the college. The M25 and M1 are busy even at this hour and I arrive at 9.45a.m. Have coffee with the director and talk through arrangements for chief executive's visit. He arrives promptly at 10.30a.m. and after a tour of the college joins in the presentations on progress to date and review of the programme for the future. He then sits in on two of the courses for half an hour and circulates among course members in the coffee lounge. Buffet lunch with college staff arranged to provide some opportunity for chief executive to meet staff. I take a fairly low-key role as the college director does not often meet the chief executive and he is responsible for the day-to-day running of the college.

Chief executive leaves at 2p.m. He visits the college about once a year, usually combining the visit with a tour of the Midland Region and regional office. I then spend an hour sitting in to observe tutors in action and an hour with each of the departmental heads to review their plans and deal with any personal issues. I am pushing hard to improve our sales training and build links between the college and the regional operations. Drop into the bar for half an hour—good way to get a feel for what delegates are thinking about the college and current issues. Make sure I drink only low alcohol beer.

Join the director at 6.30p.m. and then have dinner in the college dining room. The M1 is a little quieter after 8p.m. and I get home shortly after 10p.m.

Thursday

Spend first half-hour in the office to catch up with correspondence and prepare for appraisal interviews. Hold two discussions to cover appraisal for regional training managers. Conclude at 11.45a.m. to check arrangements for visit by Secretary of State for Employment for lunch with the chairman and the chief executive and a meeting with Youth Training Scheme (YTS) trainees. Go to reception with YTS coordinator to meet Minister. After lunch walk with Minister to the training centre for one-hour meeting with two dozen YTS trainees. Chair question and answer session and see Minister off at 3p.m. Review visit with YTS coordinator and then go to 3.30p.m. steering group meeting. I chair meeting of working group investigating what computer reservation system we should buy for the new management training centre which is nearing completion 30 miles from London. Useful meeting. Able to catch the 6.45p.m. train and get home shortly after 7.30 p.m.

Friday

Monthly meeting of employee development executive team at 9.30a.m. College director, regional training managers, head office training manager and CBT manager regularly attend together with insurance and property services training managers when appropriate and the management development and sales training managers. Agenda covers review of expenditure against budget, progress against agreed objectives, recruitment and staffing matters and new developments. We concentrate on a new interactive video for sales training, progress with appraisal training and the new management college commissioning programme. One ground rule we observe is that all employee development senior promotions should be agreed by all those present and there is some time spent manoeuvring about one appointment. Meeting always concludes with a working lunch so that the team, which is widely dispersed around the country, can take maximum advantage of having some informal time together.

Get a car promptly at 2p.m. to attend 2.15p.m. meeting at Chartered Institute to discuss my chairmanship of a syndicate as part of the Cambridge seminar. This seminar is run annually for high-flyers in the industry and the syndicate chairmen meet on this occasion to agree case study material and a common approach to chairmanship.

Return to office at 3.45p.m. having taken the opportunity to stretch my legs by walking back from the city. Spend half an hour with secretary on next week's diary and clear up correspondence, sign letters and generally catch up with what is happening. Walk over to 5p.m. meeting with personnel director to discuss progress with new management training centre and update him on progress with recruitment. Get involved in discussion with sales director on performance management, which starts in personnel director's office and continues to 6.30p.m.

Saturday Enjoy slow start to the day. Have to get out in time for a 2p.m. kick-off for the cubs' football match. I manage a team and referee matches. It provides good experience of direct coaching and training in a non-commercial setting. I enjoy a relaxing evening. I tend to need Saturday to recover from the 15 hours spent each week commuting by train to and from London.

3 The politics: power, personalities and influence

Men do you harm either because they fear you or because they hate you.

Niccolo Machiavelli, *The Prince*

Success in employee development demands at least two significant areas of competence on the part of the practitioner. The technical area, explored later in this book, concerns such matters as identifying needs and potential, producing training plans, understanding computer-based training and a wide range of related issues, not least of which is evaluation. The other area of competence concerns understanding and using organizational power, dealing with the powerful personalities at the top of the organization and matching 'developmental' principles to the ideologies of the business, which may sometimes be focused more on the short term.

This chapter sets out to illuminate what is often a neglected and little understood key skill in achieving success—that is, political skill. Often, common sense deserts the debate and stereotypes of the 'trainer's world' get in the way of understanding what actually happens in organizations. Another important issue that this chapter looks at is the fact that the view from the bottom or the middle of any pyramid is usually quite different to that from the top. Means of understanding, debating and making judgements about what is going on, and maps to chart direction and highlight political obstacles are essential in what is often the foggy atmosphere of organizational politics.

Science or art?

One of the central debates about employee development is whether it is a science or an art. Can it best be understood as 'the art of the possible' or do we improve development by analytical rigour? The debate about competencies with its concentration on disaggregation, definition of units and elements of competency, and the identification of national vocational qualifications (NVQs) is a classic statement of the analytical approach. Science and logic are paramount. Contrast this with Tom Peters' *Thriving on Chaos* which is built on a quite different ideology. Peters brings a much more holistic and narrative approach to identifying what makes an excellent company in the USA and to deriving a prescription on how to manage and thrive on chaos. This is an important issue, since large sums of money will be committed and many thousands of hours expended in management colleges and universities in the hope of improving the practice of management and all other commercial, industrial, scientific and administrative skills.

The two approaches can easily be mutually exclusive. Success in employee development, whether for yourself or for 100 000 employees in an organization, will depend on achieving a situation where strategy incorporates successfully both the analytical and the intuitive approach.

The political dimension

Employee development is a political issue in most organizations. Politics is the process of exercising power with an appropriate mandate. In democracies, this usually means with a majority at the ballot box. In dictatorships, it often means at the barrel of a gun. Political decisions are usually made so that they are consistent with some ideology or set of beliefs, e.g. Marxism, free competition, protectionism for domestic industry. Politics deals in powerful ideas that shape whole enterprises and some of the broader divisions are well known in everyday life. In order to illustrate the options for employee development the main characteristics of some of the more significant political dimensions are set out below.

The descriptions given are borrowed from political science because the study of politics and the language of ideologies are well established in that discipline. They are not exhaustive but seek to identify the main characteristics of the different standpoints. They are not intended to read across directly to existing UK parties and so the term 'radical' is used to encompass such opposites to conservatism as the socialist, Marxist, communist or similar ideology.

1 **Conservative**   Typically this school of thought is seen to be about:
- preserving the status quo. In practice, allowing people to keep the wealth they have.
- elitism through the use of wealth, e.g. buying privileged education or health care.
- viewing free competition as an absolute principle with little or no central intervention.
- maintaining law and order and a commitment to strong armed forces.

Conservatism can involve considerable change but this will flow from particular principles, such as the free-market economy. Power is used for the benefit of those who aspire to the ideology. Freedom of choice and competition for funds can lead to the decline of centrally provided education, health care and social services. Payment is by results.

2 **Radical**   Typically this school of thought is seen to be about:
- redistributing wealth in society so that those who need it can use it.

In its extreme form of Marxism: from each according to ability, to each according to need.

- retained earnings on a much more uniform basis, with high taxation and limited access to privilege in education and health (at least in theory) and high commitment to central planning and control.
- ideology overriding law and order. May have some commitment to disarmament. In some forms, such as Marxist communism, may have ideological aim to impose views on the whole world.

Radical politics is about change and will impose its manifesto once power is gained. Power is normally used by the activists to help what they see as the poorer elements of society. The general good can be regarded as more important than the bottom line. More effort and power goes into the central bodies, and the promotion of comprehensive education and free health services may be pursued.

3 **Dictatorial/autocratic**   Some of the characteristics of this school are:

- seizing and maintaining power by non-democratic means, often through armed force.
- imposing a new status quo that rewards loyalty to the dictator or ruling junta. Often confiscates opponents' wealth or 'eliminates' them.
- strong state control with little check on graft and corruption. No competition allowed outside the central manifesto.
- strong commitment to maintaining the regime and its laws, usually with strong armed forces, at least internally.

Dictatorial politics is about imposing the will of the dictator and is for the benefit of the individual or the few. Power is used for the benefit of a ruling elite. The needs of the majority are repressed and ignored. Planning and control are highly centralized and used to achieve the aims of the leader.

4 **Republican** politics is a school of thought strongly represented in the USA, Germany and France. Some of its characteristics are:

- the French commitment to equality and fraternity conveys well the central notions.
- supreme power is held by elected representatives of the people or by an elected or nominated president.
- moderate degree of central power with less emphasis on taxation; central government encourages individualistic society.
- strong commitment to the country and flag.

From these simplified descriptions of mainstream political approaches it is possible to identify some common political issues. These apply just as much to an organization or a department as to a country, and consideration of the degree to which they apply in your organization can help you to understand your situation. Consider, for example, the answers to the following questions when applied to your organization.

- Is there a strong connection between results achieved and what is paid?
- Is the organization elitist, e.g. different dining rooms, levels of management and types of car?
- Is the organization centralized or decentralized?
- Do most people follow bureaucratic rules?
- Are those with non-commercial or service skills comparatively underpaid?
- Is training and development available to anybody who wants it?
- Is the organization flat and simple or complex with many levels?
- Is there a strong ideology, e.g. 'Everyone must wear a white shirt' or 'The customer is paramount'?
- How accountable is the chief executive to a political or shareholder faction?
- Is the chief executive/chairman the majority shareholder?
- Are the boss's immediate subordinates his or her own appointees?

It is suggested you re-read Sections 1–4 above and write down those elements of the various systems that appeal to you, those that you would like to operate with and can support, e.g.

- preserving the status quo
- payment by results
- largely decentralized control
- reward for loyalty

Compare this list with your response to the 11 questions concerning your own organization. This should give you an indication of how well you fit the system, based on how you see things. A committed socialist-radical may have a hard time in a conservative bank but could flourish in a young airline or a university department. The essential point about the political process is that the view you get of anything depends entirely upon where you stand when you look. To succeed with approaches to employee development it is essential to form a realistic view of what those who hold power in an organization will support and then to match the strategy adopted to reflect this. If all senior management wants to buy a stately home as a management training centre to make some sort of political statement to a constituency, it will not be easy to sell them as an alternative a highly cost-effective correspondence course on management skills.

The chief executive and the executive directors

Not very long ago, provided an organization had a training and development policy signed by its chief executive and the executive made the right public noises, all was seen as well on the employee development front. In order to illuminate the actual political situation, it is proposed to consider in just a little more depth from a political viewpoint some of the realities in this area.

First, the 'team' as a whole. Chief executives have their own style and set of psychological and political assumptions and drives. They are usually concerned about keeping their job and improving the dividend to shareholders or whatever other results they are responsible for, e.g. bed occupancy or crime rate. They will have two groups of people with whom they work closely, one of which will produce the bottom-line results by creating and selling the products, and the other group that provides a service on issues such as personnel, marketing, legal, finance and management information systems or technology. There will be conflicts within this group. The metaphor 'Praetorian Guard' may apply to the operational directors and senior line management. Chief executives' trusted advisers may be those they have known a long time, those who have expertise in areas in which the CEO is weak or inexperienced, or those who simply 'happen' to be located near to them at head office, either physically or psychologically. Chief executives may choose a whole range of styles, from genuine consensus based on full and open discussion, to projecting a personal vision, say, of excellence, to managing the group on an individual basis with board or executive meetings being essential formalities or rubber-stamping sessions. Clearly, it is important to be aware of what style is being used, as a passionate appeal to the board on employee development would be quite futile if the usual way of working is for the CEO and the personnel director to agree the strategy outside the board meeting.

The actual process of generating and spending resources deserves some consideration. The product is determined essentially by a research and development function, a technical function such as the chief actuary or treasury director or by the creation of a service, say, from a political manifesto. There are usually, or there should be, strong links with a marketing function to ensure that customer needs are met. The line functions of production and sales generate the wealth, whether in the form of interest in a bank, insurance premiums collected, heart operations performed or cars manufactured and sold. The 'spending' departments that compete for investment in the typical industrial/ commercial organization are research and development, marketing, personnel and computer services. The legal and secretarial functions carry out largely statutory functions, and finance plans future expenditure and measures performance against budget.

Within all this, there are many complex questions that have an impact on achieving successful employee development. Ownership of the process is one. It is not unusual for the sales operations function to bid for the control of sales training and computer technology, and engineering operations often run their own extensive training operations. There is a strong tendency towards encouraging individuals to determine and to take responsibility for their own development, but this rather begs the question of providing them with the competence to do so. It is absolutely essential that the internal clients or senior executives fully support the development of their staff. Since their success depends on the staff, it should not be surprising that at this level there is generally support. However, it is tempting, say, for sales directors who are not achieving the improvements they have promised to 'bad-mouth' or criticize the training of their sales force. It is much the same reaction that we see in the parliamentary rhetoric displayed on television every day. It is essential to be aware of how the view changes depending on where you stand and to be aware of the 'snakepit' aspects of an organization. If you are interested in exploring this further, see the unusual article, 'The Clockwork or the Snakepit' by Howard S. Schwartz of Oakland University.

Returning to our chief executive, personnel will be one of anything from 5 to 15 functions reporting directly to the CEO. Some of the CEO's prime concerns are going to include:

- What will this year's profit be?
- What improvement to dividend is likely?
- What are the quarterly figures?
- Are there any press-sensitive issues on the horizon?
- How can I get X and Y to improve?
- Is my executive team strong enough and what about succession at the top?
- Why is the technology late?
- How much bad debt can I risk with XYZ company?

Chief executives are unlikely to spend a particularly significant amount of time on the personnel function and their day-to-day focus is more likely to be on performance indicators than on employee development.

Given that this sketch reflects reasonably well the pressures and demands on the chief executive and senior managers with their pre-occupation necessarily focused on business results, there are some clear indications of what needs to be done to achieve successful employee development. Some of these steps are:

- Find out who the important players are and what is important to them.
- Establish what results the chief executive wants from employee development and the degree to which these are compatible with the political interests of others. For example, a personnel director charged with introducing performance-related pay as quickly as possible and facing a difficult negotiating situation may also have a say in how quickly performance accountability training for managers should be introduced.
- Get a clear understanding of the budget parameters for employee development that the chief executive has in mind.
- Ensure that the expenditure on employee development is to within minus one per cent of the budget.
- Reach a situation where the chief executive agrees policy, direction

and strategy and is kept informed of progress but does not need to intervene on a short-term basis.

- Establish a regular dialogue with the operational directors, their executive team and appropriate functional directors, especially marketing, technology and finance.
- Establish a clear role definition for employee development within the personnel function if that is where it is located organizationally.
- As far as possible, establish links with the next generation of management through involvement in the succession process and personal contact.
- Introduce senior managers into the design stage for all new initiatives and listen to and act upon their requirements.
- Take opportunities to create a shared vision within the employee development activity, especially in decentralized operations.

In most organizations probably six to eight senior executives are of key influence in enabling the achievement of successful employee development and probably three or four are of paramount importance. These are often the chief executive, the operational executive director, e.g. vice-president (manufacture) or general manager (personal banking), the personnel director and the marketing/technology director. The calibre and 'political' standpoint of the employee development director is also a potentially important influence, though often the job is at a level that does not afford sufficient leverage in a power or strategic direction argument.

Increasingly, change and the pressure for results have been leading to greater turnover and more early retirements at managerial levels. In political terms this means that, not only must the employee development executive get the continued support of the individuals identified, but that the actual incumbents of the posts will themselves be changing, sometimes quickly. In a five-year period it will not be uncommon for an organization to have one or two major reorganizations, one or two chief executives, two or even three personnel/marketing directors and one or two technology directors. The operational director and team are likely to change at least twice. This scenario is one in which to succeed in employee development demands considerable adaptability. If the employee development specialist—perhaps you, the reader—has a strong commitment to, say, open learning or action learning it may become untenable in the short term to create satisfactory political relationships.

As already indicated, an awareness of the political process and the fact that political judgements are made as much on the basis of personal motivation, needs and power acquisition as on 'objective' facts is essential to the understanding of real organizational situations.

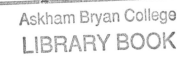

The personnel function

In most organizations the formal responsibility for employee development at board level will be with the personnel director or personnel general manager. This person will be regarded as the 'people person' as well as a member of the team responsible for business results. The personnel team will be made up of functional managers with responsibility for:

- employee development, including appraisal and succession;
- industrial relations or wage bargaining;
- salaries, job evaluation, compensation and benefits;
- communications and performance management;
- recruitment and redundancy;
- day-to-day operational personnel covering generalist personnel work.

The emphasis within personnel will depend on the particular environment. It may be highly focused on any of the following:

- identifying potential;
- decentralization of wage bargaining;
- reducing wage costs and redundancy;
- introducing payment by results through performance management and job evaluation;
- developing high-flyers;
- improving skill levels;

and will require a balance of skills in a team approach. To achieve success certain situations need to be avoided. Some personnel professionals learnt their trade and were selected for an environment where the 'enemy' was the trade union movement and the focus was on conflict and winning. The mind set was about containment and control rather than growth. It was acceptable to be 'macho' and use dominance and rhetoric as key weapons. Talk of the bottom line and settlements was used with conviction. This 1970s mentality is 'excess baggage' from a period when one observer was moved to describe the British as 'the white coolies of Europe'.

To succeed in employee development it is essential to have a chief executive who is committed and puts time into development. The personnel director needs to understand the development process, recognize its results, think strategically and sustain a 10-year view and be able to integrate the various contributions of those in the personnel function. He or she will sometimes need courage to sustain development since most real growth involves mistakes, risk, the need to practise and the time to internalize growth. One-day shots of glossy events or impressive management training centres do not necessarily produce questioning, independent, profit-oriented managers. Above all, personnel or human resource development executives for the twenty-first century will need to offer excitement and challenge to able individuals, to provide careers that promote development and growth, to express through policies and action a positive belief in the maturity of their staff and to forget the disdain for and opposition to employees that they may have needed in the past.

Going with the flow

The doyen of political understanding, Niccolo Machiavelli, advised those who aspired to success in the political world to heed the following: 'So a prudent man must always follow in the footsteps of great men and imitate those who have been outstanding.'

It is absolutely essential to appreciate that at the present state of evolution most organizations give limited power to employee development. To achieve success the exercise of organizational power or influence is necessary. This means gaining the support of those with control of expenditure and allocating time to developing and enhancing the strategies and initiatives of those who are driving the acquisition and development of skills. One useful exercise is to make a subjective assessment of the political situation and to discuss this with those you can trust within the organization. The following paragraphs identify the key steps in producing such an assessment and give a hypothetical example.

Step 1 Identify the key players in the employee development field— those who are able to influence directly the success or failure of an initiative.

Step 2 Assess the importance of the employee development input to the achievement of key objectives for the identified players.

Step 3 Assess the degree of support and ownership each player may offer.

Step 4 Estimate the strength of skill and knowledge of employee development each player may have.

Step 5 Identify the political implications for each individual.

Step 6 Identify probable future posture and actions of individuals.

By considering each individual, a useful guide or map can be produced. The following example illustrates how the process can be used for a major employee development consultancy project that might be introduced into a major organization to improve the long-term quality of the management resource. It illustrates a major project affecting some 500 managers at a cost of £1 million a year and records the employee development executive's assessment of the overall situation. Each individual is rated either a three-star or five-star player, reflecting the weight of their potential impact on the success of the project (five stars represents high impact).

Group personnel director Professional employee development is seen as a key result area over the next two to three years and will be increasingly visible. The personnel director is keen on management development and has a sound general grasp of it. He is the entry point to top management and will need to sell the project at that level. He will give strong support but cannot afford to impose his view or achieve anything less than a professional result (*five-star player*).

Employee development executive Strongly committed to employee development and the most knowledgeable in this area in the organization. If project is not successful against high professional standards he will probably leave the organization. Political position has been weakened by reorganization and devolution of authority (*five-star player*).

Project manger Strongly ambitious for the project to succeed. He does not believe that some line management or the personnel operational managers are committed. Need for more visible support from top management. If project not successful he may leave the organization (*three-star player*).

Retail operations personnel director Little or no ownership of project. He will use the output while it suits him. When he is ready, will follow his own direction. Will basically observe from the sidelines without commitment (*five-star player*).

Group personnel manager As group devolves she will need to get control of employee development or leave. Will show superficial ownership and be quietly destructive. Is not encouraging her staff to support the initiative (*five-star player*).

Group chief executive Committed to creating professional employee development for the group. Accepts advice of personnel director and employee development executive. Has final say on expenditure and strategy. Is supportive to the project (*five-star player*).

Retail operations managing director Head of largest business division. Supports use of project but also wants to create own culture for retail managers. As executive director is committed to importance of developing managers. Political impact of project central for him. He will support development but will listen carefully to his personnel director and sales director (*five-star player*).

Sales director Strong commitment to particular consultancy being used. Employee development is key for her to achieve major changes in sales operational systems. She will judge project on results and the degree to which it supports her personal strategy. Will pull out or change consultants at short notice (*five-star player*).

Consultancy chief executive Keen to ensure the project works and will do his best to do so. Contract represents five per cent of his annual turnover. His enthusiasm may waver when the next big contract arrives. Without his active involvement, quality of results required may not be achieved. He will be reluctant for his chairman to experience any failure with such a blue chip company as this client (*five-star player*).

This sort of analysis would enable the employee development executive to manage relationships over a period, to determine what to look for and to identify indicators of where political decisions may need to be made. For example, the retail personnel director and the group personnel manager could both withhold support or positively undermine the project. However, both are functionally responsible to the group personnel director and will not overtly oppose him. The retail personnel director cannot afford to lose the sales director's support but may develop his own internal or external alternative capacity to provide the same service if the sales director swaps horses. The employee development executive must retain the group personnel director's support to succeed and cannot allow the consultancy to provide anything less than maximum effort, since he is associated with the choice of supplier. He would be very vulnerable if the group personnel director and sales director did not find the output acceptable. It might be in the interests of the retail personnel director to weaken the relationship between the sales director and the group personnel director.

The group personnel manager has little to gain from the success of the project as initiated. If it were to falter and she then brought her personnel managers into the picture, strongly promoting the project in areas outside retail operations, she could project herself as a 'white knight' rescuing the project, gain credibility with the group chief executive and group personnel director and show herself as more committed to employee development than the retail personnel director. She stands to gain with little risk if she does nothing or discreetly undermines the project until the timing suits her, if the group personnel director is prepared to allow this.

This example illustrates in practice just how important it is to recognize where all the key players stand and what they are seeing. The project's performance standards and end results may be specified quite clearly and objectively. The process objectives and political interplay and accountability will be somewhat more obscure.

Setting out your stall

Most employee development takes place in political scenarios that are at least as complex as this simplified example. To succeed and sustain success in the short to medium term there are a number of essential steps:

1 Ensure that the employee development executive's contribution is compatible with what the key players want.
2 Make sure that a wide range of technical competence or products can be readily available to match business needs. Thus, approaches such as training courses, open learning, CBT, interactive video, outdoor training, action learning and distance learning should be introduced as appropriate to the important players.

3   Acquire competent staff who can get close to the customer. The hiring of staff committed and able to use non-directive approaches and tutoring can establish a development strain for several years and minimize political vulnerability.
4   Initiate a debate about employee development and market products and services.
5   Produce products that are commercially attractive.
6   Encourage as much line ownership as possible with the development resource located in operational units. Use means such as CBT to shift control of use (and ownership) to the user.
7   Collect evidence of success in terms that are politically meaningful to the key players. Make sure feedback on results is fed into the measurement systems of the operational units, e.g. units sold before and after sales training.
8   Promote what you are doing outside the organization through articles and talks at major conferences and seminars.
9   Introduce fresh ideas and expertise by using consultants and specialized products such as 'Putting People First'. Make sure you get the credit for these initiatives.
10 Know when to cut and run by changing approaches and products to reflect changing customer and political demands.

To succeed in employee development, competence in the basic developmental processes is essential. Thus, the organizational context must be managed. This involves 'the art of the possible' and that is why the political realities are so important. With strong political support but weak technical ability, employee development will survive but not flourish. With weak political support and weak technical ability, employee development will be insipid. With weak political support and strong technical ability, employee development will be a lost opportunity. But with strong political support and strong technical ability, employee development can sharpen competitive edge, increase competitive strength and ensure flourishing individuals.

Summary

The main points this chapter has covered are:

- Employee development as a political activity.
- The limitations of the analytical approach if used on its own.
- Employee development as an art and as a science.
- Political ideologies and their impact on employee development: conservatism, radicalism, the dictator/autocrat, republicanism.
- The chief executive and the functional/executive directors from a political perspective; the checks and balances on power and self-interest; the political impact of functional interests on employee development.
- What is involved in achieving successful employee development, from a political standpoint.

- The role and limitations of the personnel function and the contribution of the personnel director.
- How to analyse and chart the political reality in your organization.
- Setting out to achieve and sustain successful employee development.

What you can do

1 Identify the political characteristics of the main components of your organization.
2 Examine what you have done in the last 12 months and identify your own political standpoint and values.
3 Identify the top dozen key players in your environment.
4 Produce an analysis of the likely contribution and weight of the key players for employee development.
5 Identify which political standpoints are a threat to your own standpoints and systematically note who displays them and who is against them.

Recommended reading

Jay, Antony, 1967 *Management and Machiavelli*, Hodder and Stoughton.
Kakabadse, A., 1983 *The Politics of Management*, Gower.
Machiavelli, Niccolo, 1961 *The Prince*, Penguin Books.
Morgan, G., 1986 *Images of Organisation*, Sage Publications Inc.
Peters, Tom, 1988 *Thriving on Chaos*, Macmillan.

4 Drawing the map: vision, mission, strategy, policy and plans

No strategic plan survives contact with reality.

Anon

Thus far the practicalities of the organizational environment in which employee development takes place have been considered, together with the importance and impact of organizational power. The picture painted illustrates the powerful forces that cause continuous and significant tension and obstacles in organizations. It highlights the human needs that lie behind the apparently objective and scientific approaches claimed to be in use. Clearly, to translate this energy into a successful, focused organization it is necessary to have processes and talents that can identify the destination and the route required to harness the massive horse-power held within the organization.

This chapter examines in detail the process of moving from vision and mission statements to strategic plans, policies and objectives, through to services delivered and goods manufactured. It seeks to clarify some of the confusion often caused by misunderstanding in the use of language and to illustrate how the process of linking employee development to the main thrusts and needs of the organization takes place.

The process of moving from vision to the delivery of output can be applied at any level of the organization. Indeed, the process can apply for an individual. Development must be an integral part of such a process. If it is to succeed it must not simply reflect the vision of the employee development function.

The last decade has seen increasing efforts to line up employee development with business needs and the strategic planning process. In order to understand that process, some commonly used terms are now considered before the process as a whole and how employee development fits within it are identified.

What do the words mean?

The first step is to identify some of the key words used in the areas of vision and strategy:

- vision
- aim
- mission
- strategy
- plan
- tactics
- policy
- objective
- target
- key result area
- performance standard

Some of the main issues in identifying direction concern the creation of a picture of where the organization is headed and what the destination will 'look like', an understanding of why we are travelling and some indication of what we have to do to get there. We then need to work out exactly who will do what and when and, so that we know if we have been successful, standards of performance and feedback are important. Often the language of this process is used carelessly, so an examination of the more important words follows. It is essential that the employee development practitioner understands what these words mean.

Vision is defined in the *Concise Oxford Dictionary*, where the relevant extract for organizations is 'Thing or person seen in dream or trance, supernatural or prophetic apparition, phantom, thing seen vividly in the imagination. Imaginative insight, statesmanlike foresight, sagacity in planning'. Thus, the starting point of the process may be a quite subjective and 'unreal' aspiration towards something that does not yet exist.

Aim This is the next step and involves moving towards the target. It is defined as 'Directing of act or weapon at an object or to intend or to try to do something'.

Mission often has religious connotations and in this sense it has the meaning of 'Body of persons sent to foreign country to conduct negotiation'. It can also mean 'Task of political or other mission, operational sortie, e.g. of an aircraft'. The closest meaning to the way mission is used in strategic planning is 'Person's vocation or divinely appointed work in life'. In this context, it would perhaps be more accurate to describe it as the organization's vocation as defined by its senior officials.

Strategy is a word borrowed from the military. The closest meaning to the business context is 'Art of so moving or disposing troops or ships or aircraft as to impose upon the enemy the place and time and conditions for fighting preferred by oneself—a strategy is an instance of, or plan formed according to, this act'. This can be interpreted as so planning one's business as to have an advantage over competitors.

Plan is a 'Formulated or organized method by which a thing is to be done, a way of proceeding, to arrange beforehand'. It presupposes that one knows what has to be done and the purpose of the plan.

Policy is defined as 'Prudent conduct, sagacity; course or general plan of action to be adopted by party or person'. It clearly overlaps plan but is more general and more about direction than specific actions.

Objective is widely used in the Management by Objectives approach and is often used indiscriminately as being interchangeable with target, goal, or key result area. In fact, the 'Words' dictionary defines objective as 'goal, aim, target' as well as 'detached, impartial, impersonal'. In the *Concise Oxford Dictionary*, objective is defined as 'Belonging not to the consciousness or the perceiving or thinking subject, but to what is presented to this, external to the mind, real'. To clarify, it might be helpful to refer to objectivism in the *Concise Oxford*, which is the tendency to lay stress on what is objective. Objective, as used in the employee development field, often has close connotations with target.

Target is defined as 'Anything that is made an objective of warlike operations, result aimed at with the implication of it being a minimum acceptable objective'. In effect, the target is that which the objective seeks to achieve.

Tactics is defined as the 'Art of disposing military forces, especially in actual contact with the enemy: procedure calculated to gain some end'. Thus tactics are more immediate, more short-term and reactive than strategy.

The purpose in defining these words before considering the process of producing operational business and employee development plans is to minimize confusion and illustrate the varied and sometimes conflicting components involved, e.g.:

long term	⟷	short term
overall picture		specific actions
ends aimed at		means used
subjective		objective
pictorial		numerical
imagination		measurement
approximation		precision
direction		implementation
abstraction	⟷	focus

Since we all have our own predispositions and habits, it will be useful, before considering how to identify development needs, to run through the process of how an organization moves from vision to achievement. A typical vision might be to improve customer service. The achievement would be measured in terms of ensuring that 98 per cent of customers receive the product they ordered within 14 days of ordering it and that no more than three per cent of products mailed are returned as not wanted or faulty.

Charting the map: the process of moving from vision to results

In trying to capture the richness of a complex process it is only possible to identify the steps, illustrate by examples and show how things fit together.

The vision: the chief executive and top team will have a vision of what is possible and what they would like to see for their organization. Often this will directly reflect how they want to see themselves. It may not be easy to separate the *vision* from the *mission* since the latter is often a commitment to achieving some picture or belief. For example, a highly competitive team will want to be the best or number one. Some examples of statements of vision and mission are:

- To be the best airline in the world. *British Airways*
- I shall return. *General McArthur*
- Let a man start out in life to build something better and sell it cheaper than it has been built or sold before ... and the money will roll in. *Henry Ford*
- To put a man on the moon. *J.F. Kennedy*
- To be the UK's leading financial retailer through understanding and meeting customer needs, and by being more professional and innovative than our competition. *TSB Retail Bank*
- To be either number one or number two in every business it was in. Where it wasn't, the business had to be turned round, or sold. *General Electric (USA)*
- Customer loyalty and quality of service are essential elements of our strategy. British Gas is on the way to becoming the world's first global gas company. *British Gas Chairman*

It is interesting to note that the shortest vision/mission statement takes just three words. The longest is less than 30. It seems that stating a vision in two dozen words is entirely practical.

The strategy: once the vision is clear, a strategy needs to be devised to move towards it. The term 'strategy' is again often misused. It can in effect encompass the production of a strategic plan, which in turn is a formulated or organized method to ensure competitors are at a disadvantage. Strategic actions arising could be:

- To create an up-market financial services organization aimed at category A/B clients.
- To acquire a major US insurer such that policy income from outside the UK exceeds 50 per cent of total income.
- To become a public limited company.

Policy, **plans** and **objectives**: are the means by which strategy is implemented and may involve identifying specific issues, setting up project teams, restructuring and other actions. Some examples of these items are:

- Set up a new structure to run each major operation as a profit centre.
- Close all offices that are not on a ground-floor high-street site as a matter of policy.
- Employ over-50-year-olds in stores on customer-contact work as a policy.
- Reduce the cost/income ratio to 60 per cent within two years as a minimum objective.
- Achieve the *vision* of a slim organization by voluntary redundancy and limited recruitment.

Objectives and **targets** are closely linked and are the point at which the long term meets the short term and day-to-day tactics are necessary to meet strategic directions. The target is the result aimed at and is usually objective, quantitative and short term. The time scale will usually be no more than a year and monitoring will be quarterly, weekly or even more frequent. Vision and mission, on the other hand, might take years or decades and be monitored on a yearly basis as a minimum. Plans and objectives are likely to be made annually with monitoring perhaps quarterly or monthly.

Results or the outcomes of all this effort to move from abstract pictures to concrete reality, are then, in a good system, fed back regularly in the short term to reflect today's reality against the vision. The overall process is shown diagrammatically in Figure 4.1.

Figure 4.1   *The process of moving from vision to results*

The overall business mission and the strategic plan in most large companies and organizations are often lengthy, running to tens if not hundreds of pages, and carefully guarded so that a very limited number of senior executives have direct access to the details. Issues might be identified and publicly disseminated as follows:

- The cost : income ratio has increased from 65 per cent to 71 per cent in three years.
- The new business structure will be based on profit centres.
- Action to decrease costs.
- Action to increase income.
- The need to strengthen management.

However, the detailed plans, timings and cost have competitive commercial implications and are often carefully guarded. For employee development to succeed, however, it is essential to form a sound judgement on just what the vision and strategic plan mean for people, what impact the commercial plans have for availability of funds and what lead times are applicable to the skills needed. The cost and lead time to create a market-oriented management in a recently privatized nationalized industry might be a key strategic issue in enabling a senior management to move towards its vision of a customer-centred professional water authority.

Linking business strategy and employee development

Conventional approaches to development and training have worked from assumptions about identifying training needs based on job specifications and job descriptions. By identifying what has to be done in a job, the approach asserts, you can then identify the skills required. By then assessing the skill an individual already has, it is possible to identify the skill gap and provide training to teach the skill to close the gap. While this thinking may be necessary for individual jobs, it is not sufficient. The business situation of any organization will contain specific and essential demands. At the strategic and policy level the employee development function needs to identify and deliver products that are consistent with the vision, mission, strategy and policy of the organization.

Examination of aspects of business strategy will illustrate this overall approach to identifying need themes that will be implicit in the vision and mission of the organization and its leaders. Taking one such example: 'Customer loyalty and quality of service are essential elements of our growth strategy.' This statement was made by the chairman of British Gas in 1990. Growth as a strategy towards a vision of a global company that has a loyal customer base and provides a quality service is a situation shared with many retailers.

To illustrate the process, the growth strategy and mission to become a global company will be taken together with the vision of high-quality service and a loyal customer base but will be considered in the context of a high-street retailer. The following issues will be on the employee development agenda over a three to five year time scale.

Growth: a stated policy of growth will mean more outlets at an identifiable rate in the medium term and reasonable projections over the five-year term. The type of outlet may be changing, e.g. from small supermarket to out-of-town hypermarket, and the product may be changing from basic foodstuffs to a much wider range of consumer goods. A national organization with aspirations for global operation might have 1000 outlets in the UK, of which 900 are old-type stores and 100 are hypermarkets, and say 20 in Europe and 10 in the USA. Ten per cent growth coupled with rationalization and changing product mix could mean an additional 50 old-type stores, with a complement of 200 managerial and 1000 store staff, and 30 more hypermarkets with 250 different-style managerial staff and 3000 store staff, plus 5 management teams to run the large overseas stores. Add to this the need to replace for staff turnover and on conservative rates with the assumptions used—say 10 per cent staff turnover in stores with an average staffing of 4 managerial and 20 staff in the older stores and 8 managerial staff and 100 staff in the hypermarkets—then just for store managers and staff the recruitment and development need would be:

managers in old-style stores	$900 \times 4 \times 10$ per cent =	360
managers in hypermarkets	$100 \times 8 \times 10$ per cent =	80
staff in old-style stores	$900 \times 20 \times 10$ per cent =	1800
staff in hypermarkets	$100 \times 100 \times 10$ per cent =	1000

Thus, just for managers and store staff, this organization would need to identify, recruit, train and develop approximately 450 managers and 4000 store staff to sustain expansion and 440 managers and 2800 store staff to replace losses.

The implementation of vision and plans now starts to have an impact on issues such as demography, the availability of school leavers and women returning to work, the geographic spread of skills, the quality of retail management available, and the supply of graduates to provide store managers in perhaps 5–10 years time. The achievement of the business vision that is in the mind of the chairman will now start to require a number of employee development and human resource management strategies, policies and plans. Consider first the need for store staff and some of the questions this implies:

- What is our policy on equal opportunity?
- Do we have an age requirement or limit for checkout staff?
- Do we need different or the same skills in supermarkets and hypermarkets?
- Do we continue to recruit our supervisors from school-leaver entrants?
- Should we increase our graduate intake in the stores?

- Will our new entrants be best trained by reading texts, by using computer-based training or by in-store instruction, or should they travel from supermarkets to a nearby hypermarket to learn to use optical recognition tills?

The managerial population can pose even more demanding questions:

- Do the supervisors in small stores have the competence and potential for managing in hypermarkets?
- What is the quality of our current supervision?
- Is there sufficient potential in our stores to provide replacement for turnover and to support expansion?
- Do we want to change the composition of our management by hiring from outside?
- What is our policy for encouraging self-development, through say, open learning?
- Who will develop our managers?
- Do we acquire the employee development staff to do the job, use outside resources, have a partnership with a college, buy our own management college? How do we resource management development?
- What do we want of our specialist managers, e.g. for the delicatessen department, and what will be the role of the area managers?
- We will need fewer managers as we introduce hypermarkets. Could the hypermarket team run supermarkets as satellites and enable us to downgrade the managerial skill required in local outlets?
- Do we want retailers, marketeers, cost cutters or motivators in our stores? What combination will be necessary to get results from the school leavers of the twenty-first century?

Linking the business vision with employee development questions requires a number of strategic and policy decisions such as:

- Policy on age ranges for jobs, e.g. should over-55-year-olds now be employed on checkout tills?
- Strategy on graduate recruitment and development to specify numbers and career routes.
- Strategy on identifying and developing skills to manage new stores.
- Policy on using external consultants and management training centres.
- Policy on participating in government training schemes.
- Strategy to improve language ability for the overseas store management.
- Policy of only promoting managers who can demonstrate they are computer-literate.

As can be seen, from small acorns or simple visions, large oaks or complex strategies grow.

Let us revisit the chairman's statement for our retailer: 'Customer loyalty and quality of service are essential elements of our growth strategy.'

There are many strategic ways of achieving growth. They include takeovers or mergers, geographic expansion and new product development. Mars ice-cream gained growth by achieving 10 per cent of the ice-cream market for hand-held ice-cream in 12 months from a market share of 2 per cent—a new market of £75 million sales turnover. Buying prime sites in the high street and horizontal expansion has occurred in financial services, with banks expanding into insurance, broking and estate agency, while the insurance companies and building societies have introduced many of the functions previously the preserve of banking.

These various strategies do not necessarily involve customer loyalties. A basic strategic decision for a home service insurance company, for example, is whether to aim to sell more and more of its products to its existing customer base—and hence concentrate on holding the loyalty of that base and acquiring new younger customers from that base—or whether to deliberately target, say, high-net-worth individuals. It may go for either one or both of these options.

Concentrating now on customer loyalty, many of the strategic options may be about store design and product mix rather than employee development. Some of the issues are:

- Location: is the store easy to get to?
- Parking: is the store able to provide easy free parking?
- Product choice: can the customers buy everything they want in a one-stop shopping visit at competitive prices?
- Is the checkout process quick and streamlined?

Two points that merit employee development attention are:

1 Customer service in-store, particularly how customers are treated when they have a problem, and ensuring that cashiers at the checkouts are fully competent and able to keep things moving.
2 The overall development of staff to supervisory positions and the maintenance of high-quality motivation on repetitive jobs.

In this simplified example employee development will need to be about ensuring the organization has more skills of specific types and that the skills needed to keep customers are available to supplement the strategies of others in store design, stores location and product development. It will need to go well beyond discussion about learning objectives and arguments about reaction evaluation. Its products, the output of employee development, will need to be there at the point of sale, retaining customers on a day-in day-out basis, and available so that new stores are manned and ready to sell to beat targets on the day the store opens, or preferably ahead of the projected scheduled opening date.

To point up a contrasting situation, another chairman of a small fruit brokerage business might have a vision of a no-growth situation where he cuts back to the three major customers who have supplied 80 per cent of his profit for 20 years. Then, at the age of 70, he will be able to work just three days a week. His employee development needs are nil in comparison with the retailer. Not all businesses aim for growth. Not all situations benefit from employee development. However, for those where the business need demands employee development, and that will be 99 cases out of 100, the employee development task is central to achieving the vision and mission, since all business depends on the talents of those in the organization.

This section has concentrated on the areas of vision and mission and included policy and strategy to illustrate at the direction level what some of the considerations are. These issues apply whether the organization is a 200 000-employee multinational or a small corner shop. Most of the large organizations started small and made the right decisions about these issues, in the right environment. Later sections will consider individuals and how their visions mesh with the organization, and the chapter on identifying needs will highlight the place of employee development plans, the use of objectives, targets, key result areas, performance standards and tactics.

The role of policy in achieving success

Policy can be defined as a course or general plan of action to be adopted by a party or person. It can be regarded in its best form as a conduit or communication channel that leads from *vision* to *action*. A sound policy will identify values and give enough guidance about what is in the vision to allow individuals to make judgements that will result in actions that are consistent with the vision. Policy statements are particularly important when those who have to implement strategy are distant physically, and when reference back to those closer to the source of the vision is difficult or impossible.

Thus policy in an airline might specify that fuel is to be paid for by credit, or that unaccompanied children and the elderly will board the aircraft first. Any query on these or many other policy points can be resolved anywhere in the world by an awareness of policy. The essence of policy and its importance to success is the quality of its ability to communicate whatever the vision conveys. If it captures a vision that is really believed, e.g. that everyone, regardless of race, creed, sex or religion, should be considered equally for jobs, it can over time change attitudes and behaviour substantially. If the policy reflects lip service, it will have little effect and will be ignored. Legal sanctions to enforce basic policy will demonstrate just how strong emotions can be, e.g. the reactions in the South of the United States to the bussing of mixed race children to racially integrated schools. The profound effect of good policy statements should not be underestimated. Many people need clear guidance on what they can do.

Figure 4.2 shows a modified example of a policy statement designed to convey to sales training staff elements of a vision generated by a recently appointed employee development executive. It was based on a strategic analysis of needs carried out through discussion with the sales general manager, the chief general manager, the general manager (personnel) and a group of divisional managers. It was designed to be delivered at a conference of all training staff and was supported by a presentation with visual aids and full discussion.

Employee Development Division
Statement of Field Training Policy

Introduction

You will be aware that our approach to field training needs to be developed from the excellent groundwork achieved over the last few years. Our approach has been reviewed, starting with a two-day meeting of senior training staff to discuss and identify our future direction. This incorporated and built on informal discussion with the many users of our services. Now that I have a clearer view of what is required within the organization over the next two or three years, my first conference with you seemed the right opportunity to put to you a view of the future together with some basic statements of policy to identify some of the signposts for our route ahead.

Field training policy

1 Our primary task is to meet the needs of our customers—i.e. field operations management—to the best of our ability and making the most of the resources available.
2 Provision of the highest quality training possible is a basic requirement. To achieve this, adequate preparation time for all training officers should be fundamental to our programme planning.
3 Our products should be as cost-effective and up-to-date as we can make them. To this end, research and development needs to be a full-time activity undertaken by experienced field training staff.
4 Development of the skills and width of experience of individuals in the training division is a high priority to ensure greater flexibility in our training programmes and to improve the opportunity for job satisfaction.
5 Our planning and control systems for the National Training Programme will be improved, particularly with the aim of reducing the significant number of nights away from home experienced by too many staff.

Figure 4.2 *A statement of field training policy*

This statement was underpinned by a vision that promoted professionalism and competition with a strategic aim of being the best field training operation in the UK insurance industry within three years and to be acknowledged as one of the best in Europe within five years. In some respects, the way the staff approached the journey towards this strategic aim was more important than an objective measure of whether they actually arrived. Incidentally, the company was one of two insurance companies listed in *The 100 Best Companies to Work for in the UK* by Bob Reynolds. These companies were identified five years after the date of the policy statement example. Quality of training, promotion possibilities, ambience and communications were four of the eight criteria used.

Policy, then, is basically a form of communication and can be crucial to success. A dynamic policy should be adaptable, organic almost, for the guidance of wise men and the obedience of fools. It should be like an engineering governor, monitoring the output, giving a steer when some small corrective action is needed and shutting off the steam if the engine is going beyond its design speed or output.

Features of effective visions, missions, strategies, policies and plans

Essentially, all these instruments of communication should display features that help to transfer the ideas in the mind of the visionary to those who have to do things to achieve it. The following three mission statements represent the form such communications usually take and provide examples of what to look for in communication.

1 Charge the guns.
2 To be the UK's leading financial retailer.
3 To be the best airline in the world.

Some of the features to look for when writing or interpreting such statements are:

- **Clarity** Does the mission statement convey the vision clearly?
- **Brevity** Is the statement lean in using few words to convey big concepts?
- **Precision** Are the words exact in their meaning?
- **Unambiguous** Could anyone reading the statement come to only one possible conclusion?
- **Inspirational** Does the statement move people to man the barricades?
- **Measurement** Is it possible to check the accomplishment by measurement against the mission?
- **Legality** Would achievement of the mission break any laws, national or international?
- **Ethics** What, if any, are the ethical standards implied and are they acceptable?
- **Time scale** When should the mission be accomplished and how long should this accomplishment persist?

- **Credible**   Do the staff of the organization believe it is possible to achieve the aim?
- **Actionable**   Do people behave as if they believed the mission?
- **Background of recipient**   Will those receiving the message understand it in the same way as those sending it?

Examination of the examples chosen may illustrate some of the questions to ask. The first—Charge the guns—is said to be the mission statement given to the Light Brigade. It was certainly brief, precise, measurable and inspirational. However, it was not unambiguous. It was given by an artillery officer, to whom it meant 'put the charges in the guns prior to firing', i.e. prepare the guns for action. It was received by a cavalry officer to whom charge meant 'ride at speed towards', and guns meant 'the enemy's guns'. He clearly saw it as credible, he actioned it and one could see and measure that he charged the guns. The cost was 600 lives.

The second example is also brief, precise, measurable, legal and actionable. It can be measured against who is currently the leading financial retailer and, in fact, listing the leadership criteria would enable the organization to state if it is currently the number one, two, three or whatever. No time scale is stated so the rate of progress towards the ultimate goal cannot be measured. It would be necessary to know specifically who the opposition is for the staff to target their efforts towards achieving the mission. The term 'financial retailer' could also be ambiguous. It would be possible to define it in such a way that there were no competitors at one extreme to a definition at the other extreme which included the high-street retailers with financial products. People with a sales or retail background might also see the vision quite differently from retail, savings or merchant bankers.

The third statement is brief and clear and also precise. Not the UK, not Europe, but the world. It does not state criteria for 'best' and would have to communicate whether it means best for profit, service, on-time arrivals, speed, volume, safety or whatever. Perhaps it aims to be best at everything. This mission statement does capture the inspirational element and could easily be made credible, actionable and measurable once the criteria for 'best' are defined. Cost effectiveness and overbooking practices might cause a few problems.

In preparing your own mission, strategy, policy and plans—whether they are for a large organization, a football club, a general practitioners doctors' practice or a small configuration of people for some specific purpose, e.g. to resist the building of a motorway—the elements and features described in this section merit close consideration and discussion. The process is one of clarifying and capturing different interests so that the final statements, be they in glossy brochures or on plain sheets of ordinary paper, will move people to action in the desired direction.

An outline example of the process

The example below illustrates what the process might look like in practice for an illustrative retail bank. The stages are:

1 Vision/mission
2 Strategic business issues
3 Strategic employee development issues
4 Outline development plan
5 Resource and volume implications

To put this outline example in perspective, the bank employs 60 000 staff in 3000 branches and was formed by an amalgamation of two retail banks of 20 000 employees each and a savings bank with a similar number of employees.

Employee development blueprint for next five years

1 Vision/mission: To create an integrated bank that is pre-eminent in personal banking in the UK.
2 Strategic business issues: The main issues have been identified in the five-year strategic plan as:
   (a) Improvement of short-term (1–3 year) profitability.
   (b) Introduction of new technology to remove administration from branches.
   (c) Integrating high-street banks with savings banks with maximum rationalization of bank locations.
   (d) Shift of orientation towards sales and service.
   (e) Improvement in the quality and succession cover for management positions at all levels.
   (f) Reduction of the incidence of bad debts by increasing the quality of lending decisions.
3 Employee development strategic issues
   (a) Identify the skills needed to perform all new roles and produce resourcing plan to ensure that the identified skills are provided in sufficient volume.
   (b) Improve the quality of the top 500 managers. Identify credible successors for all jobs designated as key by the end of next year.
   (c) Identify a strategy for improving the sales skills in branches and for sales management.
   (d) Identify the development needs for each stage of the integration of retail and savings bank branches.
   (e) Identify the new roles and skills necessary to introduce new technology.
   (f) Change the direction of the bank's training college to achieve responsive and relevant training courses with a short lead time and the greater use of CBT and distance learning.
   (g) Identify key points in the organization change programme over the next three years.
   (h) Monitor and maximize the return on investment for employee development activities.

4 Outline training programme (policy objectives)
  (a) Junior branch staff: To ensure that all new and junior branch staff are able to meet service and sales performance standards within specified time scales.
  (b) Supervisory branch staff: To provide basic supervising skills on appointment and to ensure the achievement of competence in selling the bank's products.
  (c) New technology: To ensure all staff affected by the introduction of new technology have the competencies required before the branch goes 'live' with new technology.
  (d) Branch managers: To prepare newly appointed managers for their role on appointment and to improve the competence of existing managers.
  (e) District managers: To ensure all district managers are competent in their role and to prepare newly appointed district managers on appointment.
  (f) Career development: To identify the potential and likely career direction for key staff.
  (g) Succession: To identify and prepare career development programmes for individuals with the potential to succeed to key jobs.
  (h) To expand the provision of computer-based training, distance and open learning, and learner-centred approaches.
5 Resource and volume implications
  (a) Volume: The volume of formal off-the-job training should be increased by 80–100 per cent in the next three years.
  (b) Budget: Expenditure should be increased in line with this policy aim. An increase in budget from £15 million to £18 million will be necessary next year, together with an additional 40 staff who should be recruited in the current year. Thirty of these staff should be deployed in regional training centres.
  (c) Organization: It will be essential to improve the coordination from head office, to create an employee development R & D facility and to introduce learning resources centres at head office.

This example can be summarized on one sheet of paper and presented in 40 minutes. It illustrates a communicable direction and infers both the business mission and development values and vision. It is designed to stop short of detailed plans and each area of the outline training programme in Paragraph 4 would need to be backed up with detailed action plans. The process of moving from strategy to implementation through specific development structures will be covered later in the book.

Beyond business strategy—can organization development help?

There is a school of thought that advocates that management teams can assess the future condition that they wish the organization to develop and work out a strategy to get there. There is some doubt whether these organization developers are the 'pilots' who help to steer the organization in the right direction, the soothsayers who examine the entrails and pronounce like oracles on what should be done or strolling minstrels who observe what happens and then write up the tale for others to learn from. Their contribution to successful employee development can be significant but they need to be selected and used with care.

Organization development (OD) is a concept that uses simplified themes to tackle complex situations. The consultant, and most OD practitioners external to the organization, can provide a helpful broader perspective. By standing outside the politics and power situations described earlier, they can help the participants to gain a better understanding of what is going on. Much organization development activity focuses on three strategic questions:

1 Where is the organization now?
2 Where does it want to get to?
3 How does it get there?

Organization development often concentrates on role definition, values, decision-making processes, team building and the creation of feedback mechanisms or measurements of what progress is being made towards the desired objective. Clearly, this thinking relates closely to identifying both the vision and mission for the future and also where the organization currently stands, together with the steps necessary to move from one to the other, i.e. the strategic plan. Perhaps the biggest difference is that business and strategic plans are usually the province of the line executive, the accountant and the strategic planner while organization development is the field of the chief executive and team, the personnel director and employee development executive, and the external OD or process consultant.

Organization development approaches can create insight and foresight and these gifts can improve considerably the understanding and communication of top management's vision and mission. An open and businesslike approach can then create, through detailed discussion of the vision in the context of the business, two-way dialogue and commitment to detailed implementation plans. And when this situation is created and operated in a manner that is compatible with the power structure (in which some executives may wish to impose their vision rather than share a mission) then organization development can help.

Summary   The main points covered in this chapter are:

- The process of drawing a map of where the organization is going involves creating a clear vision on the part of the senior executive and the senior executive team. This is usually converted into a mission statement that identifies in broad terms how the picture can be given substance.
- The mission is then expressed in terms of strategy and strategic plans. These identify the main issues that will determine success or failure in positioning the organization in the marketplace.
- Strategy has then to be translated into action through policy statements that identify the guidelines on what is and is not consistent with the mission and strategy.
- Policy statements are accompanied by strategic and divisional plans and objectives and a process for monitoring results and using feedback.
- Employee development strategy must be totally linked with business strategy; the chapter illustrates how this is done and gives examples at the strategic level.
- The role of policy in achieving success by creating a good communications mechanism was stressed since vision has to be translated into action, often by large numbers of people who are remote from the senior executive team.
- Finally, the potential contribution of organizational development (OD) was reviewed and its role in defining, clarifying and establishing dialogue and commitment to vision and mission was highlighted.

What you can do

1 Review your organization's annual report, internal literature and videos, and public statements. Identify what senior people say is your vision and mission.
2 Collect examples of where their actions are consistent with the vision and mission and where they are not.
3 Get access to your organization's strategic plan and identify the impact of business objectives and changes on the employment development activities in your sphere of influence.
4 Identify the main characteristics of your organization, e.g. it is risk-averse, conservative and bureaucratic, and compare with what will be desirable in the future, e.g. it must be willing to take new risks, be innovative and flexible.
5 Compare every element of your employee development or training plan with the business issues and imperatives in the strategic plan. Is every activity justified by clearly contributing to an identified business need?

5 Riding the rollercoaster: managing development in rapidly changing organizations

Decisions about how to organize and deliver employee development are quite complex in organizations that are working with blurred vision and with their strategy being implemented by warring political factions. But at least in this condition the target would remain still and the rules would be known. Stability and predictability, however, are things of the past. New approaches and new paradigms are now required to begin to cope with the actual dynamics of the situations many organizations now face.

The rate and complexity of change are, as yet, far from understood. Many organization change specialists are in reality comparable to the wandering troubadour of the Middle Ages. They observe what happens and then write or tell parables for others to listen to in wonder. The technical term for this condition is post-hoc rationalization. It is reasonably safe, however, to make a few generalizations about the change process as it affects employee development.

- Change is accelerating in many areas, particularly those involving information processing and the technologies powered by the microchip.
- Change can have both positive and negative effects. In itself the rate of change is neutral. Its measurement is essentially a function of the condition at the start of the process, the condition at the end and the time that has elapsed.
- Where change has enormous impact is in the way and when it is evaluated. To say that one in three marriages will end in divorce by the end of the century is factual probability. The way this fact is seen and what is done about it depends very much on the values of the viewer.

- The management of change will require the increasing development of project management skills and flexibility in organization and employee development. The static notions of most observers of the management process prior to 1990 will need to be reconsidered to fit real situations.
- Managing, or coping, with ambiguity and chaos will become an increasingly important skill. It is no accident that Tom Peters' book *Thriving on Chaos* has been a best-seller. It strikes a chord with the times. It is in context.
- Employee development, to succeed, will have to change at least as fast as the environment to which it applies. It will need to be situation-specific, bringing precise solutions to unique organizational needs. Employee development will need to move to a different level of sophistication.
- The impact and rate of change will vary from sector to sector. The vehicle manufacture and electronics sectors, for example, experienced change early under the threat of Japanese competition and technology. The financial services industries, banking, insurance and building societies felt the wind of change through deregulation and competition in the 1980s. Management education, tertiary and secondary education, the national health service and the denationalized industries are all relative latecomers to the change process.

The overall message is that change is now a way of life. Massive changes such as the need to rethink completely relationships between East and West Europe after 'glasnost' and 'perestroika' are the backcloth against which organizations are making their strategic decisions. There is little likelihood that we will return to the way things were done in the past. This does call into question the wisdom of those dedicated to teaching and practising the solutions for yesterday's problems. The employee development function is gradually becoming more central to business success. A closer examination of just what brings about the need for change will no doubt set development in its correct context as an integral part of the general management process.

The conventional view

The conventional approach to identifying employee development needs has been mainly scientific in origin. It is crudely based on the view that you find out what is required by close examination of organization and job roles, job specification and skills required, and the identification of competencies, and then by matching what you have with what you need. Organizations find out what they have in the way of skills mainly through performance appraisal and assessment centres. Only a few use psychometric tests and even fewer actually process the information rigorously. A research study found that appraisees were four times more likely to attend a training event if it was *not* recommended for them than if it were. The typical response is then to offer a menu of courses that more or less meet some of the needs.

In parallel, the more responsive approaches of open learning, learning centres, computer-based learning, and self-directed and distance learning have developed and grown since the mid 1970s. The essence of these approaches is that they move the choice of what is needed closer to the customer with the need.

Triggers for change

To improve the strategic understanding of change and to incorporate it into the employment development strategy, it is very important to understand what is causing the change. The 'triggers' for change are outlined in this section to provide an overview and the more important of them are then described in more detail. The outline triggers described can easily be used as a rule of thumb to gain a better understanding of what is driving any change situation. This can then provide some structure for planning and understanding any change programme. Some key triggers are:

1 *The socio-economic situation*   At the level of the domestic economy this concerns the big themes. Recession, uncertain interest rates and political uncertainty about the European Community do not predict that it will be easy to obtain investment for employee development. Equally, the need to re-skill a changing and leaner productive base is clear.

2 *The political situation*   The policies and values of the government together with an assessment of its likely duration and any real alternatives will have a pervasive influence on the ground swell of change. An enterprise culture with little state intervention will promote the need for competitive and entrepreneurial skills and probably decentralization.

3 *The international dimension*   This can impact either in the sense that an international company or organization will need to incorporate these dimensions into its strategy or, certainly within Europe, the future impact of harmonization and the future of Britain's participation in the EC.

4 *The stock market impact*   For those organizations quoted or traded in the world's major stock exchanges, the effect of the London, Wall Street or Tokyo markets on share prices and takeover vulnerability might well impact on development strategy.

5 *Competition*   In the more competitive markets such as retail, finance and air transport, what the competition is doing has an important impact. Once the staff of one organization are smiling, all the others have to follow suit.

6 *Business-led change*   Changes in the business itself can be a prime trigger of employee development action. The move into unit trust selling by major composite insurance companies and the

introduction of portable personal pensions are two examples of how changes in marketing and products can flow through to development action.

7 *Corporate issues*   These are issues which are prompted by some view in the organization that large numbers of the staff should be better at something. Examples are financial awareness and running your department as a business or being better at communication through briefing groups.

8 *Organization analysis or project-driven change*   This trigger is often the establishment of a project group or the result of a persistent individual focusing effort and analysis onto some issue and then producing a blueprint for change. The issue in question might be how to change the management processes of a financial institution or the reduction of the cost-income ratio for a bank.

9 *Technology-driven change*   Perhaps the most discussed, this trigger is about the changes that have flowed from the rapid development of information technology. Dramatic examples abound, such as the paperless office or the deserted international stock exchange floor with personal dealing replaced by technology.

10 *Individual-driven change*   The arrival of a new chief executive or management team can be powerful triggers for change. At its most dramatic in takeover situations, the individual-driven change such as that achieved by Lord King and Sir Colin Marshall at British Airways can be very significant.

11 *Consumer-driven change*   Much discussed but often ignored, the customers prompt change and can have important impacts on employee development. A more educated and sophisticated customer base has been one of the factors that has pushed banks to introduce high-interest current accounts; and changes in attitudes to eating out have both prompted and been prompted by the fast-food revolution of the 1980s.

Change is a complex process, often involving many interdependent variables that just cannot be treated separately. Careful examination of the overall direction of business change and an understanding of the causal factors can at least give the employee development practitioner a closer grip on what is really happening.

The impact of change

Rapid change, or a rate of change higher than the organization's ability to cope with it readily, will have a number of significant effects on what has to be achieved for employee development to be successful. Some of these are:

- Increased demand for tailor-made and business-specific programmes to be provided by management centres.
- Less use of public or general programmes by those organizations with the resources to provide their own programmes.

- The creation of 'consortia' of major companies who then specify what they want done and appoint providers to ensure the delivery. Increasingly, these arrangements do not include the major providers.
- Adoption of action learning approaches that do not rely on the traditional analysis–solution approach. Action learning is by its very nature business-specific and ideally suitable for volatile change environments.
- Greater integration with the business planning process and a business awareness that will have to be much more focused than before. The balance between individual development and profit contribution as skill increasingly determines competitive edge will be more and more important.
- Greater flexibility and openness about the provision of learning. It is becoming increasingly futile to predict menus of training for future needs. The creation of more open approaches is a direct response to the need for greater flexibility created by the demands of change.
- The medium will increasingly become the message. Delivery by means that require individuals to cope with uncertainty and learning will be more generally necessary. The growth of outward-bound or outdoor training and action learning are clear responses to this trend.
- The ownership of development and the individual's role and requirements will become increasingly important. High investment in the provision of skills can make economic sense when conditions are relatively stable. When skill is in short supply and highly portable the situation is less clear-cut. Ford Motor Company's approach of allowing a grant of up to £250 for employees to spend on approved skill improvement activity is an example that may become common.
- Decentralization will be more widespread. One of the probable side effects could be the creation of much narrower experience for employee development practitioners. It may be necessary for them to move from unit to unit or even company to company to gain a breadth of experience in dealing with different change situations.
- Quality of development resources. The complexity of change and the lack of serious professional preparation for the task will exacerbate the shortage of competent individuals. It will be increasingly important to carry out the analysis of options for delivery and the identification of appropriate organization structure. Development of staff in the employee development function itself will be a major challenge; it will be a central preoccupation and a barrier to widescale success throughout the 1990s.
- Quality of research and development. A further issue will undoubtedly be the relevance and utility of much of the academic research and development effort. Our understanding of the change process is at best primitive and the quality of much of the literature, in terms of actually doing something in the practical world, leaves much to be desired.

Success will require the achievement of considerably increased levels of professionalism on the part of the employee development practitioner, coupled with a keener ability to understand and contribute to business at a strategic level. Commercial vision and the ability to create and understand concepts geared both to excellence and profit will be increasingly demanded. The need to ensure that individual development approaches and learner-centred concepts are channelled in the same direction as the corporate mission will demand skilful management of change processes and a developed understanding of the triggers and forces that drive change. A consideration of these triggers in a little more detail follows.

Socio-economic situations

This trigger often needs to be considered in conjunction with the purely political aspects described next. The socio-economic triggers are those generated by what is happening in society and the economy. The issues that occupy significant column inches in the financial press are also quite key for employee development, particularly at the strategic level. To illustrate the way these triggers work several particular examples are examined below. However, the specifics vary from sector to sector and it is vital for you to match the overall trends with your particular situation.

One trigger has been the demographic trend of a falling birthrate in the 1970s, which has meant fewer school leavers coming into the job market in the 1990s. This essentially social trend has been clearly highlighted for a number of years. A buoyant economy, particularly in the middle-class sector, has also meant a greater inclination for youngsters to stay in further education. The growth of service industries, with the relative decline of manufacturing, has also led to an increasing demand for customer-contact skills of a relatively unsophisticated kind. Thus, jobs such as shelf-fillers, checkout operators, sales assistants, porters, ticket-office clerks and bus conductors have become increasingly difficult to fill even though there is a significant unemployed population.

This trend reads straight through to employee development with some of the effects being:

- the employment of the over-50-year-olds in supermarkets;
- the encouragement of women returning to work into these occupations;
- the increasing creation of part-time and job-sharing arrangements;
- the improvement of induction and initial skill training;
- the provision of remedial training in mathematics for engineering trainees;
- the upgrading of customer-contact jobs in terms of remuneration available;
- increased focus on the attraction of graduates, partly to provide junior management who used to come through this route.

Changes in society and the economy have a direct impact on development and certainly trigger changes in the approach to employee development.

At a different level, local labour market studies such as that of future skill requirements for financial services in the City of London, carried out by Professor Amin Rajan and published in his book *Create or Abdicate*, can identify important skill demands and mis-matches. The Rajan study reviewed the period 1987–92 and identified key issues for human resource management. It reads directly across to specific sectors and skills within them and identifies precise estimates for the increase and number of jobs to be created and the skills required. Strategic issues such as the need to recruit and develop non-university graduates and A-level holders and the economics of developing one's own staff rather than hiring from an increasingly expensive pool can be readily identified.

A further development that should help to produce local socio-economic focus is the creation of training and enterprise councils (TECs). These institutions were designed to be local, e.g. for East London or Surrey, and aim to focus on local business needs for training and attempt to match these with national government initiatives such as the Employment Training Scheme or Modern Apprenticeships.

Increasing attention will be given to socio-economic factors, particularly at local level.

Political triggers   Often closely linked with the socio-economic triggers, these flow essentially from the political views adopted by the elected government. In the UK some examples of the impact of conservative political standpoints are:

- The provision of programmes of school-to-work experience that effectively take school leavers out of the unemployment net and provide basic skills training coupled with education and an occupation for one or two years.
- The change to the basic school curriculum in an effort to make education more vocationally relevant.
- The provisions of the Enterprise Allowance Scheme that, as part of the 'enterprise culture' political ideology, offer free business advice and counselling and a range of practical short courses covering the skills required for setting up and running a small business.
- The abolition of industrial training boards and the establishment of voluntary industry bodies also reflects a political view of minimal state intervention.

The practical effects of the political dimensions are that employee development managers need to be aware of what funding is available and how it can be matched productively to the organization's need. The creation of training and enterprise councils also offers some opportunity to influence the funding of national schemes and what can be achieved locally. This might reduce costs and also ensure that a broader range of skill development opportunities are available locally.

Political decisions, such as the privatization of industries, can also have very wide-ranging effects on the employee development needs of organizations. Companies such as British Airways and whole industries such as oil, gas, telecommunications and water have had some of their basic assumptions up-ended as they have shifted from the state monopoly situation they formerly occupied to one of being major international competitive organizations. The politically simple decision to transfer ownership from the state to private enterprise probably created more demands on employee development than any decision over the past 50 years.

International triggers

International companies and organizations may have a direct impact on the employee development strategy by requiring certain activities to be carried out locally or by an integrated international approach to some development activities. Thus, the high-flyer programme might be run from America or Holland and standards, say, for French fries and burgers (and thus the training in how to prepare and cook fast food) could be determined on an international basis.

International developments can also impact very positively. Recent changes in East and West Europe and the advent of the Single Market in 1992 have guaranteed extensive pressure for development in language skills and, more importantly, the ability to conduct business on a culturally acceptable basis in many areas previously closed to Western firms. A free European market and the probability, for example, of European banks offering their services in England or of French water companies becoming significant operators in the UK are coming much closer. The working of the various regulations and the ability to produce European managers are two challenges that have flowed directly from the Treaty of Rome and are clear examples of how international events can influence employee development strategy and trigger the need to change what is done.

Stock market impact

The indicators that are most public and no doubt occupy a not insignificant amount of the attention of many organizations' chairmen or chief operating officers are share prices, dividend and earnings per share. For some the question of who owns how much of their issued shares also looms large. Many more very large organizations such as British Telecommunications, British Gas, the water authorities, British Steel and British Airways are now subject to this discipline. Even local authorities are now effectively under public scrutiny of their performance as the quality of their service and its costs are expressed in the 'rate' for their community. This highly visible availability of market indicators, together with the excellent quality of the financial press coverage in the UK, has created a situation where performance is widely observed. The much broader share ownership and unit trust investment that now exists has also encouraged interest in financial performance. The result has been a tendency towards what is described as 'short-termism' where fund managers switch in and out of shares on the basis of market price and the ability to take short-term profit. They too are subject to league tables and scrutiny of their performance.

The effect of all this on employee development is reflected in the scrutiny that any longer-term activity then attracts. Investment to show gains in three or four years, by putting resources into developing people or products through research and development, can be subject to shorter and shorter payback time requirements. This is in contrast to some other economies, notably the Japanese, who may pay much more attention to market share and quality than share price.

Some examples of how the focus on short-term price could affect the investment in development are:

- Pressure to increase operating profitability and thus the amount available for distribution as dividend can be converted into cost-cutting projects. These in turn could recommend the sale of residential training accommodation, cuts in the support for education grants such as study for MBAs, or reduction in the staffing for employee development. An overall cut in the percentage of payroll spent on training and development is a relatively soft target for short-term savings.
- Given poor share price performance, it would be normal for the management of the company to attract substantial criticism in the financial press. This in turn would put pressure on senior management to improve the quality of operational management or even some of their own number. The usual result is for some managers to depart and others to join. This can generate the need for substantial development.

One result of the increased focus on results in the stock markets of the world has been the de-layering of many financial organizations, particularly banks. The removal of layers of management has created demands for individuals able to undertake broader roles, often associated with clearer profit accountability. In a sense, the accountability of the chairman and directors has been reproduced in microcosm for middle and even junior managers. The focus on profits then feeds through to affect the type of development being offered. It heightens the need for first-class selection processes and focuses development towards understanding how to produce and maximize profits.

Overall, the creation of an enterprise economy coupled with the means to measure performance has shifted the focus of employee development, for organizations ranging from public limited companies to football clubs to hospitals, to the provision of a contribution that gives improved profitability or organizational performance.

Competition as a trigger

Competition can be another major reason for introducing or improving aspects of development. The problem facing many large organizations is how to differentiate themselves from their competition. If the competitive situation for personal banking is examined in the UK, the 'big four' have very similar premises in most towns. They will be of a similar size, all have automated cash dispensers or share those of a competitor, and charge much the same for their services. How then can they compete? They will target market segments, e.g. students, and offer marginal benefits such as late-night opening on market day. The point at which they do compete is the point of sale. Hence the attention paid to customer service training and attempts to differentiate their services from those of their competitors.

Another area, closely allied to customer service, is the notion of Total Quality. In effect, this means providing the customers with what they are paying for—getting it right first time so that the correct transaction is carried out for the correct amount and sent to the correct destination at the correct time. These programmes generate the need for good product knowledge and concentration on competence. Competence, as perceived from the customers' viewpoint, is doing all that is required plus making the transaction human or even enjoyable.

The fierce competition across the spectrum in retailing has led to the need to update staff continually on product knowledge and sales techniques. We are considering here organizations such as Comet, Dixons, Next, and, in travel, Lunn Poly, Thomas Cook, American Express and the Automobile Association. Sectors such as food retailing and banking, insurance and building societies are also affected. One measure of change in technology-based industries is the half-life of a qualification. Thus the knowledge gained in a technical higher degree might have a half-life of four years. That is, in four years half of what has been learned would be obsolete. Competition and the need for new and competitive products puts constant pressure on keeping employee development up to date. In effect, continuous retraining is taking place in response to competition.

Business-led change

Changes in the mission and nature of the business can, over a period, exercise a profound and continuous influence over what employee development has to deliver to achieve success. Many businesses in the financial sector changed substantially over the period 1975–95. To illustrate briefly the nature of this change trigger it is interesting to examine the evolution of the Trustee Savings Bank (TSB).

1975   The TSB became a clearing bank. Prior to this it received deposits only and took care of the savings of its customers.

1976	The 73 local TSBs amalgamated into 20, thus creating larger units at much the same time as they began to offer similar services to the 'big four' clearers.
1983	The 10 TSBs in England and Wales amalgamated to become one bank. There were then only 4 TSBs, i.e. England and Wales, Scotland, Northern Ireland and the Channel Islands, compared with the 73 there had been 7 years earlier.
1989	TSB England and Wales, TSB Scotland and TSB Northern Ireland were incorporated into TSB Retail Banking.
1990–91	TSB Northern Ireland sold.
1990–91	TSB Retail Bank and Insurance established.
1991–92	Estate Agencies sold.
1995	Merger with Lloyds Bank.

In addition to this, the TSB group became a public limited company in 1986 and held its first annual general meeting for shareholders in 1987.

In parallel with this amalgamation and reorganization a number of essentially technical events took place. Some of the more significant were:

1977	Personal lending and overdraft facilities were introduced as a service to customers.
1978	The TSB Trustcard or credit card was introduced, linked with Visa.
1979	The provision of mortgages and the first commercial loans were introduced. The TSB had moved from deposit taking to a wide range of lending.
1981	The Speedbank automated teller machine or cashpoint was introduced. The TSB was becoming very similar to a high-street clearing bank.
1986	The first commercial banking branches were introduced.
1987	The development of a network of estate agency offices began and the first Home Centre in the Bank branch was opened.
1987	The TSB introduced Speedlink, which was the first telephone banking service to be launched by a UK bank. In six years, the organization had moved from the introduction of automated teller machines to twenty-first-century banking.
1994	TSB Phone Bank introduced.

The driving force behind much of this activity was a redefinition of the business from that of savings bank controlled by trustees to that of clearing bank owned by shareholders. The key changes were:

- the introduction of personal lending;
- the creation of larger branches with broader services;
- the provision of mortgage and insurance services;

- the operation of commercial business centres for small and medium businesses;
- the development of an in-branch sales force geared to achieving sales targets and turnover targets.

All these changes in turn led to the need for employee development responses, some of which were:

- The development and wide-scale implementation of courses on personal and commercial lending to introduce new skills for savings bankers. Few of those working for the TSB in 1976 had grown up with or exercised lending skills.
- Extensive technical training on lending and insurance products.
- Widespread sales training for customer services officers whose task was to sell products within branches.
- Management training geared to help managers plan and control the operation of a medium-sized branch.

Some of these changes were no doubt the result of a combination of triggers, e.g. the flotation was in a period that saw the invention and support of privatization of nationalized industries. However, the basic thrust was to change the business from a local deposit or savings taking bank (which did not even offer a cheque-clearing service) to a clearing bank offering the same services as the 'big four' on a national basis. The employee development strategy to meet these very demanding and quite rapidly changing activities needed to be able to deliver high-volume skill development programmes while also capable of responsiveness to local and individual needs.

Corporate issue triggers This group of triggers concerns issues that are perceived across an organization as important. An example might be running a branch of a bank or insurance company as a business. The widespread introduction of corporate branding or customer service training are also examples of issues that are triggered by the creation or identification of values and standards which affect the whole organization.

The creation of corporate identity and culture can be a powerful aspect of a change programme. The revitalization of the Prudential Corporation and its transformation from the image of the 'man from the Pru' with his 1950s suit and bicycle clips to the modern version of Prudential is a classic example. The existing image and the new vision of a modern international financial organization were skilfully blended by an advertising agency to create a new brand image and corporate logo. The intent and meaning of the new image was communicated to all staff simultaneously using high-profile presentations and upmarket materials. The ethics and values were incorporated into much of the employee development activity and included an internal marketing project for the function.

Customer service has received similar attention as organizations ranging from airlines to banks to telecommunications have sought to create a corporate image and corporate standards for performance. A further example of corporate-driven change is the use of group management development programmes to create a team spirit and common language across different businesses that are part of a broader organization or conglomerate. The task of communicating with dispersed managers in diverse industries and maximizing the use of talent across the organization is challenging and creates demands for employee development aimed at unification of corporate understanding while transcending national or sector boundaries.

The lack of a common corporate language can be a significant problem for large organizations. Efforts to provide development that is consistent in its approach to the use of language can be very powerful in improving communications and understanding, though the implementation of such strategies is very much in its infancy.

Organization analysis or project-driven triggers

This trigger for change involves a planned approach to the identification of what needs to be changed. An example might be concern with the way a sales organization is run and in particular an approach that integrates sales with administration and pays a basic salary to reflect this administrative focus. To change this type of situation, particularly if there is a trade union involved, would require taking a large number of people along with the change to gain commitment. The task could be approached by identifying a number of components of the area needing change as follows:

Component 1	Is the way in which area offices are organized now satisfactory? How could it be improved?
Component 2	What is the role of the salesperson? How much time is spent on prospecting, selling, follow-up service and administration?
Component 3	Could the role of the salesperson be split between front office sales roles and back office administration?
Component 4	How are salespeople recruited and trained? Are the approaches adequate? What could be done differently?
Component 5	What alternative approaches to motivation and remuneration might be appropriate to improve sales volumes?

Each of these components and any others identified could then be organized into project groups. Typically, each project would have a director and a reporting date. Members of each project would be drawn from interested functions.

Each project would report on the result of its analysis to a coordinating group that would be the decision-making body. Each project group would identify action steps to be taken and possible time scales with an estimate of resources required and possible benefits.

There would then need to be an interactive phase where the various recommendations are pulled together into a cohesive plan that would then receive detailed consideration by the coordinating group.

Throughout the process there would need to be coordination between the project directors and functional directors and a considerable liaison workload would be generated. The outcome should be a plan of action based on analysis carried out by those involved with delivering the plan, helped where necessary by consultants and secondees from within the organization itself. This generation of commitment is perhaps one of the most important gains of this approach. It is often relatively easy to form a view of what should be done and not too difficult to get some sort of consensus on a common approach. Few in a bank, for instance, would argue against the aim of reducing the cost:income ratio to 60 per cent. Actually achieving it can be another matter.

As the direction resulting from the analysis becomes clearer, two particular avenues merit special attention. First, the employee representatives should be regularly consulted. Any changes stemming from the questions posed under Components 1 to 5 could have profound effects on working practices and income. Any trade union involved in such a process should ideally be involved from the start as a full member of the process. The president or general secretary could be invited to join the coordinating committee and union members should be formally involved in the project groups. In many situations this may be idealistic but nevertheless is a worthwhile goal.

The second issue is the close involvement of the employee development staff in the process and in the planning and delivery of development actions. The employee development strategy and plans should be closely geared to deliver new skills as they are required and phased to meet the implementation programme. Some examples that could flow from the five-component projects described above are:

- Area manager training programme to define new roles and management skills required to manage separate sales and administration staff.
- Organization-wide seminars to explain the new approach and changes proposed.
- New sales training programme to improve prospecting and cold-calling skills for salespeople who will need to achieve higher sales volumes.

Again, the organization analysis or project-driven approach may include elements of the other triggers described. However, the basic shape and steps of Analysis–Proposal–Implementation–Review are quite distinctive. Project management is now central to change management and is described in detail in Chapter 6.

Technology-driven change

Technological advance has been one of the prime causes of changes in skill requirements for most of this century. The automobile engine, for example, wiped out in a few years the skills with horses that had been required for centuries. The advent of computers commercially in the late 1950s and early 1960s and the explosion of information technology in the 1970s and 1980s have been essential triggers in generating the need for new skills. These are some of the areas in which technology has triggered changes in skills needs:

- Word processing has revolutionized the use of typewriting skills and overlaps into what was once the area of printer's skills through desktop publishing.
- Spreadsheets and the personal computer have revolutionized approaches to planning and using information for control.
- Robots now carry out much of the car body-frame welding once done by hand.
- Automated tellers now dispense cash, creating new demands in the role of the bank clerk.
- Whole new industries and their associated skills now exist, e.g. video production and renting.
- Working from home with telephone, fax, teleconferencing, desktop publishing and other electronic devices is becoming more and more a possibility and a reality.

The way the process tends to work is perhaps best illustrated by an example. The task of obtaining cash and basic bank services is one that has been clearly affected. The steps were broadly:

- High-street costs and labour costs increased significantly.
- Automated tellers or cash dispensers were developed and were economic to use as substitutes for bank staff by the late 1970s.
- Functions such as providing balances and ordering statements and replacement cheque books were added.
- Cost pressures increased and technology advanced to permit the relocation of bank office administration. The use of sophisticated telecommunications, fax facilities and stand-alone and grouped computers made it possible to remove activities from the high street to cheaper off-site locations. A standing order can be initiated just as easily in a remote location.
- Developments in marketing and technology promoted direct sales and off-the-page sales of financial services. It became possible to buy goods or travellers cheques by using the telephone to place the order and a credit/charge card to pay for it.

The whole area of money transmission has developed enormously in recent decades, and the technological advances have triggered changes in employee development such as:

- how to understand and use computer printout control information, e.g. accounts overdrawn report;

- how to sell the bank's products and use productively the time saved by no longer carrying out some routine tasks;
- how to manage a branch with full back office technology installed that has relocated most administrative tasks to an administrative centre.

This one small example illustrates how the power to process information and produce control data such as automatic stock reordering for stationery has revolutionized many activities. New ways of doing things often require new skills, knowledge and attitudes and the employee development task has been to provide this. Use of the technology itself to manage learning, to provide CBT programmes and interactive video, and to provide instruction actually through the mainframe has grown rapidly. Technology can instruct a customer how to use the machine itself, as in a cash dispenser, and can also be used to provide distance learning through the computer network in the organization. Technology is undoubtedly one of the most important triggers for change that affect employee development.

Change prompted by top management   The power of the chairman and/or chief executive to create the employee development environment is very wide-ranging. The degree to which they are exercised may vary from organization to organization but the top team will hold unique values and beliefs that can permeate throughout an organization. Their actual motivational drives are many and varied but some are:

- A drive to be number one or the best within an industry.
- A driving concern with measuring performance and maximizing return on assets.
- A commitment to excellence and the achievement of high quality.
- A commitment to operating at minimum cost.
- The need to compete and take over other businesses.
- The need to take risks and gamble, say by the acquisition and selling of businesses.
- The need for recognition—it is not unknown for a knighthood to be an individual chairman's main aim.
- A total commitment to the customer and customer service.
- A commitment to the growth and development of the organization's own staff.

When a new senior executive is appointed, that person brings their own bundle of drives and needs to the job. In addition they may be cautious, conservative, bold, brash, extrovert, introvert, a marketeer, an engineer, a politician, or a surgeon, decide to leave the top team unchanged or bring in new people. They in turn will bring their personalities, skills and drives into the melting pot.

This mixture will interact with the business situation and inform the various decisions made about employee development. A marketeer chief executive teamed with a chairman focused on reducing costs and maximizing profits might well spend several million pounds on a customer service programme while pursuing extensive redundancies to reduce costs. The overall strategy of driving up the income side by pursuing greater market share while driving down costs to maximize profit is quite a common strategy.

Change at the top is often prompted by business demands or by a retirement and the subsequent promotion of a successor as chief executive. Business situations also change continuously. A period of growth may be followed by the need to consolidate and different management approaches may be necessary.

The employee development contribution will need to identify and accommodate the deep-seated motivational drives emanating from the top and produce strategies that capture the lead on direction they give.

The customer The customer, i.e. the purchaser or user of the output or services of the organization, is also a trigger for change in employee development. However, it is relatively rare to read about or observe this impact in the employee development literature. There has been a shift from notions of *trainees* or *students* to ideas about *learners*. Many employee development practitioners treat internal managers as customers and market to them. External providers similarly aim their marketing at the training manager as the customer. The customers or buying public rarely figure in the equation. They may be the recipients of customer-care trainees or some technical wizardry that thrills the computer professionals—but their views are rarely captured in the development process.

The views of customers on what products they want, what services they seek and what they think of the service is usually the preserve of market research, customer service and customer complaints, all of which will be within the marketing function. One crucial step for anyone aspiring to success in employee development is to work very closely with the marketing function and to find out what customers think of the results of the training and development. Complaints about poor product knowledge, bad selling practices, poor customer relations, badly assembled car doors, badly driven trains or heavy landings are all complaints about training and supervision.

Conversely, in a large organization the employee development function has regular direct contact with the front line employees, the car assemblers, cabin crew, bank clerks or insurance salespeople. It can build in the 'lived' experience gained from the customer-contact interface and feed this back into marketing and product development. Regular participation by the marketing director and marketing staff is a healthy sign that this conduit is open. Even better, sampling of the customers on the results of employee development should be sought. The kerbside review in selling when the trainee salesperson discusses how a call went with the accompanying sales supervisor is greatly enriched if some feedback can be obtained from the customer. Some customers will tell you how they felt about a sales interview—if asked.

The customer as a trigger for change is a greatly underexamined area. Major influences such as the Financial Services Act and the Regulation of Financial Services, with requirements such as 'best advice', are an example of customer-selling practices bringing about change. But the customer as a trigger for change in employee development strategy still has very wide scope for improvement.

Integration The 11 triggers for change described so far are one way of breaking down a complex change process into discrete components. Each component can then be viewed from the standpoint of employee development. In reality, any change situation will probably have elements of several triggers. They are interrelated and are only considered separately to aid description and understanding. Indeed, a complex change may include all the elements plus others not identified, just as a complex compound in chemistry may be made up of many elements.

We will next consider the importance of feedback for learning in a change situation, how the employee development function might itself be marketed and some issues on the evolution of employee development in situations of change.

Feedback and learning from change

One of the key elements in managing the employee development process as part of any significant change programme or project is to establish feedback links. The various triggers for change described will prompt particular development activities that will be phased in over time and might comprise a significant proportion of the employee development strategy. Ways of constantly monitoring progress and identifying the outcome of employee development should be built in to the operational control of the change project. Thus, progress reports should periodically identify what has been achieved, how this meshes in with the overall project programme or change programme and what is planned for the future. Adaptation will be inevitable and the basic guideline will be to expect the unexpected.

Feedback is central to all learning processes and the management of change is a learning process like any other. Ways of identifying and dealing with feedback have to be built in and negative feedback dealt with. The operational director might feel that the proposed timing for addressing how new roles should be conducted is too early against his/her view of the state of the morale of the senior managers. The impact and cost of delay has to be identified and the impact on the overall programme assessed. Change is a complex dynamic process and fast, open feedback loops and mechanisms provide an essential means of keeping the change on course.

Typically, the change will be managed by a coordinating group or an individual executive. It will be managed through meetings of project groups and the circulation of progress reports and minutes of meetings. Lead times will be crucial and many employee development actions will require adequate notice for designing and assembling the necessary resources for delivering programmes. Feedback mechanisms on the reality of time estimates and actual progress against the plan need to be set up early. Regular review of the employee development actions should be built into events where possible. For example, a weekend programme to review and clarify the role required of newly appointed area directors can be designed so that the outcome is reviewed and agreed with the regional director on the Sunday evening. Alternatively, the change intervention can be designed as an integral part of the operational management process with feedback built in by way of monthly reports to the executive group on what has been learned and achieved.

Action learning is a classic vehicle for tackling many change situations. It has its own built-in feedback as set members report back to their comrades-in-adversity on what they have done and what they have learned at each meeting. There is little as powerful as peer group pressure to bring honest evaluation of progress out into the open. This open feedback is then used to channel future action. The set is a microcosm of the whole organization and illustrates how the organization's staff needs good feedback mechanisms to learn and adapt.

Internal marketing of employee development

With the acceleration of change, and incorporation of many of the strategies described earlier, employee development in many organizations has adopted a positive approach to marketing its contribution. Some of the steps required are:

- Identification of market segments for training within the organization.
- Creation of a brand image that is used to identify all communications. This may include a logo and distinctive course brochures and hand-outs.
- Establishment of a professional reception area that provides good customer service.
- Creation of a customer-centred and commercial ethos.
- Development of staff to ensure the actions live up to the policy.
- Allocation of specific staff to identified areas of the business to establish a close understanding of specific needs.

- Regular meetings with key internal customers to review progress and agree new products.
- Collection and distribution of credits and positive feedback.
- Prompt action on customer complaints.
- Creation of physical facilities that meet customer expectations. For example, if four-star residential quality is what is expected and will be paid for—provide it.
- Continuously monitor reaction to products and modify where necessary.

The internal employee development function needs to be seen as professional and competitive with outside suppliers. Its literature and standard of presentation as well as its quality of products and professional staff should stand comparison with anybody—since they will be compared.

Employee development and change

One of the results of more rapid change has been a shift in the role of employee development. The earlier more static situations demanded little in terms of flexibility and commercial focus from employee development. Training was seen as a classroom activity based on five-day courses. The training menu was prepared in the autumn for the following year and activities were delivered that were predictable and eternal.

The key element in the current situation, resulting from the triggers described earlier, is the need for employee development to be focused on business results. Some of the more significant results have been:

- Development linked to project requirements and integrated with project timescales.
- Increased use of open learning and distance learning.
- The adoption of more flexible approaches to development; greater emphasis on learning and less on teaching.
- Development is more central to the business though still often located within personnel.
- More expenditure and senior management time is now focused on development.
- Change puts a premium on skills and adaptability, which provides increasingly difficult challenges for employee development.

Change has become a way of life. To survive, the new skills required have to be developed.

Summary

This chapter has concentrated on change and how it impacts on employee development. Change is now so central to management thinking that the question of how it meshes with employee development must be on any agenda concerned with success.

Eleven triggers for change were identified and illustrations given of how each has an impact on employee development. They are:

1 The socio-economic situation: how social trends and changes and the economic environment in which organizations operate can affect employee development.
2 The political situation: examines the impact of political ideology, e.g. the enterprise economy, and how this and government initiatives can be incorporated in development strategies.
3 The international dimension: considers the approach of multinationals and how international developments, especially the European Single Market, can affect development strategy.
4 The stock market impact: examines the effect of share price, dividends and 'short-termism' on development.
5 Competition: considers the power and limitations of competition and the role of development in establishing customer service and competitive edge.
6 Business-led change: examines how changes in the business, its products and markets can impact directly on employee development needs.
7 Corporate issues: addresses those issues that permeate the whole organization.
8 Organization analysis or project approaches: concerns the derivation of change programmes involving a broad spectrum of individuals, gaining commitment to a change programme and managing this.
9 Technology-driven change: perhaps the most pervasive change factor, this section examines the impact of technology and illustrates how employee development programmes have to be an integral part of achieving the benefits available.
10 Top management-inspired change: examines the drives, influence and contribution of senior management to specifying approaches to change and determining what employee development strategy is likely to succeed.
11 Consumer-driven change: identifies the lack of real contribution from the actual customer to employee development strategies and highlights the importance of links with marketing to ensure consumer needs are recognized.

The question of the use of analysis and the need to adopt an integrative approach to make sense of the complex situations involved was then described.

The importance of feedback mechanisms and the place of feedback in the process of the total organization learning from change was highlighted.

Finally, the importance of internal marketing and the process, from identifying internal markets and products through to the delivery of quality development, was described and some of the distinctive features required of development in change situations identified.

What you can do

1 Identify the major change initiatives that will affect your organization over the next two years. Review the triggers for change and produce a summary of key employee development activities required.

2 Identify the three most important of your key responsibilities in terms of the changes you foresee. Review your own experience and draw up a programme for yourself to improve your ability to cope.

3 If possible, set up a small group of colleagues or join an action learning group to experience this approach to coping with change.

4 Compare your internal marketing with the external training material you receive in *People Management*, or *Management Today*. How does it compare? Identify areas for attention and improvement for your internal marketing.

5 Review your employee development plan and organization. Is it designed to cope with change? What alternatives would make it more effective?

Recommended reading

Moorby, E. T., 'Influencing the Decade', *Training and Development Journal*, Volume 5 No. 6, October 1986.

Peters, Tom, 1988 *Thriving on Chaos*, Macmillan.

Rajan, Amin with Fryatt, Julie, 1988 *Create or Abdicate*, Witherby & Co. Ltd.

Thompson-McCausland, Ben with Biddle, Derek, 1985 *Change, Business Performance and Values*, Gresham College.

6 Project and process management in times of change

It is common sense to take a method and try it. If it fails, admit it frankly and try another. But above all, try something.

F.D. Roosevelt

One of the more significant aspects of the 1990s has been the marked increase in the rate of change organizations have experienced. Decades of relative stability characterized by unresponsive bureaucracies, lack of customer focus, local markets and complacency have gone. Competition is now global for many organizations. Technology and the media can raise items such as decisions made by a merchant bank (e.g. Barings, 1995) or a hospital to the level of national or international issues within literally hours.

These new conditions have demanded specific responses. Managements, and employee developers, now have to respond to business demands that may be difficult to anticipate, need prompt action and require a cross-functional response. These new conditions have created the need for strong project management and change process skills. Success in employee development depends crucially on delivering the skills required to survive and prosper, and these skills are often now the skills required for successful project management. This chapter will consider what is meant by project management and process management, how these fit with the implementation of strategy described in Chapter 4 and how project management is often the tool to enable both organizations and employee development functions to deliver the desired results. It will identify some approaches to developing project management skills and describe the essential components of successful project management. Training and development processes that have been used successfully will be described and the essentials of change process management will be identified.

Linking organizational strategy and project management

Chapter 4 described how a vision or picture of the future is central to the development of business or organizational strategy. The strategic plan, which is often produced on a one-year rolling basis, begins to identify the actions and results which will be required to deliver the vision and objectives. As the plan is developed, specific areas will be identified. Examples might be the introduction of new technology, e.g. scanners to eliminate checkouts in supermarkets, new roles, e.g. telephone selling of products or other specific needs. Such areas, often described as projects, can then be developed in more detail. A project manager will be allocated responsibility, agree objectives, terms of reference or 'deliverables', put together a multi-functional team if necessary and agree a budget and time-scales for the component parts. For a large organization, there may be a large number of complex, interlocking projects which will need to be coordinated and integrated. The range might cover new product development, acquisition strategy, purchase of facilities, specific skill development and many more topics. Some mechanism for integrating the progress and development of projects is usually necessary to minimize conflict and to ensure various components are ready on time. Projects need to be monitored consistently and regularly against the original strategic direction. For example, to use the vision of President Kennedy to put a man on the moon, the North American Space Agency (NASA) would have had to coordinate projects to develop the space rocket, the moon exploration vehicles, the computer technology to control the mission, the medical knowledge to ensure the survival of the astronauts, and, of course, select and train the astronauts so that they were available at the right time to deliver the mission. Within this broad prospective, even a faulty design in a small fuel system component could jeopardize the whole mission. And each ingredient had to be available to a time-scale, e.g. spacesuits had to be developed and manufactured by the time the training programme required their use. Thus a speech containing a vision—to put a man on the moon by the end of the decade—generated a vast, complex project requirement involving thousands of individuals and hundreds of teams.

Project management and process management

A project is defined in the *Concise Oxford Dictionary* as a 'plan, scheme, planned undertaking, esp. by student(s) for presentation of results at specified time'. A process is a 'course of action, proceeding, especially series of operations in manufacturing or some other operation.'

The two notions, project and process, are similar. The key distinction in the context of moving from vision to results is that the project is effectively a plan which specifies elements and objectives, cost requirements and time-scales. It has a clear beginning, elements and an end. Project management is the activity of initiating, progressing, monitoring and evaluating a task. Process management is the activity of identifying and monitoring the process or course of action (in this context) of some desired change. Project management concentrates on the 'what, who and when' of a change. Process management usually focuses more on *how* the change will be accomplished.

The skill of project management, which is this chapter's main concern, is becoming increasingly recognized as a core management skill. Many employee development opportunities are created in the course of projects. Thus the employee development practitioner needs to achieve competence in the approach itself and competence in using project management to develop individuals and teams.

The essentials of project management

Before considering the development of project management skills it will be helpful to consider some of the essential requirements of a project. These briefly are:

Identifying clear objectives   This initial stage requires clarity in the organization's vision and consequent strategic plan. Each sub-unit which is approached as a project needs to have its objectives specified in clear, unambiguous language which can be understood by a variety of project members.

Setting clear deadlines, target dates and milestones   These are essential to aid communication and in conjunction with the quality of resources available can help to clarify the work load estimated.

Preparing a project plan   This should identify the component parts of the plan with sub-objectives and time-scales. 'Walking through' the plan of the process can help to improve communications and commitment.

Project planning techniques   There are numerous approaches to planning. In the context of projects it is usually necessary to identify what steps are required, how long they will require, what resources are involved and how they interconnect. Basic approaches such as Gantt charts can be used to outline the elements of the project in terms of logical steps required. These are then displayed on a time planner showing duration of each step and when it needs to start and finish. This approach can be simple and use paper and pencil methods or relatively complex and use computer generated data.

A further level of complexity is the use of Programme Evaluation and Review Techniques (PERT), Critical Path Analysis (CPA) or Critical Path Management (CPM). These approaches use a schematic diagram to show the relationship of each step or stage and the time needed. For example, to run a training event the following steps may be necessary:

A Identify need   (5)
B Design programme   (2)
C Develop materials   (3)
D Advertise programme   (10)
E Present programme   (1)
F Evaluate   (2)

If each component requires the number of days shown in brackets, a simple way of charting this might be as described in Figure 6.1.

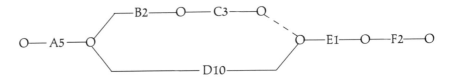

Figure 6.1   *Schematic diagram for running a training event*

The chart shows that stage D could be a bottleneck. Efforts to shorten this phase or to begin it earlier would clearly shorten the overall time-scale. In this sense, it is critical. It might be possible to shorten it, for example, by having a waiting list for the training event or by piloting the event using an approach that shortens the advertising phase.

In complex networks a computer can be used to monitor constantly critical time elapsed and thus track the 'critical path', whether it is being achieved and if the completion date is likely to be met.

It is suggested that if the reader needs to acquire operational competence in project management, the disk on project management referred to later might be helpful as also would a specialized text in this area.

Teamwork   An essential requirement for successful project management is the creation of strong teams. These may need to be function-specific, multi-disciplinary, cross-functional, integrated or some combination of these. It is essential to have the appropriate skill mix, e.g. ideas people and implementers or doers and for the team to understand how to work together effectively.

Adequate resources   The project team will need suitable resources in terms of an adequate budget, suitable environment and clear authorization procedures.

Decisive leadership and management   The main players in the project need to understand the vision and strategy of the organization and to give suitable direction and enthusiasm to the project.

Monitoring progress A key aspect of project management is the continuous comparison of actual results and outcomes with clearly stated plans. Where the project is complex, computer processing might be helpful in managing the large quantity of dynamic data generated. Regular monthly meetings to review progress and update objectives and estimated plans are a useful means of keeping in control. Perhaps the most common results of poor project management are uncontrolled cost over-runs and slippage in achieving deadlines. The Channel Tunnel provided an interesting example of how difficult project management can be. Even the *QE2* was the victim of project management syndrome when she was allowed to sail from Southampton with work associated with a refit incomplete. The monitoring of progress for some projects can be very public.

Clear communications The achievement of the many complex elements described depends to an important extent on good communications. These need to be timely, simple, clear, unambiguous, widely available to those involved and 'signed-off' by the parties involved.

Contingency planning Everything does not always go well. It can be sensible to develop contingency plans that can be implemented as soon as any substantial problem is identified. Planning techniques will often generate some of this information as plans and networks will be based on alternative systems and methods. PERT networks and careful monitoring of critical events can be particularly useful in the process of contingency planning.

Close down procedure A good project plan should include some final closing down procedure to bring the project to an end. 'Opening' ceremonies are an example of this in projects such as motorways, tunnels and buildings. It is a good discipline to include a 'post-implementation review' to learn any lessons from the conduct of the project and the successes or difficulties experienced.

This summary of the essentials of project management has been included as the project management process is absolutely key in moving from strategy to implementation. Many of the elements are essential components of good management. They can be learned and developed and this aspect will be dealt with next.

Developing project management skills

Demand for skill development in this area has steadily increased in the 1990s. Project management is no longer the domain of the civil engineer. As organizations struggle to introduce new products, organization roles and competitive values, the need to specify clearly and deliver focused change actions has accelerated.

This section outlines some of the development values and content for a typical one-day seminar for managers and professionals. It is based on a seminar produced in response to a request from a senior marketing director to improve the project management skills of several hundred young managers and professionals. The key issues were:

1 *Understanding basic project management techniques*   This was covered by using a CBT programme produced by Maxim Training Systems and titled Project Management. This disk introduced techniques such as Gantt charts, PERT and CPM and was interactive, using questions to check understanding. Study of this material was a prerequisite for attending the course. A few questions about it at the start of the first seminar soon prompted the 'grapevine' to communicate the seriousness of the prerequisite. It was never necessary to send anyone away from the seminar for lack of preparation. The programme needed about four hours study and was the only 'technical' input on techniques.

2 *Using real material*   Several case studies were used. All were based on actual tasks carried out during the three months before the seminar series commenced. They used actual material and paperwork that would be familiar to most of the participants.

3 *Syndicate work*   The course design and values were based on the use of 'live' material and issues with at least a third of the time allocated to group work. An example would be to consider examples of actual departmental project briefs in groups of six and to:
(a) review the clarity of the objectives in terms of content;
(b) produce alternative or replacement statements of objectives which make them clearer and more precise.

4 *Skill development*   Sessions were used to provide input and personal development on topics such as objective setting, planning processes and techniques, project control and team development. The emphasis was on clarity, simplicity and rigour. Groups were encouraged to review existing materials critically and then to produce objectives and plans which could stand up to the same scrutiny. The main objective was to develop a better understanding of scientific rigour and measurement whilst exploring the way in which team skills can enhance achievement.

5 *Action plans*   Individuals and working groups were encouraged to work on forthcoming, live projects. Action plans were focused in support groups and peer discussion after the programme.

6 *Evaluation*   The key evaluation was the rapid growth in demand for the course by departmental heads who approached the Training Director directly to arrange seminars for 20 participants at a time. The overall objectives of the programme were to:
(a) improve the quality of management planning and control on all new projects by the specified target audience of managers and professionals;
(b) develop a programme and content which could be used more widely in the organization;

(c) develop a common language, understanding and approach to the specification and control of projects.

The actual programme was used in the configuration displayed in Figure 6.2:

Pre-work

Complete interactive computer-based programme designed to provide an overview of project management techniques and processes.

One-day project management workshop

9.00–10.30	Introduction and overview with review of 'pre-work' assignment • Vision, strategy and identifying precise targets. • Syndicate exercise on clarifying objectives for actual projects. • Review of exercise.
10.30–10.45	Coffee
10.45–12.30	The essentials and importance of planning. • Processes and techniques of planning. • Practical task: Developing a project plan in groups. • Review of task.
12.30–13.30	Lunch
13.30–15.00	The essentials and importance of control • How to analyse variances. • Informal and formal control methods (management by walk-about). • Time management and contingency planning (The effects of optimism and pessimism). • Group exercise and review of control methods available.
15.00–15.15	Tea
15.55–17.00	Managing project teams • Building shared vision. • Selecting and developing effective teams. • Leadership styles. • Group exercise—identify requirements for effective teamwork. • Review exercise. • Preparation of individual action plans.
17.00–17.15	Review of workshop • The models used—objectives, planning, controlling team management. • Summarize outcome of group work. • Simplicity + rigour = well managed projects.

Figure 6.2 *Programme for one-day project management workshop*

Process management

This chapter has concentrated on the basic skills of project management. These skills are important to all line and employee development managers, especially in times of change. Project management as described has been concerned primarily with defining tasks and how they stem from vision and fit in with an organization's strategy. Particular attention has been given to clearly identifying resources required and how to identify programme timing requirements; in short, the delivery of the correct project outcome at the correct time and within budget.

Process management is a more recent development and concerns the management of *how* the change project is delivered. By monitoring the 'how', it can often be possible to modify the implementation of a project especially in areas such as inter-functional cooperation and integration. Process management is usually undertaken by a senior manager or management team. The person responsible sometimes works closely with an external change consultant who can provide a seemingly independent view of how the change process is progressing. He/she will usually introduce models or concepts of change management and work with the senior management in the planning and implementation of each phase of the change project. It is usual to hold frequent review meetings with the internal 'change agent(s)' or 'facilitator(s)' to pre-plan and review each phase. The executive management will be involved in a less frequent review process possibly monthly at an executive board meeting.

The skills involved in process management require a strategic perspective and a good knowledge and experience of organizational change and dynamics. This type of process management has generic similarities with the process consultation work of Ed Schein. This was widely used with small groups in the 1970s. Its purpose was (and is) to help the group deal more effectively with how it carries out the task. Clearly, when used for a large-scale project such as making explicit the desired values of a multi-national organization and getting commitment to them, the process may be very complex and demanding.

Process management involves directly the politics, personal aspirations, inter-personal relationships, power bases and powerful individuals concerned in change projects. As such, it needs to be exercised with care. The external agent may bring personal values to the process which may be damaging either to the accomplishment of the project task or to the individuals involved. It is not uncommon for the personnel responsible for process management to change when a senior executive or sponsor moves on.

Elements of process planning and review are invaluable skills for individual managers. Explicit agreement on how the group will function, for example who will go out to seek information and who will monitor progress in detail, can be very helpful.

The classic action learning approach of reviewing what has been learned at each meeting and sharing learning at the start of the next meeting can considerably enhance the performance of groups and individuals. By addressing *how* the project/change process is carried out employee development and line managers can achieve clear improvements also in terms of *what* is being done, *who* will do what and *when* the component parts can be delivered.

Ideally, a well-designed and controlled project with clear objectives and roles coupled with a process designed to review continuously how it is being delivered will lead to professional and timely accomplishment of projects.

Summary

This chapter has described some of the basic requirements for success in undertaking project management. The use of projects has been identified as one of the major developments in approaches to managing in the 1990s. It has been argued that when moving from the relatively abstract though essential concepts of vision and mission, the effective use of projects is usually essential to the achievement of desired results.

The main issues concerned in project and process management were identified as:

- The need for strong links with the organization's vision and strategy.
- The importance of identifying clear objectives.
- The process of planning and some of the techniques used in project management.
- The use of targets and deadlines.
- Resourcing, budgeting and monitoring progress.
- Controlling the project.
- Team work including team roles, selection and development of team players and how to manage and lead effective teams.
- Anticipating problems and taking corrective action.
- Communicating clearly to all those involved.
- Identifying process issues and managing *how* projects or changes are implemented.

The design of a programme to develop project management skills was considered. Key issues in design were identified and a possible programme based on one delivered to a large number of managers and marketing professionals was described.

Finally issues specific to process management were described.

What you can do

1 Review a project which you have been involved in and
   (a) critically review the clarity of the objectives (or terms of reference);

(b) write alternative statements which will make the objectives clearer and more meaningful.

2 Prepare an outline project plan for an activity of your choice. Identify objectives, duration, sequence and the critical path to achieve success in the desired time-scale.

3 Identify how you actually controlled progress on two activities of your choice. Identify whether you were optimistic, pessimistic or realistic about how long the tasks should take.

4 Review items 1–3 and identify which skill areas you need to develop personally to improve your project management skills.

5 Prepare a personal development plan in the form of a project plan to develop your skills as identified in 4.

Recommended reading

Haynes, M.E., 1990 *Project Management*, Kogan Page.

PART TWO

Implementing employee development in the organization

7 Getting specific: identifying the training needed

Identifying what has to be done to improve performance is absolutely central to success in employee development. This chapter describes widely used methods of identifying needs and will highlight the following methods or approaches to analysis.

- Manpower analysis and planning to identify the quantities of skills required.
- Conventional approaches to *identifying training needs* (ITN) for current jobs.
- The use of techniques such as *strengths/weaknesses, opportunities/ threats analysis* (SWOT) and *repertory grid* to pinpoint specific needs.
- The prospectus method or the use of the table d'hôte menu.
- The identification of competencies and the use of disaggregation to specify *national vocational qualifications* (NVQ) and occupational standards.
- Identifying needs through performance management approaches.
- Identifying training needs through the implementation of corporate mission, strategic plans, e.g. customer service, Total Quality.
- Identifying training needs through the analysis of project programmes and plans.
- The use of performance appraisal to identify individual needs.
- The use of assessment and development centres to identify potential and thus development needs.
- The place of motivation and motivated abilities in identifying needs.

The key considerations when setting up or taking over the management of an existing employee development function or a role within such a function are:

1 What has been done already and how well is it regarded by the function's customers? In many situations what is done may be the result of years of analysis and can often constitute 80 per cent of the volume of employee development to be delivered in the short term. The key question may not be what has to be done, since the answer may already be there. The question may be how fast the

organization needs to modernize what it has or to substitute other delivery systems, e.g. open learning/distance learning for formal courses.

2 How much needs to be done? The quantity of training that needs to be done is determined partly by the business needs and partly by the existing skills in an organization and any skill shortfall. The process of manpower analysis and planning is the way these quantities can be determined. An example will illustrate. An airline may decide to expand its fleet by 10 Boeing 737 aircraft. It may need 7 crews per aircraft and thus would need an additional 70 captains and 70 first officers. Its training need may be high or relatively insignificant. It would have within its fleet a ready provision of pilots with the ability to be captains. It may be using air crew to work in cabin services as stewards/stewardesses because of an earlier over-provision. Manpower planning will identify the potential numbers from business plans but not necessarily the training or development need.

3 What skills are required for current jobs? An organization that is moving from a traditional banking approach (in some cases simply paying in savings) to selling insurance policies or a subsidized educational establishment moving to a self-funding polytechnic will need new skills it may not already have; thus the skills for present-day tasks and thence the training needed will change significantly.

4 The question of what skills may be required for the future can be even more demanding, combining the need to understand the organization's vision and converting it into skills or competences that may not exist. The move from mechanical and electrical engineering maintenance to the need for automation, electronic, electrical and mechanical maintenance skills, with a lead time of three years to produce individuals with this range of skills, is a classic example.

5 A consideration of individual or learner-centred needs will encompass the learning needs of groups and individuals and focus on ways of discovering individuals' needs through appraisal systems and approaches that change the focus of identifying training needs from the organization to the individual. These might include learning resource centres, where individuals decide what they want to learn and simply book time on using a computer-based programme, or open learning approaches where the individual selects some learning method and uses it. A traditional library is perhaps the most common form of approach based on learner needs.

Manpower planning

This aspect of employee development focuses on the numbers of staff likely to be employed and the supply of staff in the marketplace. It is concerned with the population that has to be developed rather than how to develop them, but is absolutely central to identifying needs.

Manpower planning, or identifying the size and shape of the development task, can be done at the micro-level and concentrate on specific occupations such as pilots or specific industries such as the travel industry. It may take a macro-view and produce predictions for a country or even a continent, such as Europe. An outstanding example of a focused study for a commercial area was the Institute of Manpower Studies work published under the title *Create or Abdicate* and produced by Professor Amin Rajan with Julie Fryatt. This work focused on the City of London and analysed the demand and supply of skills for the five years between 1987 and 1992. It then posed questions and made recommendations on a strategic approach to human resource development. Its basic approach was:

- identifying occupational categories within areas such as insurance, banking, securities dealing;
- analysing employment trends and demand forecasts;
- identifying possible labour supply from school leavers, women working and returning, and graduates and the general working population;
- reviewing possible strategic actions.

By then analysing alternative scenarios and creating a debate in the City, this work is a classic model of how to undertake the task in-company.

To take a specific simplified example to illustrate the process: a bank that wishes to appoint a senior lending officer for commercial loans in each branch would need to go through the following process.

1 Define the role of commercial lending officer within the bank's commercial banking strategy.
2 Identify the skills and experience required.
3 Assess what skills could reasonably be expected on recruitment.
4 Design a training course for core skills and modular courses for selective needs.
5 Identify how many lending officers would be required over what period. (It will be assumed that 2000 are required in-post over the next 12 months and that 1500 will need core training; all will need a specialized module on avoiding bad debts in an economic downturn.)
6 The attrition rate or the labour turnover will also have to be established. If surveys of similar occupations in other banks, plus the bank's own experience, indicate a probable loss of 10 per cent over the year, then an additional 200 would need to be trained to ensure that, at the end of the year, 2000 are in-post and competent.

Thus, just by looking at the numbers involved and assuming courses designed for 15, the size of the need for core courses can be estimated as:

$$1500 + 200 \div 15 = 114 \text{ core courses}$$
$$2000 + 200 \div 15 = 147 \text{ module courses on bad debts}$$

By identifying occupations, gross estimates of this type can be made to reflect technology, economic trends, turnover including retirement, the impact of demography and likely skill shortages. Occupations can be studied in whatever categorization is appropriate. Some examples of categories are:

- directors
- managers
- craft workers
- technician engineers

- systems analysts
- training officers
- supervisors
- pilots

The question of quantity of skills required in occupations with long lead times for training, e.g. craftsmen, pilots, graduate trainees, can be demanding. The assumptions used are key and should be debated fully. Military pilots are a current case in point. The numbers were originally estimated to combat the possible Warsaw Pact threat. For a brief period these assumptions were made to look irrelevant by the unification of East and West Germany. Then Iraq caused a rethink of the assumptions.

The strategic response often adopted is to provide a broad base to as many entrants as possible and then to provide specialized modules as trainees get closer to taking up employment. Significant changes, such as the widespread use of automation in the automobile industry, can then be coped with more easily.

To achieve success in employee development one of the main skills is the ability to identify which occupations are key to the achievement of the business mission. By concentrating debate and analysis on these areas, the right strategic disposition of scarce resources can be made to ensure the organization is able to compete in the necessary areas.

Conventional approaches to identifying training needs

The identification of needs can range from the micro-analysis of very specific operator tasks, such as producing a microchip for an electronic component, through to how to drive a train or pilot a space shuttle. Complex processes such as managing a company or replacing a heart valve, or jobs such as technical author or bond dealer, all have to be analysed if they are to be taught. The essential process is to use some means of recording what is done so that it is possible to describe and replicate the knowledge and skill required. Methods of describing vary considerably. For example:

- A detailed explanation of how to light an oxy-acetylene welding torch would need to describe the gas supply and containers, identify the components of the torch and how they work, show how to turn on the oxygen and acetylene supply and how to ignite the flame. It would then be necessary to show the various conditions the flame might take and what it should look like and how to adjust this. Application to the metals to be welded would then have to be described and shown ... and so on.

- A study of the work of a technical author could be undertaken by analysing the inputs and outputs for the job, e.g. by studying a technical document produced and by interviewing various incumbents of the role and their managers to identify what skills have to be acquired for success.
- The success rate of first officers undertaking a captains' Command Course and the reasons for failure and success can be used to identify needs for entry to the Command Course.

All these approaches work on the notion that:

- A job can be described and defined.
- The ability and skills of a potential job holder can be identified and compared with the norm or with requirements and then any skill shortfall can be identified.
- The shortfall can be made good by the provision of knowledge or skill or the development of certain attitudes or behaviours.

They tend to regard the subject as rather inert and typically produce a training course aimed at the medium level, with remedial training for those who are significantly worse than the norm but who have to do the task. The basic logic is very appropriate to jobs that can be analysed and where the learning and behavioural change objectives can be specified clearly and unambiguously. The logic gets more tenuous as the job requirements become more complex and in the management area quite different approaches to identifying needs have been developed over the last decade. The process of identifying needs for future jobs or more senior jobs has tended to focus on identifying the competencies thought to be used by skilled exponents of the job in question. These competencies are then used to design assessment centres that seek to replicate them in exercises, activities such as leaderless groups, and the use of in-tray exercises and psychometric tests, so that the level of competence and potential in specific areas can be assessed. Training and development needs are then specified by identifying the shortfall on specific skills, e.g. planning skills or interpersonal skills.

A further approach that is widely used is to identify commonly occurring needs and then to offer courses on the basic assumption that individuals will themselves identify their training needs and ensure they are relevant. All or part of the course may be relevant as a training need. An example might be aimed at the non-specialist as well as the personnel professional and could cover:

- The role of personnel management
- The employee relations scene
- Job analysis

- Recruitment and selection
- Selection techniques and interviewing skills
- Manpower planning
- Management development
- Appraisal interviewing skills
- Employment law

This approach identifies a series of competencies that will have varying degrees of relevance to participants. One solution sometimes used is to group the skills and offer them in modules, e.g. management development and appraisal interviewing skills.

Alternative analytical techniques

There are many ways of analysing needs: observational techniques using precise time and distance measures, such as synthetic work measurement; observational techniques used in studies of supervisors and managers; highly specialized ways of investigating perception and psychological constructs, such as the repertory grid; means of analysing situations such as force field analysis; systematic ways of analysing business situations through a SWOT (strengths/weaknesses, opportunities/threats) analysis; the use of expert groups to identify the characteristics of good performance; and many others. In some respects all these approaches endeavour to be 'objective'; they describe the situation and make or record judgements on what is good or bad.

To give the flavour of these approaches, it will be useful to illustrate the range in the armoury for improving employee development. The effect of any of these approaches would be enhanced by using someone with experience and expertise in them.

SWOT

The SWOT approach involves a systematic analysis of the situation that can then be used to identify development needs. As an example, consider the case of low-volume, high-quality producer of a classic sports car in the £20 000 price bracket. An analysis might indicate:

Strengths: Good quality image and reputation for reliability. Loyal customer base who will continue to buy a virtually unchanged vehicle. Long order book makes production control straightforward and stability of design means few production changes. Low volume has permitted the retention of craft methods. Good second-hand value of product.

Weaknesses: Delivery times may lose new customers. Reliance on craft methods has limited the introduction of new technology. Pricing and competition limit unit profitability and overall profit is poor because of low volume. Purchasers tend to be middle-aged and market penetration in the under-35-year-old market is very poor.

Opportunities: Because of the attractiveness of the traditional design, the output could easily be doubled if automation were introduced and price could be increased by 10 per cent. An increase of 30 per cent per annum over the next five years would be achievable. There is little competition in the market though the Japanese competition is giving exceptional value for money in this segment.

Threats: Essentially, that the younger market will commit itself to the readily available high-technology products in the absence of the availability of the British product. Poor maintenance organization and high interest rates will escalate tough trading conditions and could cause cash flow problems.

Training needs: In broad terms, a decision to introduce a strategic plan of 30 per cent per annum growth to pursue a mission of being the highest-volume quality two-seater sports car in the under £30 000 market would require:

- Improved ability in the marketing and finance areas;
- Up-graded production engineering skills to introduce and maintain automation;
- Re-skilling of craft workforce to work to more mass-production standards;
- Development of production assembly skills;
- Development of parts supply skills;
- Introduction of a more commercial approach by middle managers;
- Introduction of a technician engineer training scheme and retraining young specialist craftsmen.

Each of these areas would have to be considered against the business plan and projections to identify precise skills needed. An assessment of the skills of the workforce would then be required to identify the short and medium-term training needs.

A helpful way of analysing a complex situation is to use a two-axis diagram, as shown in Figure 7.1. Depicting clusters of strengths,

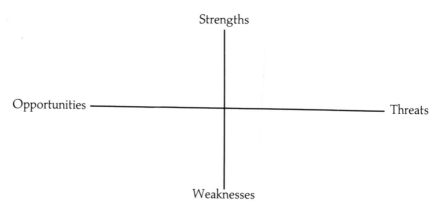

Figure 7.1   *A two-axis diagram to simplify a complex situation*

weaknesses, opportunities and threats will quickly identify the need for particular remedial action.

Items that are both weaknesses and threats, e.g. poor quality of young counter staff and inability to attract quality young entrants, would quickly highlight strategic weaknesses.

Repertory grid   A quite different approach is the use of the repertory grid. This technique seeks to identify the constructs that people have in their minds to describe certain situations. An example would be a project to identify the key managerial characteristics required for the successful management of a travel company's retail branch. The following is the process in outline. Each manager interviewed would be asked to:

1   Select 10 managers that you know well.
2   Select three from this group.
3   Select two who differ from the third in some significant characteristic.
4   State that characteristic or construct.
5   Identify which choice, i.e. the two or the single manager, represents 'good' performance.
6   Select three new managers and repeat when process is exhausted for the first three.
7   These constructs can then be ranked to give some indication of relative importance.

Thus, it may be identified over a sample of 25 managers that their constructs for describing a good performer are:

● Ability to communicate
● Commitment to high-quality merchandizing
● Ability to keep a distance from individual staff—not 'one of the gang'

These constructs can then be used in interviews, appraisals or assessment centres or, as in this case, in development centres to identify individual and group training needs. In this example, examination of the data showed that no manager had, as a construct, the commitment to maximize profit. This construct was key to the company's mission statement at that time and was brought into very strong focus in the development workshop.

The methods described and many other proprietary approaches and conceptual models seek to identify specifically for organizations, groups or individuals what their needs are in order to move from the situation, position or skill where they start to some desired or normative standard of performance. A useful analogy is that of the à la carte menu from which a party of four might select four different starter dishes from a choice of ten. The provision of food to meet specific needs reflects the process of finding out what training or development should be available to meet needs. In many ways, open learning and CBT offer a pick-and-mix approach where the customer can choose from a wide range of popular sweets or programmes. To take the analogy a little further, there is an approach to identifying needs that is very similar to the table d'hôte. This will be considered next.

The prospectus or fixed menu approach

While the purist might argue that individuals are unique, with their own unique mix of learning styles, motivated drives, motor skill abilities and learning or even training needs, reality in meeting needs is somewhat different. You can always have a lobster, fresh from the sea, cooked to your specification and served at 7.45p.m. with a bottle of Sancerre—if you can pay for it. To provide 1000 canteen meals between 6p.m. and 7p.m. is quite a different proposition, especially if the per head cost must not exceed £3.15.

A significant proportion of training provided is in fact channelled through courses of two to three or five days duration where cost and bedroom occupancy rates may demand as much attention as behavioural performance objectives. The approach described as 'fixed menu' is the one used in most management colleges and polytechnics and in the large-scale operations carried out in hotels by companies or organizations offering commercial courses. Many advocates of what they see as more enlightened approaches will criticize the 'shotgun' approach and advocate the 'rifle' or individual approach to identifying needs. However, there is little doubt that probably half of all training provided in the UK is off-the-peg and the approach demands some closer examination.

The essential process is to identify blocks of skill that will attract a significant audience and to analyse and/or identify from experience the content and likely audience for specific activities. The objectives of the course are specified so that attendees may select what is appropriate, either themselves or more usually in conjunction with their supervisor or manager. It is not unknown for the course content to reflect the predilections of the course tutors available—e.g. the amount of time spent on case studies, role plays or video feedback is usually influenced by the institution's experience.

To give some size and shape to the menu and the range of choice the following might be typical.

A residential college

1 Range of one- to two-week courses on management development designed to be interlinked and to cover the on-appointment to manager stage, the middle manager stage and the senior management level (which might be two to four weeks in duration). All managers, whether from retail, computer operations, sales, investment or property services, attend the same course.

2 Range of technical courses, typically 8/12 in number, all starting on

Sunday and finishing on Friday. In a bank they would cover such topics as:

- An introduction to commercial business
- The role of the securities specialist
- The practice of banking

3 Range of management courses, primarily of one week, covering such topics as:
  - The role of the manager
  - Effective communications
  - Staff development

4 Marketing and sales, again all five-day courses, on:
  - Managing a selling operation
  - Approach to marketing, market research and product development

5 Courses specific to current needs that may be three or five days:
  - Successful project management
  - Running the bank as a profit centre.

An independent management college/ university

1 General management programmes—as residential college.
2 Human resource management programmes—one-week courses covering such items as:
  - Managing change
  - Performance management
  - Leadership
  - Interviewing and selection
3 Marketing and sales—basically similar to residential college programme but longer and with a more senior target population.
4 Finance—one-week course on such topics as basic finance for non-financial managers, and finance for financial directors.
5 Specific/specialized programmes—these will again be five-day courses mainly on such topics as project management, information technology and Total Quality. Essentially the same as in specific in-company residential centres but longer.

The independent management college/university will also make a feature of its undergraduate work, research and Master of Business Administration (MBA) programmes. In some ways this is comparable to the table d'hôte menu in a restaurant with a Michelin star. Excellent, as long as the menu is to your taste and the food agrees with you.

A specialist training course organization

The approach of these organizations is varied. One might specialize in two- or three-day non-residential courses in city centres and offer a range of courses for practitioners and junior managerial staff spanning the following types of activity:

- Training officers
  —Instructional techniques
  —Identifying training needs

—Evaluation of training
- Personnel officers
  —Compensation and benefits
  —Recruitment and selection
  —An overview of training

The skill in this approach to identifying training needs is to combine analysis and learning event design and delivery with marketing. The package is then put together in units of one, two or three days or one, two or four weeks and targeted at specific audiences. Market forces determine what dishes remain on the menu. The content, or most of it, will be relevant to most of those attending; and, it is argued, those attending events with participants from a number of companies and organizations will gain greatly from other course participants.

This approach has been described in some detail because it is so widely used and in many managers' minds the product it projects is closely related to the whole sphere of employee development. For some managers development means five-day courses.

Off-the-shelf courses can be tailored more closely to the needs of specific organizations and it is reasonably common for college tutors to become familiar with specific organizations or industrial sectors (e.g. banking and finance). In any menu-driven approach to analysis the meeting of needs must necessarily be rather approximate and individual relevance has to be traded off against cost per head. In this it is not dissimilar to the dilemma facing our chef in deciding the balance between à la carte and table d'hôte.

Competency approaches to identifying training needs

Much of what was described in the previous sections on identifying training needs and SWOT or repertory grid and similar approaches had its roots in the 1960s. The competency approach is perhaps more of a 1980s phenomenon. Its roots were in a major project on management training undertaken by the American Management Association in 1979/80 through McBer and Company, a consultancy headed by David McClellend. It identified a generic competency model and its uniqueness was essentially that it developed its description of competencies by studying managers who were outstanding performers when compared with the standards of performance in their own job. This focus can be contrasted with approaches that develop competencies from theory, expert opinion, job analysis or some form of disaggregation from an overall purpose statement.

The approach was written up in a book called *The Competent Manager* by Richard E. Boyatzis, president and chief executive of McBer and Company, which was published in 1982. The importance of the competency model in the United Kingdom lies in the fact that since the mid 1980s its basic conceptual approach has been adapted by the Management Charter Institute and the Training Agency is using a modified version to define competencies for national vocational qualifications. Through industry and sector lead bodies, these NVQs will form the bedrock of the vocational education system for the next several decades. To give a flavour of the approach, Boyatzis identified the job competence assessment method as a five-step process:

1 Identification of criteria measure—which is simply choosing a suitable measure of job performance.
2 Job element analysis—this involves identifying a list of characteristics that are seen as leading to effective or superior performance. These are then weighted for importance by the managers, studied and grouped into clusters of similar activities, such as directing subordinates or leadership. (This process has marked similarities with the repertory grid approach but uses different methodology.)
3 Behavioural event interviews—these identify a detailed description of a number of critical incidents on the job and record the interviewee's behaviour, thoughts and feelings. This is then produced as a typescript and coded for various characteristics or competencies.
4 Tests and measures—these are used to test specific competencies identified and to relate results to the job-performance criteria. The competencies that are validated for superior performance are listed.
5 Competency model—relationships between competencies and job performance are determined to produce a validated competency model. Once the competency model has been established it is necessary to assess which competencies need to be developed.

The overall process can be summarized as follows:

- Identify and describe the competencies needed for successful completion of a task.
- Create an understanding of the competency by producing understandable and testable descriptions of criteria for performance.
- Produce means of assessing whether the competency can be demonstrated at a satisfactory level.
- Experiment with the use of the competency to demonstrate acquisition of basic skill, e.g. practising different approaches to a golf swing.
- Practice using the competency, e.g. once the precise grip and swing have been identified, modify previous behaviour such that the current competency can be used consistently.
- Apply the competency to the job—once the level of competence has been maintained consistently it can be applied to real-life performance.

Advocates of this means of identifying needs claim it makes a major step forward by identifying the competencies of successful practitioners and then providing the means to test the current level of performance of aspiring practitioners. Thus individual plans can be developed. It is thus much more precise than the earlier methods so long as individual delivery systems to meet needs are available. It is rather like identifying the 20 most popular ingredients to ensure a successful menu and then offering the choice of combinations of these in an à la carte menu. To become totally competent as a diner you would have to demonstrate the ability to enjoy all the combinations on the menu. It does depend on the identification of the correct 20 ingredients and on ensuring that nothing is missed in the areas of 'art', e.g. the way the chef uses the highest-grade olive oil to cook the meat.

While it might be seen as an improvement on previous approaches, the competency approach is clearly being interpreted at the 'management is a science' end of the spectrum. There has been a significant amount of disquiet as to whether the 'art' or intuitive or holistic end of the spectrum is sufficiently represented. The competence approach could be seen as inflexible and overly analytical. It describes competencies in a very jargon-based language using prescribed formats. Assessment of whether an individual can demonstrate competence is then made against the prescribed performance standard format. The approach adds little to our knowledge of how to develop individuals. The mechanistic view of performance it takes and the hoops individuals have to go through to 'demonstrate' their competence at various levels takes little account of the situation-specific nature of many jobs. Indeed, the concept gives little recognition to the way in which most performance standards at senior level are as much a function of the personality and brain preferences of the individual as any predetermined competencies requirement.

The development aspects of the competence approach are far from clearly defined. Delivery systems for development will probably need just as much attention in the future as that so far devoted to defining job competencies. It is interesting to observe that the centralist approach to definition of competencies has occurred at the same time as the focus for development is moving more and more towards the individual. In many senses the jury is still out on the competency approach. It is likely, in the words so often used by Reg Revans, that the approach is necessary but not sufficient.

Performance management systems

Performance management systems (PMS) is another relatively recent approach that has been used closely with approaches to performance-related pay. The basic approach is to identify, define and promote the use of best management practices and by defining roles and performance standards to enable the accurate monitoring of performance. This clearly provides a means of appraising performance and directly relating performance to pay.

The essence of the approach is to use a powerful statistical/mathematical computer programme to make the subjective data as objective as possible. The process is, first, to identify the performance areas that are key to success. For example, a bank may use the following areas:

1 Achievement of business targets
- Commercial lending targets
- Fee and insurance commission income
- Volume of output
- Meeting deadlines

2 Performance areas for management practices
- Managing and motivating staff
- Planning and organization
- Judgement and decision making
- Marketing and business development
- Providing customer service

Each area would be further broken down into 8–12 managerial practices with specific objective measures and standards that would then be reviewed periodically. A practical example of this breakdown, for 'Managing and motivating staff', is as follows:

(a) Review job roles and organization and delegate specific accountabilities to staff that are precise, understandable and measurable.
(b) Monitor business performance weekly and review with all key staff monthly.
(c) Encourage all staff to use their own initiative and create an environment where mistakes are used to learn from and are not an issue to be feared.
(d) Assess individual training needs quarterly and identify and implement individual training plans.

3 Self-development
- Determine the incumbent's commitment to and achievements in his/her own self-development.

4 Overall performance level
- This is determined by an agreed formula which weights performance in each area to produce an overall evaluation or score.

Each area is assessed against a numerical rating by both the immediate boss (direct evaluation) and the 'grandfather' (indirect evaluation). The types of scale used are:

1 Achievement of business targets
(see Figure 7.2.)

Target	Not Achieved	Partially Achieved	Achieved		Exceeded
e.g. Lending	1	2	3	4	5

Figure 7.2 *Business target achievement*

2 Performance areas for management practices
(see Figure 7.3.)

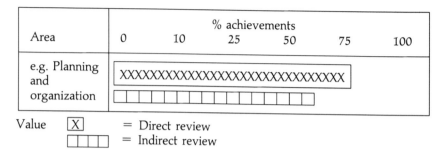

Figure 7.3 *Performance areas for management and self-development practices*

3 Self-development
The same evaluation scoring method can be used for self-development as for managerial practice (see Figure 7.3).

4 The overall performance level score
This is computed from these various ratings.

The approach allows for identifying needs at several levels. To illustrate, an individual may achieve an overall performance level of 50 per cent from the direct review and 60 per cent from the indirect review. The self-development might be at the 40 per cent level on both evaluations. The business results could be a mixture of achieved and partially achieved ratings. The latter would indicate areas of weakness that might reflect difficult business conditions or a lack of skill or application on the part of the manager. The effect of special circumstances can be incorporated by rating the circumstances from 1 to 5, with 1 being especially favourable circumstances, e.g. low interest rates, and 5 being very difficult circumstances, e.g. high interest rates with recession locally.

Thus a score of 1 for business conditions with a partial achievement rating would begin to indicate the need for action. This could be a training need. A detailed analysis of the managerial practice areas, which might show for example a rating of 50 per cent for commitment and energy but only 10 per cent for planning and organization, would start to flag very clearly a training need.

Thus the PMS method, which is certainly a very numerically sophisticated approach to performance appraisal, can be used to identify individual needs in a fairly precise way. It has definite similarities with the competency approach. The creation of a computerized data base, that in reality might apply to several thousand staff, offers the possibility of very detailed and sophisticated analysis, which could be fed directly into a training plan for the organization. For example, a profile could be identified for decision making as follows:

	Average profile %
Senior branch managers	75
Branch managers	25
Assistant managers	50
Senior supervisors	50
Securities clerks	90

If the organization employed say, 2000 branch managers, it would be surprising if decision-making training was not required for at least 1000 of them in some 50-plus courses, or one a week if traditional course-based approaches are used for the next year. A close eye on the performance ratings next year should indicate a significant improvement for the 25 per cent average percentage profile for branch managers or an urgent investigation would be necessary for this area of competence.

This approach is not yet being fully exploited and, like the competency approach, it clearly lies at the objective or scientific end of the spectrum. However, it does offer a useful way to define and measure the overall skills required and changes in culture and organization. It is built on face-to-face feedback and creates a felt-fair attitude towards performance review and payment for performance. It is reasonably costly to introduce but it can be argued that the saving in time usually spent on conventional appraisal, together with the potential improvements in motivation and direction, considerably outweighs the up-front costs and computer provision.

Identifying training needs directly from the corporate mission and strategic plans

One further method of identifying training needs is the direct identification of a need by senior managers in support of their strategic vision. One of the best-known examples was the drive for customer service initiated by British Airways. The need for delivery mechanisms to ensure the achievement of major changes in the way staff regarded the customers and behaved towards them was clear. The key features of the 'Putting People First' programme that was chosen to meet this need were the concentration on self-understanding, on the basis that staff need to understand themselves to serve others, the high degree of theatre and professionalism incorporated in the presentation, the mixed composition of the audiences which integrated air crew and ground crew, pilots and stewards, and the very overt support of the programme by Sir Colin Marshall and his management team. This particular approach, though widely written about and admired, is comparatively rare in the UK. It illustrates very clearly the power of a clear mission allied to appropriate development approaches.

Identifying training needs through the analysis of project programmes and plans

One of the most noticeable results of the impact of change has been the proliferation of project groups to tackle major strategic issues. A derivative of this is the high demand for project management training described in Chapter 6.

The process follows a fairly clear pattern and has a direct impact on the creation and identification of training needs. To illustrate, a hypothetical example will be briefly outlined. It reflects the process that all major banks are experiencing.

Cost pressures and competition have created a strong inducement to remove all unnecessary administration from the high-street bank and to carry it out in less expensive out-of-town locations. A common solution is to centralize the administration in a convenient location. The telecommunications and information technology now available make this completely feasible. The task is then to group branches and link them to an administrative centre, to install the technology and create a new type of branch with minimal staff and sometimes banks of automatic cash and deposit machines. The new administrative centres have to be set up and the management of the whole process established. A project might have an objective as follows:

To convert all 2000 branches to new-style operation over a three-year period and establish 200 administrative centres in line with the implementation programme.

Some examples of the training needs would be:

1 To ensure that all senior branch managers, who are responsible for approximately 10 branches and one administration centre each, understand their role and how to manage a group of branches profitably.
2 To train all users of the new technology so that they can demonstrate competence at the time their branch is scheduled to be converted.
3 To ensure that all managers of the new administration centres are competent to manage the new role and technology.
4 To introduce sales training for all staff in new-style branches to ensure that maximum profit advantage is taken from streamlining the administration.
5 To ensure that all administrative staff with customer contact are able to maximize telephone sales opportunities.

These examples identify some of the needs that would have to be phased in with the project plan over the three years. It would clearly be of limited use to train in Year One those managers who would be taking over an administrative centre in Year Three. This approach to identifying needs demands that a representative of the employee development function is an integral part of the project team and can contribute to decisions about resourcing and timing so that skills are available when they are required. Many organizations are increasingly managed through projects and it is not uncommon in large organizations for them to work to two, three or even four-year time scales. Matching the flexible and demanding needs identified as a project unfolds with the prospectus, designed up to 18 months before its December courses are implemented, can present interesting challenges in achieving success in employee development.

The use of performance appraisal to identify training needs

Many organizations operate appraisal schemes that are designed to provide a platform for regular discussion on objectives, achievement, development needs, future career direction and potential. The typical scheme will identify areas where the appraisee has performed well and where improvement is necessary against agreed objectives.

Overall performance is typically rated on scales like this:

> A – Exceptional
> B – Above agreed standard
> C – Met standard in all major respects
> D – Approaching standard expected
> E – Below standard performance
> F – Unacceptable level of performance

Potential is explored by discussing the appraisee's readiness for promotion, e.g.

> Q = Qualified for immediate promotion
> WE = Qualified with experience within two years

There is usually a summary of any development needs and a record of any development provided during the year.

Analysis of the record of appraisal discussion provides a good source of data for identifying the needs and expectations for employee development. The appraisal will often record what the individual and his/her boss have identified as the specific needs for the job. It is not uncommon for the demand for specific training needs to exceed the supply to such a degree that a waiting list of two or three years might occur.

By simply listing all needs identified and grouping them, say for senior managers, middle managers, junior managers and so on, an accurate list of personal needs can be identified and programmed. In one piece of research I carried out, involving the analysis of 50 appraisal forms, the unfortunate conclusion was that individuals stood a greater chance of attending a course if it was not recommended than if it was. This was established by analysing actual attendance at all courses run during the year with recommendations made in the previous year's appraisal round.

Appraisal can also give indications of training needs for those with potential, particularly when appraisers are encouraged to identify what development needs exist to help the appraisees achieve their potential. Performance appraisal from the individual's perspective is covered in Chapter 12.

The use of assessment centres and development centres to identify potential and development needs

The assessment centre approach was initially developed to identify potential and was essentially a selection process. In the last decade it has been used increasingly for development and, as such, offers a potential approach to identifying development needs. The assessment rationale is as follows:

1 Identify successful performers of the jobs that are subject to the assessment.
2 Analyse what skills and characteristics they display.
3 Develop exercises and tests to assess these characteristics and identify the performance achieved in the exercise by high performers. Examples of the exercises are the Leaderless Group, In-Tray Exercise, 16PF Test or Myers–Briggs Type Indicator.
4 Run an assessment centre with trained assessors to observe and categorize the performance of individuals whose suitability is being assessed.
5 Provide feedback on performance to assessees.

The development workshop is an adaptation of the approach and is designed to give feedback and use the exercises to develop abilities during the workshop. A typical assessment or development workshop would last three or four days, and for assessment the ratio of assessor : assessee would be 1 : 4. For a development workshop a ratio of 1 : 2 or at most 1 : 3 is more usual and the process is used to identify specific individual needs. An example might be a general manager who was over-aggressive in meetings. The need was to learn how to control meetings using process skills. Discussion and preparation before the next two or three exercises, together with review, enabled the manager to practise timing and using group processes in order to get the agreement of the group relatively easily through skill rather than bluster.

Assessment centre methodology, coupled with the use of psychometric instruments can provide a powerful means of identifying individual training needs.

Motivational needs and training needs

The essential logic pursued so far works on the assumption that there is some definable level of skill or competence for a job or organization and that the existing level of skill of individuals can be identified and compared with the desired or necessary level. By comparing the two it is possible to identify training needs and design suitable training events, courses or experiences.

There is a school of thought that offers a different perspective. This argues that all human beings have things that they are motivated to do and that the skill lies in matching what has to be done by the organization with what the individual wants to do and is good at. In effect, rather than taking the job and role as a given to which the individual is matched, it looks for ways of finding jobs that will enable individuals to use their gifts. The main exponents of this approach are Art Miller, Founder and Chairman of People Management Inc., whose approach is SIMA (systems for identifying motivated abilities), Don Clifton, Chairman of SRI/Gallup, who as founder and CEO of Selection Research Inc. set up a company specializing in the selection and development of people, and John Cleaver, president of J.P. Cleaver Company. All three are Americans.

Each in his different way seeks to identify themes or motivational drives and use these either to predict and counsel on appropriate future actions or to match individuals to jobs. All offer powerful means of identifying development needs for the individual.

A challenge to conventional wisdom

This chapter has sought to capture the main strands of thought and practice in the identification of training needs. One approach that does not follow this pattern, or the motivational pattern briefly outlined above, is action learning as espoused by Reg Revans. It proceeds from different assumptions but is totally underpinned by scientific method and rigorous intellectual concepts. In essence it adopts the following principles:

1 Comrades-in-adversity working on real problems contribute their 'lived' experience to the solution of those problems.
2 Individuals learn only by questioning and taking responsible actions on problems that matter.
3 Ownership and sponsorship of real situations is essential to learning.
4 People work best in sets of six individuals meeting regularly and taking action on what is discussed.

The conceptual base is quite different in that it gives responsibility entirely to the learner and his/her comrades. All one needs to bring to the set is a real problem, integrity and a preparedness to change. The identification of need is intrinsic to the process. The only analysis it needs at the introductory stage is an acceptance of the need for individuals to grow and a belief in their ability to recognize their own problems.

It works, and on a large scale, but the analytics and controllers described in Chapter 3 on power and politics may find it hard to digest.

Summary

This chapter has concentrated on identifying what has to be done. It has reviewed various methods of identification and given examples of the mainstream approaches. As a counterpoint it has described some of the more recent developments and the place of motivational themes and action learning in the framework. The main approaches covered are:

- The identification of the quantities of skills required in the future to replace those who retire or leave the organization, to provide the skills to manage the organization in the future, to produce future products and services and to introduce and use new technology. This requires the use of environmental, strategic and manpower analysis and planning.
- The conventional approaches to determining training needs, which involve identifying the performance levels and skills necessary to undertake a task successfully, assessing the individual's or organization's current level of performance and deciding what skill, knowledge, attitude or experience needs to be provided to move from the lower to the upper level.
- The use of techniques such as strengths/weaknesses, opportunities/ threats analysis (SWOT) and the repertory grid.
- The prospectus or one-week course approach commonly used to package a group of skills that approximately match a market need and can be run economically and in an administratively tidy fashion.
- The identification of competencies based on the work of Boyatzis and the AMA, where performance standards and competency standards bring together the competencies displayed by successful performers, the job requirements and the ability of individuals.
- How performance management systems can be used to specify managerial and non-managerial work processes; the use of sophisticated quantitative and probability techniques to measure performance and identify performance shortfalls.
- The corporate mission and specific initiatives such as customer service programmes and Total Quality approaches and how they can lead directly to identifying development needs and the design of large-scale corporate development programmes.
- The use of project plans, which can provide fertile information on training and development needs; how a project plan can be analysed and the training and development needs identified and phased in with the project programme.
- Performance appraisal, a well-tried method of comparing actual performance with agreed performance objectives and standards. Through discussion between job holder and boss, with a review by the 'grandfather', realistic needs for development can be agreed and actions planned to meet them. An analysis of all the development needs identified provides an aggregate view from the job holders on what development they need.
- Assessment and development centres or workshops, which are used

to identify the characteristics of good performers and from this to design exercises, tasks and tests to determine how potential incumbents compare with the performance that successful job holders demonstrated on the exercises. Development workshops produce individual development plans both at the workshop and after it.

- Motivated themes approaches, which advocate that people will do best at tasks that let them use their gifts and gain satisfaction.
- Finally, action learning is described as an approach to identifying needs based on individuals with real problems and ownership working with their comrades-in-adversity to find solutions.

What you can do

1 Prepare a one-page summary of the business issues and development and training needs that face your organization. Quantify as far as possible.

2 Create opportunities to discuss with your peers and line management the priority and relevance of the needs identified. If possible, get a reaction from your chief executive and senior management.

3 Produce an inventory of the methods of analysing needs you are familiar with and have used. Which gave you most significant results and greatest satisfaction? Do you need to extend your range of skills in identifying training needs and, if so, how will you do it?

4 When identifying needs, do you identify performance standards linked to business results? Examine the three most important needs in the employee development area and identify three performance standards for each.

5 How much of your training is substantially the same as it was 12 months ago? (Describe it as a proportion to the nearest quarter, i.e. $\frac{1}{4}$, $\frac{1}{2}$, $\frac{3}{4}$ or all of it.) Can you satisfy yourself that the training needs this training is designed to satisfy have remained unchanged?

Recommended reading

Boyatzis, Richard E., 1982 *The Competent Manager*, John Wiley & Sons.

Lewis, A. and Marsh, W., 'The Development of Field Managers in the Prudential Assurance Company', *The Journal of Management Development*, Action Learning Special Issue Volume 6 No. 2, 1987, MCB University Press.

Rajan, Amin with Fryatt, J., 1988 *Create or Abdicate*, Witherby & Co. Ltd.

Training Agency, Qualifications in Training and Development—A Consultation Document 1990, Training & Development Lead Body.

8 Making the case for the money

*No one would remember the Good
Samaritan if he had only had good
intentions. He had money as well.*

Margaret Thatcher

This chapter will examine how to go about making a case for the money to develop and deliver an employee development plan. It will show how this process relates to strategy and identified needs and takes account of the power situation in competing for limited funds.

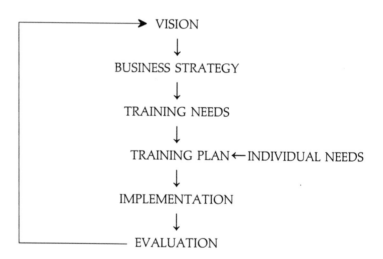

Figure 8.1   *The logic behind successful employee development*

In considering the logic for this book (Figure 8.1) it would have been possible to consider evaluation before making the case for the money and indeed Chapter 10 on organization could have preceded Chapter 7 on identifying needs. The most frequent situation for someone working through the process of making a success of employee development is one where the function already exists and is subject to an annual budgeting process. That is the logic that will be followed here. The most significant force in this situation is usually inertia and the considerable commitment that will exist in support of what has happened before. The case for the company training plan and hence for the money will usually have to be made in this environment. It will be necessary to modify the organization rather than create it from scratch. It will be rare that the route to success will permit the complete destruction of what existed.

The chapter concludes with a substantial example of how to present the case; before this it examines the financial aspects of training and development, various ratios and measures, the power of the customer, and how to present the case for scarce funds. The view of the line manager, the finance director and the individual employee are all explored. The hard discipline of a zero-based budget approach is explained, together with a thorough examination of ways to manage the budget. The overall aim is to get all the funds the organization can reasonably allocate to employee development and then to control expenditure accurately. Thus, by maximizing the contribution of employee development while minimizing the cost, a firm base will be created for current expenditure and that of future years.

Ensuring relevance

The essence of any successful sales approach is to enable the buyers to realize what they need to buy. Employee development has to be sold to the senior management of a company in competition with the demands of all the other 'spending' departments, such as marketing or information technology, and the insatiable demand of the 'producing' departments (such as retail sales and manufacturing) for staff to produce the product. People buy goods or services to meet what they feel are their needs and so the case-maker has to identify these needs. The process is as much about ability to feel the core values of the organization as analytical technique. Some examples follow.

Strategy and vision are essentially about the values and aspirations of the senior managers and can give valuable clues to what the executive group will buy. A strategy that flows from a vision of being the best in terms of profitability and quality of service over a sustained period will tend to support:

- Recruitment of high-calibre generalist graduates.
- Financial awareness training and development.
- The development of high-quality management talent.
- The introduction of Total Quality and customer service programmes.

However, a vision which is about the achievement of some high technology success such as the production of Concorde or the TGV train might put its emphasis on:

- Recruitment of the very best aeronautical or traction engineering graduates.
- Introduction of extensive technician-engineer programmes.

- Development of high-quality project management talent.
- CAD-CAM training for supervisory staff.

Thus the vision-mission-strategy process must be examined to identify the key components and specific areas which the case must address. Training and development needs have to be quantified in detail to produce a plan that can be converted into specific resources needed. The investment then has to be converted into training days so that the cost can be estimated. A simplified example might be:

1 Introduce customer-care programme over a six-month period.
2 Three-day event necessary.
3 5000 staff to attend in groups of 50.
4 100 events required × 3 days/event = 300 days.
5 Each event requires 2 tutors, so 600 tutor days required = 100 tutor days/month would require 5 tutors minimum in the team.
6 At a residential cost of £200 per delegate, and £1000 per day per tutor, this programme run residentially would cost £200 × 5000 = £1 million for hotel and food, plus £600 000 for tutors and, say, £400 000 for travel and administration: total £2 million. This might be expressed more palatably as £400 per head. Some shrewd planning could eliminate the residential requirement and bring the cost down to £200 per head. A programme design that reduced the tutor requirement to 1½ tutors and simplified administration could bring the cost down to £150 per head. To achieve a healthy customer-care workforce could cost less than providing coffee and tea for a year. Perhaps more significantly, consider whether it would be better to improve customer service at a cost of £750 000 or to replace 200 PCs with more up-to-date models.

These are the sorts of alternatives and decisions that the case has to address. The desired returns need to be expressed in terms that can be understood and need not necessarily or even usually be in terms of return on investment. In fact, employee development was an area in which one of the major car manufacturers did not require a return of x per cent on capital requested for expenditure. It was almost the sole exception.

Development as a financial investment

Mr Micawber created one of the most popular descriptions of finance when he said: 'Annual income twenty pounds, annual expenditure nineteen pounds, nineteen shillings and sixpence, result happiness. Annual income twenty pounds, annual expenditure twenty pounds and sixpence, result misery.' His grasp of cash flow and the basic principles is exemplary.

At a national level, Britain has consistently underinvested in education and training compared with our industrial and commercial competitors in the USA, Japan, West Germany and France. The case needs to be made in a context where as many as one in four of our sixteen-year-olds are not literate, where we cannot produce sufficient teachers and there is great ambivalence about the responsibility of employers for the school-to-work phase. Education and much training has been seen as a cost and is only just beginning to be regarded as a commercial weapon. In making the case for a larger share of the national expenditure, the spending Department for Education and Employment needs to generate close links with Trade and Industry and Defence. We cannot close the trade gap if we do not have both the capital and the skill to do so. To succeed in a national strategy we need to follow very similar disciplines to those facing any commercial or industrial state or private organization.

At the company level, the most straightforward marker for expenditure is percentage of payroll spent on employee development. The payroll element is declared annually in the annual report and accounts and is, therefore, readily available. The expenditure is less easy to define. The budget will typically include salaries and employment costs: e.g. pension contributions for staff; the running costs and rental/loss of interest for any training centre; the cost of buying/leasing technology; the rent for accommodation and training rooms; the cost of distance learning materials and other direct costs such as travel and hotels; the payment for educational courses such as MBA or actuarial professional training, together with any residual cost for employment training schemes; the support of instructors in the community and the use of technology. All these costs, excluding any allowance for the cost of trainees' time, would be in the order of 2–8 per cent of payroll.

It is a useful exercise to try to establish the typical percentage in the industry your organization works in. The proportion may vary because of the nature of the industry: e.g. because of the high cost of pilot training an airline might spend 6–8 per cent while a financial services organization might spend 3–4 per cent. Some high-technology companies dealing in information technology spend in the range of 8–10 per cent and defence institutions such as the Army could be argued to spend about 100 per cent in peace time, though decade-on-decade this is clearly not the case.

In making the case, the choice of which ratios to use and whether, for example, to include trainees' wage and salary costs or the net cost of training after corporation tax relief or the appreciation on the management training centre depends on the audience and its financial sophistication. It is possible to make a case on plausible assumptions that a £10 million training centre with the possibility of change of use to a hotel, in the right location, could pay for itself if sold at the right time in the next 25–30 years. For some training, it may be possible to include all sorts of offsets such as government grants for relocation or training schemes.

The following points should be considered when making the company case.

- What do competitors spend?
- Does the organization want to show a high expenditure or not?
- Is cost reduction an important consideration?
- Who has the power to increase the expenditure?

The business performance measures that are appropriate will vary from sector to sector. If at all possible the case should key into these and demonstrate the contributions of activities. Some measures might be:

- Increase market share from X to Y.
- Increase hospital bed occupancy to Y per cent.
- Decrease cost:income ratio to 60 per cent.
- Increase sales from six to eight insurance policies per week per sales-person.
- Ensure collection of Y per cent of poll tax.
- Run 95 per cent of trains to arrive within 5 minutes of due time.

Careful examination of the business plan and listening to senior managers who are oriented towards performance measurement will provide clues to what they are prepared to buy. The financial analysts will often supply useful insights into what return on investment (ROI) is acceptable and what size of investment might be sustainable in the short/medium term. Remember the power of inertia. An organization will need to be in real trouble to suggest cuts of 30–40 per cent in expenditure. A few are, but this situation will be quite clear. An increase in excess of 25 per cent is going to require substantial justification. In real terms, maintaining last year's expenditure and increasing it by up to 10 per cent should be feasible, if the business strategy requires it.

Some examples of specific performance criteria for employee development will illustrate how business issues can be expressed in measurable terms which can then form the basis for a thorough evaluation of the activity.

1 To ensure that for all senior branch managers:
   (a) they are evaluated as at least competent at appraisal;
   (b) the average overall assessment for the performance management system increases from 55 per cent to 60 per cent or more.
2 To contribute to the creation of a financial retailing culture that is sales-driven by providing sales management courses that increase sales on average by 20 per cent in the 3 months following the event.
3 To introduce a 'fast-track' approach for senior succession, so that:
   (a) the top 50 key jobs are identified and for at least 40 of these jobs there is a successor identified as ready to succeed immediately or within one year;
   (b) career management for the next level of 150 jobs is undertaken to agreed corporate standards.

4 To improve the cost effectiveness of training and development by:
   (a) reducing the cost per day of residential training from £120 to
       £100 by the end of next year;
   (b) developing more cost-effective means of delivering training and
       development and demonstrating the cost advantage over existing
       methods.

Performance criteria and standards are political as well as objective
issues and should be discussed to ensure that they reflect what the
powerful customers want to see happen.

The individual is also a party to what should go into the training plan
and be paid for out of operating expenses. Trade unions have taken an
increasing interest in the skill of their members—for many individuals
the biggest investment in their life after their house is the cost incurred
to create the skills they have. As employee development is increasingly
seen as central to economic performance the individual will be
increasingly represented in the planning process. Ford Motor Company
has agreed with the Transport and General Workers Union an approach
which allows grants of up to £200 per employee per year to gain extra
skills. The decision point on how the money is invested is thus moved
firmly towards the customer. Incidentally, in a company the size of
Ford, every 10 000 employed would have the capability to invest £2
million if the scheme was fully taken up. In the event, about one in five
of Ford's UK employees have taken advantage of the scheme. Some
10 000 grants were made to employees at a cost of £1.8 million to the
company in the first year. While approximately one in five applicants
wanted to use the grant to gain additional academic qualifications, some
28 per cent wanted to improve their foreign language skills. By far the
most popular language chosen was German—Ford has a major plant
near Cologne.

Another example of the potential influence of the individual will be the
use of technology and distance and open learning. The creation of
learning centres for computer-based training and interactive video and
the use of open learning at the Open University or Open College, will
require careful consideration of the individual's buying preferences and
will cause a shift in how expenditure is thought about. The purchase of
400 work stations or sufficient resources to service an internal learning-
resource borrowing programme are both capital decisions in the order
of £500 000. Their usage will depend very much on how well
individuals take to the approach.

Thus the probable motivation, commitment, choice and involvement of
individuals are key factors in making the case. There are few things
more embarrassing to the maker of the case than the creation of a white
elephant, and moving the decision making to the individual inevitably
increases the pressure on the person responsible for decisions in the
case to get it right.

The power of the customer

In employee development the customers have a key interest in the product because it can add directly to their competence and worth. Within companies or other organizations the worth of the activity is created in the minds of the users and their opinion is in many ways analogous to the vote. Empty conference rooms or learning resource centres or cancelled action learning groups are possible results of the customers voting with their feet. Strong competition in the marketplace has created a situation in many organizations where employee development activity has become a profit centre rather than a cost centre. The effects of decentralization have accelerated this and also impact very strongly on what case for finance is made and to whom. Each of these two issues merits further consideration.

Cost centre or profit centre?

There has been a significant shift in the UK in the perception of employee development and how we think about it. In the early 1980s, the training function, as it was then usually known, was seen as a cost. It did not sell its products internally or within organizations and did not generate income. Similarly, schools and universities were subvented from the central Exchequer essentially as a cost. This way of thinking did little to focus the training management on cost effectiveness and efficiency unless they were naturally so inclined. Interestingly, many of the commercial providers of development were set up as charities or trusts and were (and some still are) non profit-making.

The conceptual change happened fairly quickly, mainly in the first half of the 1980s. Employee development came to be regarded in a similar way to other commercial activities and the notion of a profit centre began to be applied, especially to discrete units such as management training residential centres. The move was towards minimizing costs and maximizing income. Thus users were charged specific prices for services and some, in theory at least, could turn to other suppliers if the cost:quality ratio of the product supplied was not considered satisfactory. This shift considerably sharpened the focus of those providing employee development. Many welcomed the opportunity to become more professional and commercial. Immediate impact was felt in the marketing of employee development, which became a key internal task. It was increasingly possible to compare cost and product with outside suppliers and indeed to follow some of the early pioneers and sell a proportion of the organization's resource to outside customers.

In reality, much of the 'profit' was actually a surplus or contribution and restrictions were put on the ability to sell products, e.g. to competitors. Thus comparative day-rates were produced to reflect a bundle of external costs for similar training and the performance of the unit could be compared with them. A considerable improvement in the degree of focus on producing products that customers were prepared to spend their sometimes hard-earned budgets on was achieved.

Centralized or decentralized organization

There was a considerable shift towards decentralization in the 1980s and this has meant essentially that the decision-making process is closer to where the manufacture or provision of a service takes place. Individual organizations have set up local or regional personnel functions under the umbrella control of a group personnel director. The decentralized unit will act on the provision of employee development for its own local needs. The advantages include greater relevance of the development strategy and more focused identification of needs. The disadvantages will include a tendency to be parochial, increased overall cost as work is duplicated and an increased likelihood of political factors having a disproportionate influence.

The need for integration and collaboration in a large organization can be very demanding and a strong integrative effort will be necessary for topics which are of corporate-wide importance, such as the development and career management of the top cadre of management.

Different perspectives

It was said earlier that what you see depends very much on where you stand. When it comes to consideration of the case for the money there are a number of views which have to be incorporated to gain in effect a consensus for the commitment of funds.

First, there is the line management view. Line managers usually focus on very specific outputs and their performance will be judged on the quantity and quality of what is produced. Employee development will be a means to an end to enable the achievement of outputs. Line managers will be concerned with the total human resource and how the skills at their disposal compare with what is needed. Their evaluation will be immediate and hard-edged, in terms of sales gained or lost, customers checked in or any one of a thousand measures of performance. Time on development will be time spent away from producing.

Line managers will not usually be concerned with how needs are met and the finer points of tutored courses or learner-centred methods will not usually interest them. They are decisions the employee development people are employed to get right. Cost will probably interest line managers, particularly if they have control of expenditure on development, which is often not the case. They will listen to what their staff say about what they receive and will base whether they give or withhold line support on their judgement of the professionalism of the employee development staff, their experience of what they have received before and their assessment of the relevance and likely delivery of what is being promised.

Second, the view of the finance directors and their function will have some weight. It will focus essentially on bottom-line impact. They will not usually focus on technical content. Concern will be with how the proposal compares with the previous year, how accurately the budget was estimated last year and whether there were any major variances, what the total trend for the budget is and whether there is any need for an across-the-board cut because the aggregate budget has increased too much. The financial decisions will be driven by next year's profit projections and share performance may be an issue if take over is a possibility.

The finance function may also drive the basic assumptions to be used in making the financial case. If they are working to a four per cent inflation rate, for example, it would be unwise to base the case on a different figure. There is considerable debate in the training press about evaluation and return on assets. While many of the concepts are intellectually interesting, the case-making and budget approach of most organizations is an altogether cruder affair. Many of the expenditure decisions are simply extrapolations of last year and the key is to try to anticipate all eventualities at the planning stage. One-off cases for funds during the financial year are rightly subject to much tougher scrutiny. Unless the chairman or chief executive wants a customer-care programme, you can expect a tough time from the finance director if you ask for £2 million in mid-year when the half-year results are £10 million down on projections.

Finally, the view of the individual merits consideration. The concept of development will vary in their minds, from being a right every employee should expect, to a bonus of a week's holiday at the organization's training centre in the country or in a hotel on the south coast. Dialogue to orchestrate individual views can enhance the case, and judicious use of newspapers, magazines, videos or other media can help to create a climate where expectations are raised. This can only support the provision of funds. Promoting the notion of the internal customer and enhancing the role of the individual in debating the case has been long overdue. Involvement by trade unions, especially in youth and technical training, can also help to ensure that the voice of the individual is given proper consideration both in generating the case and in deciding how much should be spent.

Using ratios

When producing a case for the money there are a number of rules of thumb which can be very helpful. Some of them are outlined below. They are intended very much as illustrative and you are encouraged to develop your own up-to-date and specific data for your own situation.

Cost per day of training
At its simplest this is:

$$\frac{\text{Total expenditure on training per annum}}{\text{Total number of days training per annum}}$$

This ratio gives a good guide to the trend in cost of training and indicates improvement in efficiency of delivery. In financial services the ratio might be in the order of £150 per day. It is a crude ratio which incorporates both residential and non-residential training and the cost of activities such as CBT.

Training cost as a percentage of payroll

This is:

$$\frac{\text{Total expenditure on training in the year} \times 100}{\text{Total payroll for the year}}$$

Again, a crude indicator. As long as the way the expenditure total is calculated is consistent it can be compared with other organizations in the sector and nationally. A three to four per cent figure might be the order in finance and perhaps five to seven per cent in air transport.

Budget variance

This is the comparison between the budget for each cost heading and the actual expenditure. The overall figure should be kept as favourable, i.e. underspend against budget if possible.

Training days per trainer per annum

This is a useful measure of efficiency of scheduling. The ratio is:

$$\frac{\text{Total training days per annum}}{\text{Average tutoring staff per annum}}$$

The total training days is a function of number of events × duration of events × attendance and a total in excess of 1600 days would be creditable. If you assume 10 people per course, this requires 160 days out of 200 in the classroom per member of staff, which clearly would be very demanding.

Average training days provided per member of staff

This gives a useful guide to level of activity. The ratio is:

$$\frac{\text{Total training days provided per annum}}{\text{Total number of employees}}$$

A figure of 2–3 days per annum per individual would be typical in finance and 3–4 days would stand comparison with most other organizations. To illustrate, for an organization with 30 000 staff this upper figure would be 120 000 days. At £150 per day this would be £18 million per annum.

Some of the ratios can be adapted for CBT to identify, for example, average hours per month per work station. A further useful ratio is the percentage of key jobs with an identified successor.

There are many other ratios and various ways of using them. A useful comparison for the cost-per-day ratio is with the average cost for one day of non-residential training from an external supplier. The typical rate in mid 1995 was £300–350 plus VAT for an individual and £110–140 per individual for a group in-company. A one-week residential management course would cost in the region of £1500–2000 per head and gives a good comparator for a residential management centre that, given a virtually guaranteed high utilization, should be able to operate at less than £1200 per individual per week. An 80 bedroom centre would then expect an annual budget not to exceed £96 000 × 50 weeks = £4.8 million. Given a utilization of 80 per cent, i.e. 64 bedrooms filled per week, and a day-rate target of £160 per student (i.e. £80 residence and £80 for tutoring), this would give a maximum income or budget of 64 × £800 × 50 = £2.56 million. Thus the plan can adopt a range of assumptions and estimate a cost of £3 million ± 15 per cent with a high degree of confidence in achieving this.

The development of ratios with simply obtainable up-to-date information can provide powerful data both for making the case and controlling expenditure.

The shape of the case

The format, length and amount of financial information required will depend largely on the audience. The steps involved are similar to those required for any report and presentation:

- Gather facts on the present situation and what will be required.
- Convert this to concrete plans and costs.
- Identify the audience and what particular business issues are of interest to them.
- Determine the level of financial justification the audience normally requires.
- Identify their jargon and use it where appropriate.
- Decide on the length of the case and stick to it. If these decisions are usually made on two sheets of paper per agenda item at the board meeting—that is what you have got: 1000 words.
- Lobby all the key individuals. Get their views on the plan and incorporate them in the final draft. Few things improve the likelihood of acceptance more than ownership.
- If you make a presentation, keep it short.
- Make it very clear exactly what you are asking to have approved.

To illustrate the approach, an example is outlined below. A possible lay-out for the contents is shown in Figure 8.2

The key points in presentation are:

- The audience
- The shape of the case
- The length of the document
- The financial data
- The interests or 'hot spots' of the decision makers.

The case described in this example used the language and jargon common in the organization, focused on the staff 'in the engine room' of the bank, i.e. the branches, and on management training and development.

The full 35-page bound version would be used for a presentation at a board meeting and as a blueprint for the employee development management team. The four-page Section 5 and the one-page executive summary would be used for the group chief executive and the one-page overall summary would be for internal dissemination. The degree of financial data was quite detailed and interspersed throughout the case.

		Length in pages
1	Introduction	½
2	The business issues	3½
3	The training investment last year	3
4	The training implications of the business issues	
	Branch staff	2
	Branch supervisors	2
	Branch managers	1
	District managers	1
	Regional office staff	1
	Head office staff	1
	Computer services	1
5	Organization and budget issues	4
6	Overall summary	1
	Appendices	
	(a) Courses scheduled for current year	2
	(b) Total regional training days last year	1
	(c) Manpower data	8
	(d) Proposed employee development reorganization	2

Note
Section 5 was printed on a distinctive colour in the report and was written so that it could be read either on its own or as an integral part of the overall report. A one-page executive summary was then produced.

Figure 8.2 *Sample contents page for the case for the money*

Back to basics

One common tendency in budgeting is to take last year's figure as a base and then to increase this year's budget to reflect inflation and increased activity. Since the demand for employee development almost always exceeds supply and waiting lists are the usual safety valve if the product is right, this is quite tempting and easy to rationalize. Thus there is some demand-pull normally present. Commercial effectiveness often operates in the opposite direction where the aim is to produce the same or more product or service at less cost. Decision making is far from clear when outputs are intangible as in the case of most staff activities.

One approach to combat this tendency is the *zero-based budget*. In this approach the assumption is made that nothing is carried forward. Every function starts with a 'zero base' and has to justify every expenditure area with an indication of priority. This process considerably sharpens the debate when done rigorously. It also helps to produce a meaningful exchange and highlights what decisions have to be made. What often happens is that budgets, and therefore plans, are cut arbitrarily—say by 10 per cent across the board—or a staff freeze prevents the recruitment of staff. Managers act to protect their best interests and deliberately overestimate by, say, 15 per cent so that a 10 per cent cut in real terms is a 5 per cent increase. With employee development, the way of adapting the plan to accommodate a shortage of resources is simply not to develop sections of the workforce or to have very long waiting lists for popular activities.

With zero-based budgeting each area is examined afresh and what needs to be done this year is identified. A range of activities and costs might be identified as shown in Figure 8.3.

Product induction for all new salespeople	–	£0.5m.
Sales techniques for all new salespeople	–	£1.2m.
Advanced sales for financial consultants	–	£0.25m.
Refresher course for salespeople with 5 years' service	–	£0.75m.
Unit trust training for all sales staff	–	£1.0m.
Experienced agents sales development	–	£0.5m.

Figure 8.3 *Activities and costs of a training plan*

A similar range of needs might be identified for area managers and district managers and various other categories. Each activity would be given a priority and it might be decided that two-thirds of the proposals will be adopted. These needs can then be compared with resources available and a plan produced that realistically reflects what is needed. It may be closely related to last year's expenditure or a considerable change in expenditure may be appropriate—up or down.

This sort of approach focuses attention and highlights the process:

- Identify business needs
  ↓
- Produce employee development proposals
  ↓
- Decide what is appropriate and affordable
  ↓
- Implement an agreed plan geared to business needs

Managing the budget

To achieve continuing success for the plan it is essential to monitor and control expenditure. Successful exposure to reality is an essential ingredient of any such planning process and long-term credibility for future plans will doubtless be affected by the soundness of earlier plans. The basic steps in the process are:

- Establish a sound base by producing an accurate plan.
- Ensure information used is reliable and accurate.
- Obtain timely, accurate information on progress.
- Carry out a regular review of actual expenditure against the plan.
- Take prompt action to control any significant variance from planned expenditure.

Considering each step in a little detail:

Establish a sound base

The analysis described in this book indicates the need to ensure relevance to the business plan and business needs. The previous year will provide a guide, often quite a useful one, as to what is needed. Estimates of volume of activity required will be key factors in determining the base as will a close knowledge of major elements in the plan. For example, if a large amount of rented accommodation is hired in hotels, the managers who do the hiring will probably have a keen view of likely price movements and what they can negotiate over the next year. Each element should be exposed to debate with those closest to the action. Establishing a sound plan is rather like rehearsing all the elements of a battle in your head before it happens. The better the experience and judgement of probabilities, the more likely the plan is to be accurate.

Accurate information

Control and corrective action depends on accurate information. At a basic level, this requires that the manager understands the use of cost codes and that close collaboration with the finance function is established. Monthly budget reports record expenditure by using codes against cost headings. If these are incorrect then the information does not help control.

To take a simple example, the cash flow budget estimate for supervisory training for January might be £100 000. The outcome is shown as £150 000, a significant adverse variance. On investigation, £20 000 of this amount was found to have been carried forward for November and £25 000 was for a sales conference for supervisors, organized by the marketing function and incorrectly coded to the employee development budget. Thus the 'real' situation for January was a spend of £105 000 against a budgeted amount of £100 000. It can take a significant amount of effort and liaison to ensure the information is reasonably accurate. Inaccurate information is at best useless for informed decision making.

Timely information Another basic requirement is timely information. Ideally, information should be in real time, i.e. information is up-to-date as of yesterday's close of business. Some businesses achieve this, particularly where immediacy has business implications such as in retailing or information technology, but it could be unrealistic to hope for this in employee development financial management. The minimum acceptable is data that are accurate and received within about 10 days of the month end.

Regular review In managing the budget, regular meetings to review performance are essential. Monthly management meetings can incorporate the budget progress review as a standing item. By holding the meeting, say, on a fixed day that is a few days after the last month's figures are released, an up-to-the-minute review is possible using the organization's financial timetabling. Variance analysis can be used to concentrate attention on any item of overspend in excess of, say, five per cent and the reasons for this can be established. If necessary, national action can be agreed in a geographically dispersed organization within days of the figures being available and implemented immediately. Given strong commitment to operating on a commercial basis, it is rare for there to be surprises, but the discipline of regular review keeps the focus on cost effectiveness and performing to plan. With an objective of performing to within one per cent under budget, it is important for the employee development management to control what is happening and to be seen to be managing commercially.

Prompt action Feedback and corrective action are essential ingredients. Any overspend or underspend should be traced back to the plan and assessed. Strategic priorities sometimes occur during the year and the overall plan may need to be rebalanced by redeploying staff, hiring consultants or a management college or cancelling part of the programme at short notice. Action taken needs to be based on strategic requirements and not 'short-termism' but sometimes has to be taken promptly and decisively.

Financial management of the budget is the other side of the planning coin. To survive contact with reality, the plan has to be driven to cope with changing circumstances. Once the case is constructed and made and the finances are allocated, employee development has to be implemented and enabled for success to be achieved and this step is described in the next chapter. Before that, a full example of a case for an employee development plan is set out in the appendix to this chapter.

Summary

This chapter has set out to identify the key factors in making the case for the money to carry out employee development. In doing this it has examined the potential audience for the case and the characteristics of successful case-making. It examines ways of ensuring a persuasive case is prepared and then implemented. The main areas covered are:

- Linking the case to the main preoccupations of the buyers by examining the organization's strategy, and identifying what employee development actions are essential for the achievement of business success.
- Presenting employee development as a financial investment so that the case can compete effectively with other 'spending' operations. The needs of the individual and how these can be identified and reflected in the plan and the increasing importance of choice and the views of the customer were considered. The use of performance measures and standards together with means of comparing the size of the investment in development and some useful ratios were identified.
- The power of the customer, the role of cost centres and profit centres, and the implications of decentralization were described.
- Different perspectives on the case were presented by considering how the line manager will be more concerned with operational results whereas the financial director's perspective is concerned with bottom-line results, cash flow and performance against budget. Individuals may view development as a personal investment in themselves.
- The use of ratios in preparing the plan and persuading decision makers was explained. Means of identifying how your particular situation compares with others in your industrial/commercial/service sector, such as percentage of payroll spent on development, were examined.
- The shape of the case in terms of presentation, audience, length, relationship with the business needs, identification of key individuals and lobbying for support were looked at, together with an example of format and content. The aim of this section was to ensure that the decision makers bought the case and provided the funds.
- How to focus on essentials and identify real priorities using zero-based budget concepts was applied to the planning process. The objective of providing only what is required at a cost relevant to today's needs was highlighted. Managing the budget by creating a sound financial plan based on accurate information that is used regularly to identify variances is essential.
- Approaches to making sure the financial information used is accurate and available promptly so that corrective action can be taken against agreed business priority areas were described.
- One of the best ways of getting the employee development plan accepted is a track record of cost effectively delivering what the business requires, on time, in terms of what operational managers expect.

Overall, the thrust of this chapter is to discover and present whatever information senior management require to enable them to buy the case. Selling the case is about enabling the buyer to buy.

What you can do

1 Produce on one sheet of paper a case for the training plan that identifies the main business issues, the essentials of the training that will be required, the resourcing and the budget proposals.

2 Identify what current ratios and measures are relevant to your organization and compare them with your own data. Important examples will be your percentage of payroll or turnover spent on training and indicators such as 'at least five days' per year spent on management training courses.

3 Identify three key issues on employee development in your environment. Systematically check out where key players stand on them. An example might be the degree to which choice of development should be 'open' and under the control of individuals.

4 Identify the most significant omission in what your organization proposes to do on employee development over the next 12 months. What could you do to rectify this? Try to draw up an action plan with performance criteria and sell your plan to your immediate superior.

5 Identify the main expenditure on employee development planned for this year under no more than 12 headings. Identify the current expenditure for your organization or unit and any areas of significant variation. Identify the causes of the variations and what needs to be done to put the plan back on course.

Appendix to Chapter 8

An illustrative case for an employee development plan

Company background
United Cars plc is part of a multinational vehicle manufacturing company with headquarters in Detroit. It was established in the UK some 60 years ago and is now part of the Northern Hemisphere regional operation. It produces passenger cars, lorries, buses, and tractors and agricultural equipment. In 1995 it made an operating profit of £400 million in the UK and this was regarded as average performance in comparison with its main internal rivals—West Germany, East Germany and Spain. Its total employment dropped from 70 000 in 1985 to 40 000 in 1995, over half of which is located at its Midlands plant which was opened two years ago and built on a green-field site. The company has some of the most advanced technology in the industry in operation here, in stark contrast with its original plant.

Profits declined regularly from the 1985 high of £600 million at 1995 prices and 1995 was the first year this trend was reversed. The 1994 profit of £300 million was widely regarded as unacceptable. Market share worldwide had slipped on average but only marginally. Europe is the main market for the UK production and most models' market share declined by two or three per cent over the last five years. The outstandingly successful small hatch-back produced in the Midlands plant, however, achieved 53 per cent market share.

The parent had authorized a massive involvement in training and development in 1992–94, most of it in support of the new plant and to develop competitive management practices. The years ahead will be tougher as the general depression in world markets bites into investment. However, training is a well-supported function worldwide and many of the current decision makers have grown up through the company's training programmes over the last 20 years.

The training plan that will be put to the UK board, with a nod to functional counterparts in Detroit, will concentrate on key issues. It will probably be one of six agenda items and will get at most 45 minutes airtime. However, the paper presenting it will have been carefully reviewed by specialists in each functional director's area so the discussion is likely to be to the point and informed.

Employee development plan objectives

The main objectives for the 1995/96 employee development plan are to:

- Ensure that the skills required are available.
- Reduce the overall budget expenditure from £21 million to £18 million at 1995 prices without any decrease in standards. This is a 14 per cent decrease without allowing for inflation or some 18 per cent if inflation is 4 per cent. In year 2 and year 3 (i.e. 1996/7 and 1997/8) on current information it is anticipated that the employee development budget will need to be increased at about the rate of inflation—estimated at 4–5 per cent per annum at this time.
- The cost of training and development will be continuously monitored to improve effectiveness and reduce costs incurred. Special attention will be paid to obtaining and maximizing government and regional subsidies and using new training technologies such as computer-based training and teleconferencing with Detroit.

The investment proposal

The company's zero-based approach to budget was used as standard operating procedures require and the overall summary is shown in Figure A8.1.

	£m.
Staffing costs	3.2
Premises—rent	2.2
Internal services, e.g. information technology	1.2
External training	2.7
Consultants	1.8
Computer-based training/interactive video	2.9
Open learning	1.0
Employee skill programme	2.0
Educational support	1.0
Total	18.0

Figure A8.1 *The investment proposal in summary*

The detailed case is available for discussion but the overall key points are these.

The reduced investment of £18 million is approximately 3 per cent of the annual salary bill which for 1995 was £605 million. Our competitors are, to the best of our knowledge, investing 3–4 per cent in the UK and 4–5 per cent in Germany. In the UK the staff head count will be 105–115 for employee development and administrative staff in-post, a reduction of 10 over last year. The internal profit centre charges for premises and information technology are based on 1995 utilization. The item of £2.9 million for the CBT and interactive video includes the production of an extensive range of programmes on quality and the purchase of learning centres. The consultants will be used mainly to introduce Total Quality in our old plant. The employee skill programme, introduced last year, has been a great success and the £2 million will support the same level of activity this year.

The main business issues at which the employee development plan will be aimed are:

1 To drive up product quality by an integration of Total Quality approaches with improved management training.
2 To ensure the high level of technician engineer skills required to keep the advanced body and engine assembly robotic technology at full economic efficiency are available.
3 To enable the company to attract young entrants in the face of demographic changes that are making the attraction and retention of young employees increasingly competitive.
4 To ensure that the operator level skills are maintained at a high level.
5 To improve the quality of management for succession and to develop and retain those with high ability in the face of decreasing numbers of promotion opportunities.
6 To make the most of the skills of our employees.

A quarterly review of the progress against plan will be carried out with plant management and any variations against budget in excess of £100 000 will be referred to senior management. The overall aim of all employee development activities will be to contribute to improving profitability.

The employee development plan—1995

The plan covers 10 broad areas of activity. For each, the main elements of the training policy are outlined and then specific proposals for 1995 are identified. These, following usual practice, are not shown in detail since this will change in response to conditions at the time in what is a responsive and rapidly changing industry. All implementation will be carried out in close consultation with operational management and priorities will be adjusted as required. The following then are the broad areas of activity, in no particular order of priority:

Management and supervisory development

The employee development policy for this area is that:

● Management and supervisor training will be to an agreed corporate pattern and delivered in the UK by two nominated management centres.
● Priorities and needs for operational management are a divisional responsibility within corporate guidelines.

- Action-learning principles, in view particularly of the introduction of Total Quality, are to be incorporated with the off-the-job programme.
- Successors for 80 per cent of all identified key jobs must have individual development plans by the end of 1996.

The main elements of the plan will be:

1 To provide and develop the corporate introduction to management, middle management, production management and senior manager courses. To redesign the trainee production supervisor programme to incorporate more open learning and CBT and reduce the formal component from 20 days to 10 days over a 6-month period. The throughput for the management courses will be approximately 500 per year and the average duration of the courses attended will be 6 days. This will require approximately half the external training budget and will be delivered at Rugby and Buxton management centres. Approximately 100 production supervisors will require the trainee production supervisors programme and altogether this will need 8 man-years of professional employee development resourcing and administrative support.

2 Appraisal interviews and the performance improvement programme will identify a range of needs that will be met by internal and external resources. Some of the main issues for 1995 were customer care and client liaison, the use of computer-aided design, understanding and using personal computers and spreadsheets, financial control and project management. These issues will demand some £0.5 million on external courses and approximately 7 man-years of internal resources, especially for supervisory training.

3 The recently introduced approach of assigning internal employee development consultants to assist local management in identifying needs and implementing change strategies will continue. It was regarded as particularly successful last year in focusing effort. To provide an adequate service, guided by the volume of cost savings identified last year, it is proposed to deploy 8 man-years of resource in this area.

Technician engineers Technological change has had a major impact on quality at the Midlands plant and the technical capability to design, purchase, install and operate high-technology robotics and electronics engineering is increasingly vital. The employee development policy for this area is that:

- Sufficient technician engineering students will be recruited and sponsored to meet all projected manpower needs from our own resources. This will require 25–35 students per annum throughout the 1990s.
- Existing employees will be encouraged and trained to upgrade or broaden their skills. The main elements of the plan will be:

1 To recruit 30 technician engineering students in 1996 and to investigate methods of sponsorship for the future.
2 To extend the CBT programmes and open learning material currently available.
3 To investigate in collaboration with Detroit and the product engineering division, production engineering division and strategic planners, the likely skill needs in detail for 1995–2000 and in outline for 1995–2005. Develop a clear description of the mission required and a strategic plan to cover the whole human resource management input to this area.

This will be a major study and overall, including plans to improve considerably the mentoring of young engineers, will require an allocation of 10 man-years for implementation. This reflects the concerns, indeed demands, from plant management and engineering management to ensure we are competitive in this area. Our marketing people also strongly support this area, as reflected in the current campaign showing our vehicles being built by robotics.

Total Quality Total Quality has been introduced worldwide over the last two years, largely to ensure competitiveness with Japanese producers. The main policy item for this area is that all employees must attend a one-day programme as a minimum requirement and demonstrate understanding of relevant quality performance standards.

The main elements of the plan for 1995 are:

1 To run ½-day, 1-day, 2-day and 5-day modules such that, by the end of 1995, 75 per cent of all appropriate staff have attended and achieved satisfactory performance standards.
2 To introduce new CBT/video programmes to ensure that quality performance standards are fully understood and met.

It is estimated that the Total Quality programme will require 10 man-years of internal resourcing supported by consulting help in substantial measure. Most of the consultant budget will be spent in the area.

Operator training The policy guidelines are that:

● All families of jobs will have had the required competencies identified in terms consistent with the Total Quality programme standards.
● No operator will work on the production line until 100 per cent under test conditions has been demonstrated.

The main elements of the plan will be:

1 To complete analysis of all jobs by mid 1996.
2 To provide a two-day programme for all production supervisors covering competency standards and on-the-job training techniques.
3 To establish off-the-job training facilities in all main skill areas, e.g.

body finishing, welding on assembly, engine construction, to provide induction training for all new employees.

It will be necessary to adapt the specific content in conjunction with production engineering and plant management during the three-year life of the programme. Twelve man-years of resourcing will be required, using CBT where appropriate.

Professional and commercial staff

Policy guidelines are that:

- The UK should be self-sufficient for information technology staff and provide cover for 50 per cent of predicted shortfall in Spain, Italy and Eastern Europe.
- The UK should aim to be a major development area for finance staff.

The main elements of the plan, reflecting a directive from Northern Hemisphere management that the UK should be the centre of excellence for this area of competence, will be:

1 Establish a training centre with a design output of 80 systems analysts and computer-aided design specialists per annum. Work with the National Computing Centre.
2 Produce on-line training programmes for the use of information technology.
3 Create a centre of excellence with the City University. Establish a chair in finance and recruit 24 high-calibre students in year one for the finance function.
4 Establish links between the Information Technology Training Centre, the City University and the Rugby Management Training Centre. Produce a tailor-made project management programme for IT staff.

This element represents a major initiative and will require eight man-years of resource commitment and £1 million setting-up costs from various elements of the UK budget with a subvention from the Northern Hemisphere budget.

Graduate training

The policy guidelines are:

- Graduates will be a major resourcing activity for future middle management. The level will be set at 100 and 12 specified universities will be targeted. Salary level will not be allowed to be an obstacle.
- The balance between arts and science will be 50 : 50 with robotics and manufacturing engineering graduates being prime targets. The graduate programme will be based on 4–8 weeks' induction, depending on function, coupled with support for obtaining professional qualifications in all disciplines, e.g. engineering, finance. All graduates will work in engineering, marketing, finance and production and will be placed in permanent jobs within 12 months of joining. Mentors will be identified and trained for all graduate trainees. The programme will require 2 man-years of resourcing and

a commitment of at least 5 days during the year on the part of 100 mentors, i.e. 2 further man-years of management time.

Computer-based training/interactive video

The policy in this area is that:

- Conventional training will be replaced by CBT whenever it is practical and a 20 per cent cost saving can clearly be achieved.
- CBT/IV should be freely available in learning centres at times convenient to the trainees.

The main elements of the plan will be:

1 To continue to identify where CBT can contribute cost effectively and produce a minimum of 100 hours of CBT material and 10 hours of interactive video.
2 To establish, administer and equip 20 learning centres with 6 stations or computer booths each.
3 To produce video films in support of Total Quality and as a resource to the company's UK training establishments.

The current year required considerable investment in hardware to extend the availability of CBT at a cost of £500 000, and material to be developed for CBT will require 6 man-years of resourcing and approximately £500 000. The video films and interactive video will require a similar amount.

Open learning

The main policy points are:

- To make learning more widely available but focused on business objectives.
- To encourage individuals to learn in their own time.
- To improve motivation to learn by encouraging individuals to become fully involved in determining their learning needs.

The main elements of the plan will be:

1 To investigate how open learning can be integrated with existing programmes to reduce costs.
2 To introduce open learning approaches such as the Open University's Effective Manager and Women into Management programmes for at least 100 participants in each.
3 To promote open learning and distance learning by obtaining an extensive range of materials such as audio cassettes, books and open learning programmes and promoting their use within the organization.

The resourcing required will be two managers, plus administrative assistance, together with an investment of approximately £1 million in open learning resources. This will be largely a non-recurring setting-up cost and will be available over the entire three years of the planning cycle.

Employee skills programme

The ESP has been a major success. The board last year approved the introduction of the programme, which allowed all eligible employees to apply for a grant of up to £250 to develop individual skills.

The policy objectives were:

- To involve employees in their own development.
- To encourage the development of the skill base.

The programme mainly involved dissemination of information and the operation of the approval and grant-provision process. In all, one man-year of resourcing was required to process 12 000 applications and the grant funding requested is £2 million. This programme has been enthusiastically supported by the trade unions involved.

Young people   The difficulties surrounding their availability, educational level and employment have been a matter of concern in the UK for some time. When negotiations took place on the location of the new plant and the availability of development funding, commitments were made about young people. In the UK the school-to-work situation is the subject of various government initiatives, such as Modern Apprenticeships.

The policy objectives will be:

- To obtain the quality and quantity of youngsters required to achieve the business plan.
- To provide employment for local youngsters where possible.
- To be regarded as a model employer in this area.

The employee development plan will require the following:

1 The recruitment of 400 school leavers nationally, 200 in the Midlands, to follow a programme including 4 weeks of induction training, weekly day release for educational study, off-the-job training and planned work experience. Extensive use will be made of CBT and distance learning.
2 The scheme will run for a minimum of two years and to obtain Government funding will need to be open to inspection.

The programme will need six man-years of resourcing and approximately half the cost will effectively be subsidised.

General   There will be expenditure required on developing our employee development staff, for whom our agreed vision is that they should be the best in Europe. This is included in the budget estimate for staffing.

Action   The plan as outlined has been designed to ensure that the skills required to meet the three-year business strategic plan are available. Every effort to maximize cost effectiveness will be made and the quality of our employee development will not only stand comparison with our main European competitors—it will also cost less per employee. The board is asked to *approve* its implementation and the investment requested.

9 From plans to action: options for implementation

Once the plan has been approved and the necessary finance allocated, the next stage to consider is implementation. In most dynamic processes of planning the question of implementation together with how to organize the function and get the development skills required is considered at the same time as the case is developed. The context of the case, its relevance to the business plan, the choices on implementation and how the delivery mechanism is organized can be thought of as four strands woven into a rope. Weakness in any strand can lead to fraying and a useless rope. Equally, a well-woven rope is much stronger than the sum of its parts. Relative weakness in training skills in a strategy closely aligned to business results can produce satisfactory results. Highly skilled development consultants who are not quite in tune with the business can easily be moved to the periphery.

The various elements and options are considered in this chapter. It must be stressed that most of the choices that have to be made are within the context of an existing situation and will be about degree rather than absolute choice. For example, there is the use of open learning combined with conventional classroom training courses or the integration of action learning with conventional change-management programmes, rather than a choice between open learning and all other methods. There are some basic choices which can have important strategic effects and the more important of these are:

1 Standard trainer-centred courses *v* learner-centred events.   This choice is essentially about whether the plan should deliver 'bottoms on seats' or be segmented. In an airline context the former might be achieved by a chartered flight to transport 300 holiday makers to Benidorm with set lunches, and the latter by the use of business class seats with choice over meal times. High-volume training where large numbers of people need similar or identical knowledge and skills can best be accomplished in some organizations by a treadmill of courses at a training centre or regional centre with training staff who have a very limited range of highly developed ability, e.g. insurance product knowledge and sales skills for new insurance salespeople.

2 Glossy packaging v utility.   As with most products, training and development may appeal more to some customers when it is gift-wrapped. Thus, concentration on brand-image, glossy presentation and handouts and a high degree of showmanship can be taken to excess, as can utilitarianism and a concentration on learning. The sales conference in Malaga in contrast with the Outward Bound course using tents and dormitories point out two extremes. Clearly, the aim will need to be to make the most of both options.

3 Country club management centre v high technology learning delivery centre.   The texture, quality and style that the organization requires can affect what options are chosen. If managers have become accustomed to four-star hotels as a minimum, as part of how the organization thinks about staff, a week at a teacher training college that is superbly equipped with CBT and learning resources but which does not have television, bathroom and coffee-making facilities en-suite might cause a few learning problems.

4 Training delivered by the organization v learning managed by the learner.   This is perhaps the most profound choice. Large sections of British industry still regard training as attendance at five-day off-the-job courses. This logic leads to the menu-driven approach often delivered in residential colleges. There is clearly a demand for the product. There have also been some imaginative developments in the learner-centred area with a great growth in open learning through the Open University, Open College and MBAs by distance learning.

5 Research and development v buying off-the-shelf.   Perhaps one of the most fundamental choices, this issue is about dedicating staff whose full-time task is to develop and produce new products so that the staff delivering employee development or facilitating it have the best support available. The other alternative is to buy what are in effect proprietary products and to seek to make them fit the organization. The many off-the-shelf products, which range from time management courses to MBA programmes, all suffer from the same potential defect. In catering for the maximum possible width of market, they necessarily lack specificity and fit for particular segments of the market.

These five basic choices are likely to run through the individual implementation programmes and affect the employee development executive's vision and how this relates to other development staff and line management.

Options for employee development

Given the backdrop described above, some of the options open to an organization are:

1 Recruit and maintain its own employee development organization.
2 Develop its own employees to carry out training, e.g. banking skills or sales training.

3 Recruit specialists from outside either on contract or for permanent careers.
4 Use specific colleges for identified training, e.g. a management college for middle-management training or a computer centre for systems analyst training.
5 Enter into a partnership for all the organization's management training with a business school, university, or management centre.
6 Enter into a similar arrangement with a major consultancy.
7 Purchase ad hoc services from management centres or consultants.
8 Create own faculty of academics, consultants and industrialists who commit an agreed portion of time to an organization.
9 Use open learning in conjunction with any of the foregoing options, using either own staff or sub-contractors.
10 Similarly, use CBT as a major delivery mechanism in conjunction with other options.
11 Totally sub-contract the employee development function to a managing agent, using competitive tendering.
12 Move the identification and delivery out of the specialist function to the line. This can be promoted through action learning, then use of coaching and mentoring and the use of line managers to deliver training.
13 Promote the use of external educational resources.
14 Shift the choice to the employee as in the Ford Motor Company approach, using a grant of up to £200 for employees to improve their skills.

The pros and cons of these options will be explored next, and how these choices can impact on the success of employee development will be highlighted.

Internal employee development function

Using the organization's own employee development function as the sole or primary resource for delivering the plan is an approach that was widely used until quite recently and many organizations still pride themselves on self-sufficiency. A company may have virtually no employee development staff who have worked for another organization.

Advantages

- Staff know the organization, its history, politics and products.
- Senior management know the employee development staff and their past contribution.
- Employee development will be seen as reinforcing existing values and will essentially be non-threatening.
- A strong appreciation of the culture and product can considerably enhance the introduction of new approaches such as CBT and open learning.
- Staff are trusted by employees.

Disadvantages

- Employee development skills are limited to the experience within the organization.
- Long service can lead to conservatism and complacency. This can be a major brake on implementing change.
- New talent and the introduction of skill levels not previously attained by the present organization can be inhibited.
- Development and introduction of new ideas or alternative approaches can be difficult.
- The operation may adopt essentially amateur values without the exposure to challenging views from outside.

Most organizations opt for some balance with a core of existing staff supplemented by some of the other options described. The key question must be: does the function cause the development required to happen quickly enough and in sufficient quantity? One of the main challenges is to develop a career route and development experiences for those involved so that the growth from direct trainer or tutor through to training or development consultant or manager can be achieved. This will be considered in Chapter 10.

Another key issue in using this option is the way that those in the function are regarded. It is said that the prophet is often without honour in his own land. If the employee development function, or what ten years ago might have been regarded as the training school, was seen as a dumping ground for failed sales supervisors or a place to put a worthy line manager in the later years of his career, then would it be reasonable to expect it to be highly regarded as a mainstream contribution to achieving the business plan? One way to counter this sort of image is to have high-calibre staff seconded into employee development as part of their career development. One financial services company as a matter of policy kept a proportion of its training establishment for high-flyer salespeople who had been identified as having potential for junior management but needed some broadening.

One of the strongest arguments for recruiting staff from outside the organization is to broaden the range of skills available or to improve the depth of skill and development in employee development. In an organization in relatively steady state, this might see the integration of 10–20 per cent of the staff from outside over a two-year period. New skills such as CBT design or an open-learning background coupled with recruitment of managerial or employee development consultancy experience, or specific practitioners such as interpersonal skills trainers, would be typically involved. A similar proportion of internal staff might be recruited in the same period.

In a time of rapid change, or a changeover from a static, conservative business to a growth or aggressive customer-responsive one, it might be necessary to replace most of the existing resource if the skills required to operate in the new fashion are not available. As much as 80 per cent of staff might need to be recruited from outside over the one- or two-year term. In this mode, or using this variation of the own-employee organization, employee development would be transformed quite rapidly. Typically, external staff will also be used extensively on a consultancy contract basis.

Consultants   One of the major growth areas of the 1990s has been the use of consultants, as organizations struggle to cope with rapid change. Employment on a part-time consultancy basis has now become quite common.

Advantages

- The best talent for specific areas such as customer service can be hired for specific periods without including them in the permanent head count.
- Peaks in demand can be managed by using mid-range consultants for basic training, e.g. sales or supervisory training.
- Specific skills can be brought in for specific products, e.g. producing a video training package.
- Approaches such as performance management can be introduced using proprietary packages; this cuts the need for development time and makes use of consultants' cross-industry experience.
- Training the trainer, especially at the more skilled and experienced end of the range of experience, can be focused specifically in-company.
- It may be politically more acceptable for an external consultant to identify employee development needs and action required than internal staff.
- The use of an organization development or process consultant as a sounding board, or to help with a change process, can be very valuable. The consultant brings an objectivity by not being involved in the political process and can facilitate difficult change processes.

Disadvantages

- Consultants can be expensive and fail to achieve real change in what employees do. Failure to understand the environment can lead to a rejection by line management.
- Their approach may be too detached; they may fail to understand fully the mission of the organization at an emotional level.
- The advantage of their specialization, say in time management, can lead to blindness in other areas. The insensitive installation of *management-by-objectives* was a classic example of this.
- Their use can push against the integration of employee development with the business needs and can undermine the internal staff.

Consultants can make a significant contribution. They can broaden the base of the employee development that can be offered, carry out analytical and project work that often might go by default, and then produce proposed solutions for discussion that may already have some consensus of support.

The choice of which consultant to use is clearly crucial for success. Steps in the selection process would ideally include:

1 Drawing up a specification document for an 'invitation to tender'. This should help the organization seeking assistance to clarify its requirements and provide a sound basis for any future relationship.
2 Deciding on who should be invited to tender, having firstly identified a short list of the best consultants in the area for which the tender is sought. Investigate the following:
   (a) the consultant's track record;
   (b) their experience of your type of sector, organization and the work required;
   (c) which specific individuals will provide the consultancy help;
   (d) the organization's client list;
   (e) which clients would be available as referees;
   (f) the quality of the administrative support available;
   (g) the size of your contract compared to the turnover of the consultant's business.
3 Invite tenders and select a short list to present proposals to you.
4 Visit two or three preferred suppliers. In particular, check that the inter-personal relationships are workable.
5 Discreetly check out the chosen supplier.
6 Ensure that internal customers are comfortable with the preferred supplier and the quotation for the work.
7 Set up mechanisms to monitor progress and implementation.

Management college   Ad hoc use can be made of a management college or a partnership with it entered into. The provision of junior to senior management training and education in-company provides a particular challenge. The ability to develop skills across a range, including disciplines such as finance, personnel, marketing, information technology, legal, property and administration, and specific applications within, say, portfolio management, merchant banking, turbine manufacture or hospital management is demanding. The usual response is to use a specialized management centre and to hire the centre to analyse, design and deliver a course or courses for particular problems or staff. Thus, a college might run the organization's middle management course or its financial training. The choice in the UK is basically among business schools, universities, private management centres, management centres run by consultants, and a few company centres that make their training available to outside customers. At the more junior end there is a wide range of independent providers that will be considered later.

By 'ad hoc' is meant the occasional use of courses in an uncoordinated manner—this usually occurs when managers see a brochure or know someone who has attended the course. The next level of customer-provider relationship is where organization-specific courses are run at a centre as described above. When this option is used, the organization typically relates to one or at most two providers. Perhaps the ultimate way of using this strategic option is a partnership where the organization works with one management centre to identify and develop a whole range of courses, advisory work and consultancy and works with the centre as if the staff were its own.

Advantages

- Access to a broad range of staff who specialize in particular areas and often have national standing in their topic. Areas such as marketing, IT, finance and strategy are typical examples.
- The staff are usually dedicated to teaching and learning and should be competent in learning design.
- The whole environment provides the opportunity for cross-fertilization with other industries and sectors, particularly where managers attend courses with a cross-section from other companies.
- The use of the centre itself. Many are in very attractive surroundings and provide an environment conducive to learning.

Disadvantages

- The style of the centre may not be consistent with the organization. Each centre has its own style. A reflective and indirect approach may not suit a hard-nosed results-driven multinational.
- The staff may not have had substantive industrial or commercial experience and may be too academic. All centres run the risk of becoming 'ivory towers'.
- Since few companies would typically provide more than 10 per cent of the centre's business, there might be a tendency to lose interest in the client. Off-the-peg courses that can be easily sold are much less trouble.
- The values of the centre, particularly in the university sector, may be more about research and publication than about improving managerial performance.

Since these centres provide a significant proportion of the senior management training delivered in the UK they demand consideration. One of the central issues in this area is the problem of 'language'. Each organization tends to develop its own language and the time wasted on clarifying such simple examples as strategy, policy, objectives, targets, key result areas, performance standards and competencies can be considerable. Working closely with a centre to ensure a common basic language is used, which can be adapted and understood within the organization, can bring significant bonuses.

The recent shift towards concentration on outputs and action is also encouraging, and attempts to focus the substantial resources that these centres have to provide meaningful employee development should be well worth the effort sometimes involved.

Private providers   Private providers of training offer a variety of services. They include Employment Training, 'returner' training for those rejoining the job market, and specialist courses such as the use of psychometric tests. There is also an extensive range of short courses, such as Training Officer Development Programmes.

In general, there is a wide range of short specific courses readily available for the small to medium firm. Larger organizations may use the courses for areas where they have a one-off need or insufficient demand to run a course in-house.

Advantages

- Courses can be found for individual needs identified through appraisal or by individual managers.
- Tutors can specialize in topics such as effective presentation and incorporate wide experience of different industries.
- Course participants can mix with those from other companies, institutions, sectors and gain a breadth of experience.
- Courses can be sampled and then run in-company at reasonable cost without one-off development cost.

Disadvantages

- The language and concepts used may not readily fit the company.
- The content may not match the need very precisely and some of it may be irrelevant.
- Transfer of learning back at work may be difficult if support is not provided.

External providers offer a very wide range of predominantly off-the-job courses. The quality of the product may vary, just as it can with in-company delivery. It is sensible to check out the quality of training using one of the course evaluation indexes. It is possible for the smaller firm to devise a plan that could be delivered entirely by private providers or in combination with the public education sector. They do offer an economic means of meeting individual needs and may provide as much as 10–25 per cent of the training delivered by large organizations with their own training function. A glance at the list of user organizations carried on the back of many course brochures will quickly illustrate the width of coverage for this implementation option.

Distance learning   This option, together with open learning, lies very much towards the learner-centred end of implementation. Both have been gaining ground over recent years.

In essence, distance learning is that which is done at a distance from the tutor, trainer or teacher, although there is contact and review with someone. The simplest medium used is books and work assignments. Distance learning can be based on books, company-produced notes or booklets, audio or video cassettes, magazines, articles, film (more rarely), computers, either personal or on-line, and computer-based or interactive material. It was possible to study for a degree through distance learning using the Commerce Degree Bureau of London University 30 years ago and language courses have been available for a similar period.

Advantages

- The learner decides what to study and is often more motivated, having selected the approach, to complete the study.
- The overall cost is substantially less than conventional methods. No travelling or residence is involved. For knowledge-based aspects of learning, the cost is probably less than a quarter, on average, of conventional classroom methods.
- Access can be provided to very high-grade tutorial staff who can mark assignments at their own convenience.
- If a significant number of students is involved, the material can be produced to a very high quality economically. Examination of some of the language courses available or reference to the Open University material will illustrate this.
- To the organization, the fact that the students will pursue much of the learning in their own time makes the approach particularly cost-effective. Large numbers of trainees can achieve learning with a relatively modest commitment of training staff.

Disadvantages

- The lack of interaction with other trainees, except through something like a summer school, can be a problem for some subjects.
- The lack of face-to-face contact with the tutor can mean it is much more difficult to help individuals who have learning problems.
- The lack of peer contact and the demands of a course programme require a great deal of commitment and discipline on the part of the learner.
- If there is a large target audience the content may be less focused than might otherwise be possible. Distance learning materials for diverse industries might miss or underplay certain sectors. For example, in banking, the specialist currency dealer might not obtain such ready access to material as in a more mainstream activity such as lending.

It can be argued that much formal training is a very expensive way of getting people to read and discuss material. Clearly, learners differ in the way they structure their learning, and skills that are manual or interactive cannot be learned only from books. However, the pedestrian plod through overhead transparencies showing Hertzberg's or Maslow's principles, or the photocopied notes used by some teachers could be tackled very much more cost effectively by distance learning.

An example is the type of project management course described in Chapter 6. One of the demands in such a course is to understand the technique of critical path analysis and the programme evaluation and review technique (PERT). The art of managing a project is dynamic and requires a wide range of skills. A simple way, given the facilities, is to use a CBT programme for all trainees to study before meeting for a one or two-day course on the practicalities. Knowledge has to be tested at the start to ensure everyone has done the work and all are starting from a common base. It only needs one or two participants to be sent away, perhaps back to Scotland or Exeter, for not demonstrating a reasonable grasp of the CBT content for the preparatory work to become an integral part of the course, though in the particular course being described this was never necessary. The importance of project management and the organization's limitations in reaching high standards were sufficiently known for it not to be necessary.

Open learning Open learning is a relatively recent notion and refers to the openness of access to learning. The UK has had notable success with its Open University and Open College, which have made the route to obtaining degree qualifications much more accessible, both to people who could obtain basic entry qualifications but not a place at university and to those who could not, because of their personal circumstances, attend university. Collaboration with the BBC has created a large-scale distance learning delivery mechanism, access to which is much more open than was possible just a quarter of a century ago. Open learning is of crucial importance, both to the individual learner who wishes to succeed in self-development and to the organization that wants to capitalize on the great wealth of untapped ability on its payroll.

Advantages

- Access to learning is provided for a wide population who might otherwise be excluded.
- There is more opportunity for individuals to tailor a learning programme to their needs.
- Using a delivery mechanism such as the Open University provides access to high-quality learning material at reasonable cost.
- Learning can be opened up to disadvantaged groups such as women returning to work or women who wish to enter management.
- The motivation and thence abilities and skills of people can be tapped and channelled into areas that the normal company programme does not cover.

Disadvantages

- The concept may be mistrusted by managers who want to specify just who should learn what, and how, and when they should do so.
- The standards achieved may not be as well recognized as the more conventional certification approaches.

- The language and business focus may be seen as missing, as the 'open' approach is necessarily more diffused in its target population than some company training.

The combination of distance and open learning can be very powerful and an extremely useful way of tackling those strategic problems in implementation which are caused by:

- lack of time to release people;
- the cost of travel and subsistence involved in providing conventional training to staff dispersed around the country, as many are;
- the potential shortage of skilled tutors and mentors.

An example of the imaginative use of open and distance learning in a commercial environment is the 'LEAP' programme operated by the Midland bank. Staff join a club and undertake to hire, free of charge, a minimum specified number of resources per year for development. A handy analysis scheme helps them to locate where their development needs lie and the approach then provides an index to material for loan. Thus, if an individual felt that the area of time management was a problem, an action plan and progress report might be built around videos on the 'Unorganized Manager' together with a CBT diskette on time management and the book *The One-Minute Manager* by Blanchard and Johnson. This sort of approach can be used for literally tens of thousands of staff, given the administrative staff and the investment in resources together with management support. It could actually be run on an investment of £10–15 per head plus a similar amount for administration, given some basic assumptions about usage.

CBT and interactive video

This is one of the most recent options, being available practically for commercial purposes since the early 1980s. Computer-based training uses computer hardware and specialized software to deliver training and learning programmes through the computer monitor. It can be used on a stand-alone basis where the minimum requirement is a processor, a monitor and some means of loading the disk. Alternatively, it may be used on the mainframe computer, employing the terminals involved in normal commercial operations. In this case, training usually occurs at specified periods in the day. This approach is particularly appropriate for dispersed operations which are highly computerized such as banks, building societies and retailers.

The approach has been further developed so that the computer can manage the learning programme, giving us computer-managed training. In this, the learner might be instructed to refer to other media such as a book or video and carry out an assignment. The computer programme might then test the student before he or she can proceed. At its more sophisticated, it could refer the student to a particular resource, say a chapter in a book, and then retest a specific aspect of the competence required.

This technology can be linked with video players, thus opening up the use of visual material as an integral part of the programme. As the name suggests, interactive video permits the user to interact with the video material and the computer programme. In a simulated sales situation, for example, a video clip might be used. The learner is asked to decide how a potential purchaser would react by selecting from:

A: Asks further technical questions
B: Raises an objection on price
C: Gives a buying signal

The learner then pushes the key indicated and the programme would play the appropriate video for the response chosen.

The whole approach is highly flexible and reasonably priced. As the technology improves and becomes cheaper, the cost advantages of the approach will clearly improve.

Advantages

- Programmes can be tailor-made and used at dispersed locations, in some cases using mainframe computer installations.
- The approach is readily assimilated by a generation brought up on computer games and introduced to computers in schools.
- The learning design can be very effective and contain integral testing and monitoring.
- It can considerably reduce the cost of providing knowledge and a limited range of skills, particularly for large-scale operations.
- It can provide standardized material which can be easily updated just by replacing the diskette.

Disadvantages

- It does need the hardware investment, a significant front-end cost if technology is not already in use for some other purpose and the delivery is not on-line.
- Some people do not like using the technology, particularly those who are not familiar with it.
- Like all technology, it can be an expensive white elephant if not used.
- The quality of many programmes leaves much to be desired in terms of creativity and interest. Poor CBT can be little more than electronic page-turning.
- Many generic programmes are of limited specific relevance and the high cost of initial programming tends to encourage this. For example, a programme on sales for financial services which actually concentrates on a building society is of limited use to an insurance company.

As a very crude rule of thumb, a one-hour programme will require 100 hours of programming effort; but, for large-scale application, once the hardware is in place, it might achieve the transfer of knowledge at something like 20 per cent of the cost of conventional conference-room approaches. There is little doubt that the use of CBT as a delivery system will continue to increase over the next decade and be a major delivery mechanism. The challenge will be to integrate it strategically with other aspects of delivery to produce flexible and responsive systems which cater for the needs of individuals while meeting the business requirements of the organization, all at an economically acceptable price.

Action learning

Action learning is different in kind from most of the other options for implementation but merits consideration in this section. It is not, except in the most general sense, an approach that is derived from the business plan. It is a means of developing the questioning ability of all levels of staff so that action to overcome problems can be identified and implemented. It needs to be consistent with the vision of senior management and, for real success, that vision must contain a genuine commitment to improvement based on making the best use of the abilities of those in the organization.

Action learning has been an option since 1945 on a very limited scale, but was more widely adopted after 1965. The approach was developed by Reg Revans to encourage comrades-in-adversity to work in sets of some six people to overcome real problems. It is free from the various steps in analysis in that it focuses on the 'lived' experience of those participating and their immediate problems. These problems might in themselves be strategic: e.g. how to reduce a £1 million outstanding debt in an insurance company, or what the Belgian Bank in Brussels should do to establish a successful relationship with EC headquarters, which are located in Brussels.

Advantages

- Action learning focuses specifically on actual problems.
- It is relatively economic to implement in-company and will often be adopted and continued by managers in their own time.
- Benefits are readily identified and action is taken as part of the approach.
- It can enable managers to take responsibility for their own development and be used directly to improve the performance of individuals or groups.

Disadvantages

- It can generate frustration if not supported by top management.
- It can be seen as difficult to control and thus politically threatening by some senior managers.

Action learning may be organized either by internal staff or by consultants. To some degree, once the process is launched in a sizeable organization, it can be self-sustaining if managers are prepared to act as set advisers for groups of their subordinates or peers. It is essentially about applying rigour and logic to problems, about sharing skills and then having to meet peer expectations. Learning occurs through taking action. The set may require any contribution of resources relevant to its particular problem or problems. Thus a set could ask for a discussion on finance, each member could use a CBT programme on financial ratios, the group might watch a video on cashflow and discuss it with an accountant, or even ask one of its members to read an article on zero-based budgeting and present the essence of it in the context of a specific problem.

Mentoring and coaching

Another option that can be more learner-based is the use of a mentor or coach. The mentor is usually a more senior colleague or manager from another function who is prepared to act as a guide or role model for the individual. Mentors share their experience and get involved in career guidance and discussions with the trainee. Typical ways of using mentors are for a senior engineer to guide a graduate engineer through the period required to qualify as a chartered engineer or for a senior manager to be available to a young or middle manager who is on a development or MBA programme.

The organization can set up the scheme with a launch event to highlight the skills and responsibilities involved and then leave the relationship to evolve in whatever depth is necessary. In many ways, mentoring may be regarded as the modern equivalent of the relationship that existed between master and journeyman in the craft guilds. In essence it provides help with on-the-job training that is individually focused.

Coaching is a more focused and sometimes more short-term approach, where the coach seeks to use everyday experience to improve performance. Coaching may be one-to-one or one-to-many and can consist of subordinate coaching boss as well as the more usual boss coaching subordinate. Examples of coaching occur in team or individual sports: the football coach encourages players and guides them in how to execute a set-piece such as a corner, or a golfing coach works on a professional golfer's swing to help the golfer achieve excellence. Faldo's winning of the Open Championships in 1990 after receiving a guru's coaching on his swing is an example. In management, coaching may take place by listening to and then discussing a presentation or by a kerbside conference in which a sales meeting is reviewed to improve performance.

Advantages

- Real work is used so there is no problem of transferring what is learned.
- Feedback can be immediate and practice to remedy faults can often

be carried out on the spot.
- Access to current high-quality experience is provided for less experienced individuals.
- It can be much cheaper, as no outside expert, travelling, accommodation or even, in some cases, loss of production, is involved.

Disadvantages

- Since the approach is opportunistic and involves taking risks, mistakes may be made that cannot be controlled as in the classroom.
- Learning may be disrupted as work situations put pressure on good quality learning.
- Bad habits can be transmitted, though observing bad practice can sometimes be put to advantage.

To make mentoring and coaching work as strategic options requires a real commitment to development on the part of the organization. On the other hand, since as much as 90 per cent of development takes place at work, it is a way of focusing effort on the most fruitful and productive means of developing skills.

Career management   Extending this theme of using experience to develop skills, a sound career management approach can make a very significant contribution to providing some of the skills required by organizations. As a strategic option it requires setting up a unit to make sure it happens and positive support from managers who make selection decisions. The process in outline is:

(a) Identify the future skills and competencies required for all key jobs in the organization over a sensible planning horizon.
(b) Identify those staff with the potential to fill these jobs.
(c) Identify the ideal career paths for jobs.
(d) As vacancies occur or new roles are created, compare the requirements of the jobs to be filled with the career needs of those identified as having potential.
(e) Appoint staff, not only on the basis of immediate contribution, but also by taking account of broadening appointees' careers by using carefully selected experience.

The management of careers may be carried out informally or with some formality. Performance appraisals that include an assessment of potential, assessment centres and succession plans are all important indicators of where to put in effort. Some examples of how career management can provide growth in skill and experience are:

- Managing a small or medium-sized overseas subsidiary to gain general management experience. A youngish actuary might not be the best general manager on the market to manage an overseas subsidiary, but a chief executive in 15 years' time will probably make fewer mistakes and better decisions if given the chance to practise on a smaller scale.

- Experience under the age of 30, of all aspects of personnel management, as provided to many of its staff routinely as part of career management by an organization like Ford, gives a strong base to build on.

Advantages

- Broader experience is available for senior jobs.
- The organization has a better basis for making judgements about promotion.
- Some skills can probably only be learned in this way, e.g. how to integrate the efforts of a senior team of executives.

Disadvantages

- It can sometimes be difficult to get the timing right and the individual may not wish to follow the direction indicated.
- Some staff may be lost by giving them increased responsibilities.

Overall, career management or management development has an enormous contribution to make that is rarely achieved to anything like its full potential.

Graduate schemes The recruitment and development of graduates is a further option. Conventional wisdom is that graduates will provide an above-average intellectual resource of high-quality young staff who have already successfully coped with a number of academic and personal challenges. Many graduate schemes set out to attract staff who will provide the middle and senior management backbone of the company. Because of the possible significance of their contribution at the top of the company or organization, their selection and career management demands attention. The graduate scheme will need to provide a good general introduction to the organization or a scheme to get the best out of high-flyers—preferably, both.

Advantages

- The scheme can provide a corps of reasonable known academic and intellectual talent, the size of which can be determined and recruited fairly accurately.
- The organization can determine the courses the graduates take and shape the output of the scheme to provide the cadre of management it needs.
- It can be more cost-effective than recruiting on the open market, especially in highly technical areas where the best talent can be attracted.

Disadvantages

- If the recruitment or induction is not done well or competitors deliberately target three- or four-year experienced graduates, high attrition can cause the investment to be wasted.

- It can be difficult to attract high-calibre graduates in the production, manufacturing and retail environment.

Overall, most large commercial organizations compete for graduates in a fiercely competitive market in a bid to get the quality of talent they require.

Secondment and external activities

Secondments to charitable or educational establishments or similar activities can also be used on a limited scale. The requirement is often for managerial ability in a context that can be quite challenging to individuals who have spent all their working careers in large organizations.

Advantages

- The experience of staff seconded is broadened beyond their organization's values and norms. Often the use of initiative is a key requirement for the secondment.
- The opportunity to manage a project with high public visibility can sometimes be obtained.
- Some secondments can be used to develop specific competencies in potential high-flyers. For example, six months working on setting up an inner-city self-help group can provide invaluable practical experience to a highly technical manager who is less effective in interpersonal skills.

Disadvantages

- It may be difficult to channel newly acquired entrepreneurial skills on return to the organization, especially if they are required for the next job but one and not the available vacancies.
- The secondee may not wish to return to organizational life.

In some cases, secondments and external activities can provide a useful addition to the armoury of options available for implementation.

The education system

The education system will be an integral part of the development plan and can perhaps best be considered within these phases:

Bridge from school to work: This phase would cover the provision of basic vocational skills and sometimes some remedial skill training in areas such as mathematics and literacy. Typically, the trainees would be school leavers on the Employment Training Scheme or the Modern Apprenticeship Scheme.

Vocational training: This would encompass those setting out to acquire vocational skills through the qualifications administered by such bodies as the Business and Technician Council or the City and Guilds Institute. Day release, block release or sandwich study subsidized by the state and financially supported by the employer is the usual way this is provided. The training will range from quite basic to degree level and would include national certificates and diplomas.

Undergraduate: This level is supported by many organizations through sponsorship schemes whereby individuals are provided with financial support through grants and work experience in the summer vacation. This sponsorship will sometimes be an integral part of the graduate recruitment strategy.

Postgraduate and professional: A few companies will support a small number of high-potential trainees following an MBA course, usually part-time or through distance learning, or taking professional qualifications with one of the many institutions, such as the Institute of Actuaries or the Institute of Banking.

Advantages

- A broad range of courses is provided and resourced by the state.
- There is an element of subsidy or grant support for some educational courses.
- A college or university can be used as an extension of the organization's employee resourcing.

Disadvantages

- Staff may be lost to other employers when they compare terms and benefits.
- The skills provided are very portable and the organization cannot guarantee any return on its investment.

Creating a faculty

One way of obtaining the benefits of specialization and a choice of resources while retaining control and focus on business needs is to create a 'faculty' of internal and external resources for the organization. This can be achieved by securing the commitment of selected academics, consultants and businessmen to provide, say, a minimum of 20 days per annum to the organization. Some of this will be spent each year on getting to know the organization and keeping in touch with developments. This element in effect would be in the nature of a retainer with, say, 15 days spent contributing in some way to programmes.

Advantages

- Experts in particular fields and in the business of the organization can be retained. Thus, a financial organization concerned to create high customer service standards and introduce Total Quality, with a need to improve lending performance, could be quite precise in specifying the skills it would wish to have in its faculty.
- It broadens the employee development skill base while creating and maintaining some identification with the organization.

- It can be much cheaper and quicker to use someone from the faculty to develop, in a relatively short lead time, programmes that are specific to the organization.

Disadvantages

- For the faculty to work really effectively, the staff would need access to commercially sensitive information.
- The main employer of individuals in the faculty, if they are not self-employed, may find the arrangement clashes with their needs.
- The faculty or dedicated network would have to be continuously managed.

Setting up a training centre

The next step is to create a training centre for the organization. There are 50–100 such centres in the UK, the bulk of them concerned with managerial and supervisory training or technical training such as banking or selling.

Advantages

- There is a cost advantage to be obtained over hiring hotels, given the occupancy is managed successfully.
- By having its own centre, an organization can ensure that its future plans and strategies are not discussed in public bars and lounges in hotels.
- It can be used to create a core of employee developers and can ensure a high standard of facilities.
- It can be used as part of an overall strategy to ensure the use of a common language in the organization's training and management processes.
- If it is located conveniently for the organization's head office, the involvement of senior managers may be increased.

Disadvantages

- Since the centre will usually be dedicated to one organization, the cross-fertilization of attending public courses or being in residence in a management centre serving a variety of organizations will be lost.
- Unless there is a strong contribution from outside, the centre can become parochial.
- The danger of the centre becoming, or being regarded as, an 'ivory tower' will exist. Strong contact with the operational work of the organization needs to be maintained.

By setting up or operating its own centre, an organization is able to create a focal point and provide the physical means of implementation using an appropriate combination of the options described.

R&D capacity

Part of the process of implementation may, and usually does, require the development of new products and approaches. The options in this area are:

- buy products that have already been developed, e.g. a 'Time Manager' programme;
- develop your own products by expecting those already involved in diagnosis or delivery to produce new products on an as-and-when possible basis;
- establish a full-time R&D capacity in the employee development function. Such a capacity enables a small group of staff to develop the rather specialized skills in this area and to explore new methods of meeting needs. This capacity would need to be closely allied to the computer-based training and interactive video units and collaborate closely with any open learning or distance learning that is part of the strategic employee development plan.

Advantages

- A specialized unit can work on projects to produce high-quality products on time and without the distraction of operational development responsibilities.
- A centrally produced response can be made available on a geographically dispersed basis with proper briefing on its use. The effect is to achieve a much more professional delivery and image in the eyes of the customer.
- The development of products and approaches can be scheduled and reductions in unit costs obtained. An example of the advantages of an R&D capacity was the greater control and quality achieved in the large-scale training in some organizations for the Financial Services Act.

Disadvantages

- The need to take some of the best deliverers and facilitators off-line is a marginal disadvantage.
- Tension may occur between operational employee development managers and R&D people, e.g. regional training managers with immediate demands on them for responses can clash with the more detached view of the developer committed to perfecting the product.

Research and development can be used to achieve major enhancements of the professionalism of an employee development organization.

Ingredients for success

In moving from the plan to implementation one of the key judgements is how to deliver the plan. This requires a knowledge of the various options and skill in matching them to what the customer requires. Each component of the employee development plan will need to be derived from the business plan and options for implementation discussed with line managers so that commitment and support is gained. Some of the more recent or radical approaches such as interactive video or action learning will have to be deliberately marketed.

The quality of the employee development staff and how they are deployed will be key elements in achieving success. The next chapter examines these issues.

Summary

This chapter has outlined some of the main options available for implementing the training and development strategy. It has compared the use of employed staff with consultants and outside suppliers and considered the various means of delivering employee development, ranging from the conventional conference or classroom instruction to action learning and computer-managed learning. This area of training is one where perhaps the widest literature exists, going into detail right down to how to prepare and deliver a lecture. Some of the most relevant and recent references are listed under Recommended reading at the end of this chapter. The main areas covered here are:

- Unless the employee development function is being set up from scratch, the usual situation is one where selecting how to implement the plan is an ongoing process and a significant proportion of the methods and options used will be the same as in the previous year.
- To achieve change this mix of options and methods needs to be monitored continually and changed to respond to business needs.
- The basic situation and probably the most common is where the organization recruits and develops its own staff to implement development. These staff may be technical specialists, e.g. salespeople or bankers, or people developed from within the company or recruited with specialist employee development skills.
- These resources may be supplemented or supported by consultants, management or technical training centres or polytechnics/universities. The staff hired will bring specific skills.
- Going a step further, an organization can enter into a partnership with a college or consultancy such that the outside staff work closely with the employing organization as if they were part-time employees.
- The further option of running a training centre, using the organization's staff supplemented by a faculty run by the college director, was also explored. Here the impetus for choosing, assembling and maintaining the faculty lies with the organization rather than an external resource.
- The use of open learning and distance learning were described and the advantages and disadvantages explained. The possibility of focusing on the individual learner and the great increase in the breadth of learning resource which could be made available were highlighted.
- The application of modern technology was described by concentrating on computer-based training and interactive video. The potential cost advantages of CBT and computer-managed learning

together with the on-line application of CBT were described, with some cost considerations.

- Action learning was outlined as a quite different option based on a different learning paradigm. Ways of integrating action learning concepts with the demands of business strategy were identified.
- The roles of the coach and mentor were described, with the focus on learner needs and learner-led approaches that move away from off-the-job courses and seek to use work experience for development, as does action learning.
- Career management, or efforts on the part of the organization to manage careers and development, so that the skills and experience it will require are developed in a more orderly fashion was outlined. The particular cases of graduate training schemes and secondments were explored and the advantages and disadvantages highlighted.
- The use of the national education system, ranging as it does from non-examination subjects through vocational qualification to graduate, postgraduate and professional qualifications, was examined to identify how it could be used to achieve success.
- Finally, the option and need in larger organizations to develop its own employee development research and development function was advocated with a description of its contribution to increased professionalism, better products and improved delivery lead times and project management.

What you can do

1 Review the options described in this chapter and the options actually in use in your organization. Explore any that are not used and assess whether they could make a contribution.
2 Identify the costs of using two or three of the delivery methods described for your organization and compare with an estimate of using a different method for each.
3 Review the articles in the latest issues of *People Management* and identify which developments in terms of delivery methods are attracting attention. Are any of the approaches described of relevance to your own situation?
4 Rate the acceptability of the options described in this chapter for your organization on a scale of 1 to 5, with 1 = not acceptable and 5 = commonly used.
5 Identify any other delivery options that you use and compare their effectiveness with those described.

Recommended reading

Bentley, Trevor, 1990 *The Business of Training*, McGraw-Hill.
Lewis, A. and Marsh, W., 'The Development of Field Managers in the Prudential Assurance Company'. *The Journal of Management Development*, Action Learning Special Issue Volume 6 Number 2, 1987, MCB University Press.

Moorby, E. T., 'Mentoring and Coaching' in *The Gower Handbook of Training and Development*, second edition, 1994, Gower.
Rae, Leslie, 1983 *The Skills of Training*, Gower.

10 Putting it all together: organizing the function

A place for everything, and everything in its place.

Samuel Smiles

We have now considered vision and strategy, power within the organization, the identification of employee development needs and making the case to use the organization's resources against competing demands. It has been stressed that all this is a continuous process where the luxury of starting from scratch is rarely an option. The various ways of delivering development were examined in outline only, as there is a considerable literature in that area. This chapter deals with some of the options for organizing the delivery of development. It describes the various roles involved and the scope of employee development. The issues of centralization and decentralization, coordination, and profit or cost centres are then considered. The actual deployment of functional specialists and the use of part-time staff and networking is covered, before the strategic issues of setting up a new organization or changing an existing one are explored. Finally, the areas of attracting and selecting professional staff and the relationship between personnel and employee development are discussed.

Where does employee development fit?

There are a number of options for locating the function within an organization.

1 *Reporting directly to the chief executive or board of management*   This option is rare except in those organizations where employee development is also a mainstream activity. Thus, in a human resource consultancy, a college or a training and enterprise council, where the strategic results of the organization are expressed in terms of employee development, the function might report directly to the chief executive. Succession planning and senior management resourcing reports directly to the chief executive or chairman in some organizations.

2 *Reporting to the personnel director or vice-president (Human resourcing)*   This option is probably the most common in

manufacturing and commercial operations and in many service organizations. It usually represents a situation where employee development is regarded as a specialist sub-division of a personnel function which spans manpower planning, compensation and benefits, line personnel, recruitment and placement, salary administration, industrial relations, communications, job evaluation and disciplinary procedures and includes employee development.

3 *Part of the line function*   In a decentralized or smaller organization parts, or the whole, of the function might be under the control of the line manager. Certainly, the great bulk of most employee development will be carried out and controlled by line management. Examples of where this relationship would exist are:

- An off-the-job production welding school to train production operators.
- A sales training centre in a division of an insurance company.
- In-store training in a retail store.

4 *As an integral part of professional development*   For many professions, qualification requires a period under the direction of an established professional. It would not be unusual for actuaries, engineers, accountants, solicitors, architects and surveyors to control the professional development of young staff.

5 *Reporting to and controlled by specialist functions*   The three most common areas where employee development is located functionally are sales and marketing, information technology and engineering. Other examples might be nursing in the National Health Service or Royal Electrical and Mechanical Engineers in the Army. The balance here is frequently based on political power and the wish to control functional staff. The trade-off is often between knowledge and experience of the functional skills, e.g. selling against the development and training skills required for learning design and delivery. The basic paradox always concerns the reality of employee development being a managerial responsibility of the direct supervisor, individuals' accountability for their own development and the benefits that can be contributed by a skilled employee development professional.

Switching to the domestic situation, few would deny that parents are responsible for educating their offspring or that one generation has a responsibility for developing the next. Equally, all individuals reach a point where they must take responsibility for their own growth. But in the complex pattern of modern society few parents could achieve business objectives *and* educate and develop their children. We therefore use full-time educators to undertake, essentially on a sub-contracted basis, the provision of knowledge, skill and attitude as defined by the national curriculum, which in very broad terms is the training and development plan derived from the ruling political party of the day.

Employee development roles

In any employee development function there will be a number of roles. They may be undertaken by one or more individuals or several roles may be combined and filled by one individual. This section will describe the more common roles; if they are then compared with what has to be delivered, they can be combined into a pattern or mosaic appropriate to a particular situation.

Reception

The contact point with the customer is often the receptionist. This role is to project the image of the function and to ensure that all visitors to a training centre or department are made welcome, whether it is a room in a factory or a management training centre in 400 acres. The receptionist needs to know what is going on and where facilities and courses are located, and be able to deal with all levels in the organization.

Administration

The administration role for a large operation can be a significant organizational and financial task, spanning the following activities:

- Organizing the circulation and accuracy of information about future activities, programmes and courses.
- Designing the marketing format for all literature.
- Controlling the optimum use of facilities, e.g. conference rooms, bedrooms, open-learning resource centres.
- Operating an efficient booking system to maximize the use of facilities.
- Dealing with cancellations and changes to the programme.
- Distributing joining instructions and support material.
- Operating an accounting system and a financial planning and control system. Control of the budget, monthly expenditure and cash-flow statements, and continuous control to maximize utilization should be integrated.
- Ensuring that all facilities are prepared properly, e.g. that the correct video recording and playing equipment is where it is required at the right time.
- Where there is a dispersed operation or an open-learning scheme operated around the country, ensuring all materials are assembled and dispatched to where they are required.
- Providing basic clerical and administrative support to the employee development professional staff.
- Where there is a residential aspect of the function, e.g. in a training centre, the administration function might include the provision and supervision of catering, domestic services, maintenance and bar staff, i.e. all those aspects of hotel management that are required.

Technical support

Employee development has increasingly involved the use of technology. Some of the equipment in common use is:

- overhead projectors

- video recorders and cameras
- television
- sound and vision recording studios
- teaching walls with associated electronic controls
- mainframe computers and personal computers

Any sizeable organization for employee development would need a technician on hand or at least very readily available. When CBT and interactive video are being used some quite sophisticated technical support may be required, especially from software houses or the organization's own information technology function.

Direct trainers The delivery of training is undertaken by either employee development staff with titles such as instructor, training officer and lecturer or by non-specialists. The role essentially involves the following:

- Identifying what has to be conveyed and producing a plan or programme.
- Managing the learning by delivering the programme. This might include the use of lectures, discussion, role play, video feedback, practice, demonstration or any other delivery technique.
- Following up if this is part of the programme.

The direct trainer will often have some technical skill which is being transferred, e.g. selling, jig-boring, hairdressing, and the role will usually be concerned with face-to-face delivery to individuals or groups and focused on specific skill areas. It will sometimes be an integral part of a broader role, e.g. training adviser or training manager.

Tutor mentor This role is similar to that of direct trainer but uses more remote methods (i.e. not face-to-face). The tutor might manage the learning process on specific items of a programme and meet the learner from time to time to review progress. The Open University tutor is an example of this role. The overall programme design will be the responsibility of someone else and the tutor delivers segments of an overall plan or strategy.

Training adviser This role is the first where a broader experience and contribution is involved. Titles may include senior training officer and principal lecturer and the role might include some or all of the following responsibilities:

- Identification of employee development needs in consultation with an internal or external client.
- Selection between alternative options for delivery and presentation of proposed programmes to clients.
- Preparation of a training plan for an area of the company or an in-depth functional area, e.g. financial services pension consultant.
- Evaluation and validation of programmes and adaptation where necessary.

The main distinction between the delivery role and the adviser role is that the former focuses more on learning delivery whereas the adviser is more concerned with analysis and design. In the smaller company the two roles would almost certainly be integrated.

Consultant The employee development consultant might be an internal staff member or an external consultant. The consultant would be expected to have broader experience than an adviser, either more in-depth or experience in other industries. The role could include the following:

- Diagnosis of development needs in the context of the overall business situation.
- Identification of strategies and plans to overcome the problems and obstacles identified.
- Presentation and agreement on the approach with the client.
- Overseeing or delivery of some or all of the strategy and plan agreed.

Examples of the consultant role might include an internal employee development consultant who specializes in an area of the organization, e.g. pensions, and can provide a service across the range from pension management through pensions administration to the development of pensions sales consultants. Another example might be the consultant who has implemented customer service programmes in three airlines who joins a bank to introduce a similar tailor-made programme for all employees.

Training specialists There are many specialist roles as new technologies and approaches are introduced. Examples are the programmer for CBT programmes, the interactive video script writer and producer, the author of distance-learning texts, the learning-style specialist and the educational psychologist. The need for particular roles depends on the decisions made about delivery options, and specific specialist functions are derived from the organization's context and strategy and the business or strategic plan. The role may need competence in aspects of the other roles described.

Training manager/ employee development director This is the broadest specialist role and will normally include the following major aspects:

- Identify strategic employee development needs and prepare a strategic employee development plan.
- Gain commitment to the employee development function throughout the organization.
- Prepare, gain approval for and monitor and control the development budget.
- Ensure that the resources necessary to implement the plan are available.
- Recruit, develop and motivate the employee development staff.

- Monitor delivery against agreed direction and correct where necessary.
- Provide direction to any residential training facility.
- Represent the organization externally on employee development issues.
- Identify in conjunction with colleagues the strategic plan for the personnel function.

The essential requirement of the managerial role is to provide a vision and strategy for the function and to ensure its direction is consistent with corporate needs. The role may require the exercise of the competencies needed in other roles.

Specific roles in many organizations may require aspects of the various roles described. They are meant to be indicative and a starting point for dialogue.

The scope of employee development

Employee development is typically located within the personnel or human resource function. It will invariably cover training policy and delivery and may cover management and career development. It can be extended to include external recruitment, internal recruitment or promotion, assessment centres, performance management systems and performance appraisal. If one exists, it would usually include a residential management centre or other training centre, though the principal or director could report directly to the human resource director. In a smaller organization it could make sense to include employee communication within employee development. External activities such as relationships with training and enterprise councils, non-statutory industry training organizations and suppliers of training and development services would also be within the scope of the employee development executive. The following sections consider the scope of employee development and the usual organizational requirements and interfaces.

Training policy

The definition of policy and standards of performance is a core aspect of the function. The identification of standards to be met either through a centrally controlled programme or a devolved or decentralized operation is central to the scope of employee development. Its influence would normally span all levels of the organization from chief executive to the most junior. However, where specific aspects of training are under the control of a function, e.g. sales training, or are decentralized, there will often be the need to negotiate the boundaries of the scope of employee development and standards.

Training delivery

The delivery of training will usually be clearly within the scope of the function. Four distinct types of delivery would be:

- Central delivery, which might be carried out in a classroom, conference room, hotel or regional centre. The content will be specified and delivered within policy guidelines.

- Residential centre delivery, which might range from management training to technical training. There may be an interface between training and, say, management development and often the need for integration with the training policy and coordination aspects.
- Regional delivery, where the delivery is decentralized. It will usually be controlled by a central development function but may have sufficient autonomy to develop its own products and occasionally policy.
- Computerized delivery, which might be through personal computers or mainframe. In the latter case, in particular, close liaison with the information technology function is essential.

Coordination This aspect of the role is particularly important in decentralized or regionalized operations. It is essential to ensure the maximum advantage is gained from local development and that development is delivered within the policy and standards specified.

External training The use of external providers needs to be coordinated and controlled. In a large organization this aspect can cover quality assurance where the experience of using different providers can be monitored together with coordination. One classic example is the two-day seminar on, say, appraisal where a dozen people from different parts of the organization book independently. It might be much more cost-effective just to send one or two.

Recruitment and assessment This is an area where opinions about what should be included within employee development begin to clash. One school argues that selection is an integral part of employee development and that, particularly in the case of assessment, the development aspect is of major importance. Any development aimed at maximizing individuals' strengths and motivation must necessarily include these as an integral part of the activity. The opposite school is founded in notions of matching people to jobs through personal specifications and job specifications that look at jobs to be filled rather than people to be grown. Recruitment is usually located outside the employee development area.

Career management This term is used to describe the actions aimed at ensuring that potential is identified and that people are developed to meet future managerial needs. It is the management of experience. It is sometimes referred to as management development and concentrates on identifying individuals for roles. It may require a longer time scale than day-to-day employee development, focusing perhaps on which junior managers should attend a development programme for middle management jobs they might occupy in two to five years' time. The activity will often include the design and operation of a performance appraisal scheme, which will itself identify development and training needs.

Graduate selection and development can also be included in this area. The main interfaces are with operational personnel managers who will often be closely involved with appointment decisions locally. The management development function may be split from the training function and report either to the employee development director/ manager or the personnel director. Occasionally, especially when focused on senior managers, it reports to the chief executive or chairman.

Performance management systems

A development of the late 1980s, performance management systems take performance appraisal a step forward and define the management process in much more detail, using some form of managerial competence model. These systems may be aimed at motivation, reward, development and organizational role clarification and could arguably be located in compensation and benefits, employee development or even operational personnel once the scheme is launched.

Personnel operations

This is perhaps the most significant interface to manage. The local personnel staff will usually have a close relationship with local management and see themselves as brokers for employee development and the other areas of human resource or personnel management, e.g. compensation and benefits. They may or may not be competent in particular areas. They may be skilled 'gate-keepers' able to manage the interface situation or skilled 'wall-builders' dedicated to keeping others out. The way in which this interface is managed in a human resource function is probably the best indicator of the professionalism of the whole operation.

External relations

There will usually be a strong need to have links outside the organization. These may be with the Training Enterprise Councils (TECs) with regard to youth training such as the Employment Training Scheme, or with external providers such as management centres or consultancies. Many industries have organizations such as the Insurance Industry Training Council (IITC) and the Association of British Insurers (ABI) in insurance, together with professional educational bodies such as the Chartered Institute of Insurers (CII). Typically, there will be 'informal' groupings such as a group of insurance training managers that meets biannually. All these external contacts, together sometimes with national contacts such as the CBI or TUC or international bodies, can form useful inputs to the organization's employee development function.

In considering how to introduce or change an employee development function, careful strategic consideration needs to be given to where it should fit within the organization, where its scope and boundaries will be drawn and the roles that will be carried out within this remit. These are issues that can have a significant impact on whether success or rejection is the ultimate outcome. The political in-fighting within the personnel function and the larger waves from decentralization strategies or changes in key personnel can rock or effectively sink the employee development function. Some of the broad issues are considered next.

Key strategic organizational issues

The size and scope of the employee development function will be determined within the context of other key issues, some of which are:

Centralization   Organizations tend to oscillate between centralization and decentralization. The vogue in the early 1990s in the UK was away from centralization though all organizations tend to identify certain issues that still demand central attention, no matter how strong the pressures for devolution are. The advantages that centralization offers include:

- The ability to ensure that all component parts of the organization work in the same direction.
- The effective pooling of research and development effort so that major development projects can be used to effect across the corporation.
- Planning and control of functions so that, in a complex organization, planning can be undertaken to a common standard. Control systems, especially those for financial control, can then be used to control diverse organizations and businesses.

Decentralization   is the process of devolving planning and control. It has been seen as the optimum reaction to competitive market conditions, particularly in a political climate that promotes free enterprise. The decentralized unit will be responsible for most of its activities and the advantages are generally the mirror image of those for centralization. Some of these are:

- The decentralized unit is closer to the business customer and should be able to respond more quickly and with greater relevance to market needs.
- It should be more focused and able more easily to plan and communicate its strategic vision and mission.
- It will create its own identity but in doing so may experience friction and conflict with other units in the organization. Typically, there is conflict between the central head office seeking to monitor corporate standards and the pursuit of narrower objectives by the operating unit.
- Decentralization is most appropriate for manufacturing, delivery or service organizations with a relatively short-time horizon for development and planning.

Clearly, centralization and decentralization rarely exist in pure forms. It is common to have an organization where there is a central employee development policy unit and, where the organization has a residential management college, this may be a corporate resource. Decentralized units work within the overall framework and will receive some services from the central unit. A high degree of central control can improve the cost effectiveness of delivery of employee development but often at the cost of flexibility and service to particular customers or parts of the organization. There are strong arguments for a centralized employee development research and development capability.

Research and development　Many organizations actually have a minimal R&D capacity for Employee Development. Development is left to operational units or they buy the results of the R&D of others in a package, e.g. 'Putting People First', Kepner Tregoe Decision Making, Accelerated Learning, and the myriad of implementation packages based on research. There are considerable advantages to be gained by setting up a dedicated employee development R&D unit, some of which can be:

- Specific applications can be developed that are immediately relevant to the organization, e.g. a specific sales process.
- Lead times can be much better controlled.
- Full-time commitment to the role produces better quality products and often more lateral responses to problems.
- Briefing and skill development can be controlled and delivered by the organization's own staff who understand the context.
- Rapid response to specific needs can be achieved.
- Competitive edge can be developed and the market take-up controlled.

A close link with customers is essential, just as for any product, but the establishment of employee development research and development can considerably enhance the professionalism of the function.

Project organization　With the advent of rapid rates of change, one of the strategic issues that needs to be considered is the permanency or life expectation of any employee development organization. One way of viewing organizations is to set them up with little recognition of the turbulence they face and to copy other forms of organizing for apparently similar situations. This is, essentially, to view the organization as a static entity based on inflexible principles such as specified numbers of levels or direct reports. An alternative is to view the employee development task for the medium term as a project task. By defining business output and standards of performance it is possible to derive an organization that will need to flex and change over time. It might be necessary in the early stages to concentrate on managers and to develop technical skills, and then to provide high-volume sales training. Some technical training, say in how to use automated accounting computers, might need to begin after three months and end after six months.

Thus, it may be sensible to consider the employee development organization in two components; a core or basic organization that will continue for the foreseeable future and a variable element which might last for the whole or part of the life of a major business project, such as the introduction of an automated administrative back-office for the network of a retail bank. The project itself might last three or four years, with the employee development effort needing to change and adapt during that period.

Dividend improvement and cost reduction   Many organizations are under severe pressure to improve or maintain the level of dividend payable to shareholders. In areas where the organization is vulnerable to takeover, the share price will also be a carefully watched index of performance. It is common for consultants to be employed whose brief is to cut costs. The simplest ways of doing this are de-layering, i.e. taking out levels of staff, amalgamating units and cutting staff, and simply taking existing plans and, after suitable challenge meetings, cutting what is proposed by 20 per cent (or whatever is the most plausible cost figure). This pressure may impact directly on the employee development organization by removing manpower. The task then is to rethink priorities against available manpower.

Functional delivery   The organization may need to take account of fragmented or specialized needs and determine how best to provide a service to a large legal department, say, or a division made up of architects, surveyors and civil engineers. These specialist applications are devolved functional units and need to be recognized and dealt with by the organizational approach adopted for employee development.

Profit centre, cost centre or just there?

There are basically three ways of treating the costs involved in employee development. The first is simply to regard the cost as an overall investment and apply normal financial control and reporting procedures to the expenditure incurred. The second is to establish employee development as a cost centre and to allocate a proportion of all costs and services used to it. Thus, a cost centre would include accommodation, rent, computing and pro-rata allocation of security, etc. The cost centre can then show a surplus or deficit against budget. The third level is to operate as a profit centre and this involves the generation of income and transfer pricing for services used. Using this approach, a charge is calculated to reflect all the conventional costs, such as salaries, rent and cars, together with items such as marketing and research and development. A day-rate for consultancy and rate for each day of training programmes can then be devised and all services used can be 'charged' to the customer. This will incorporate all administration and reception costs and can produce a 'price' that is comparable with that charged on the open market. An element of profit can be included in the price and the difference between income and costs is the profit or surplus generated.

The profit centre concept is most likely to be used in a situation where decentralization is strong and, in theory, the customer will have the right to buy services such as employee development either from internal suppliers such as a management centre or from outside. In practice, the need to balance the intangible benefits of internal employee development with ad hoc outside price comparison usually means the concept is applied with a light touch. However, the treating of employee development as a profit centre has many advantages, which include:

- Increased focus on what the customer wants.
- Awareness of the features of external suppliers as a competitive alternative.
- A more commercial business-oriented approach on the part of employee development staff.
- A facility to pay employee development staff on the basis of results and commercial performance.
- More commercial approach in budgeting and financial control.
- Improved marketing generated by the need to be competitive with outside suppliers.
- Where agreed at the policy level, the opportunity to sell products and facilities on the open market and generate actual profit. Examples are the marketing of customer service programmes by some commercial organizations and the use of residential centres on a letting basis at weekends.

The question of how to charge for services is important for the atmosphere and culture for employee development that is to be created. A positive commitment to profit generation and the use of commercial comparisons can considerably enhance the acceptability of employee development. For example, the day-rate cost for a residential centre designed to operate as a four-star residential hotel unit can be readily compared with the day-rates of a bundle of similarly located hotels; and the cost of two- or three-day courses can be monitored against similar non-residential provisions by half a dozen selected suppliers.

Alternative approaches to employment

Flexibility in approaches to the basis on which staff are employed can be increasingly important. Some of the options are as follows.

Full-time employment   on the employee development function staff. This incurs anything from 15–40 per cent of salary as annual employment costs for items such as pensions and relies heavily on correct selection decisions and a predictable future demand for the skills employed. The range of skills available can be rather limited and it can be difficult to utilize them fully.

Secondment   from within the company. This approach can help flexibility by facilitating the use of individuals with specific skills for an agreed period. Examples might be the secondment of bankers as tutors in a management centre. Shorter-term secondments of those with specific skills, such as a six-month secondment for an information technology project supervisor to investigate the best equipment to set up learning centres, can also considerably extend the range of skill available and increase flexibility.

Part-time employment   With changes in job patterns many employee development staff now seek variety and independence. Contracts designed to provide, say, 100 days of consulting per annum on specific aspects of management training can be negotiated at rates considerably more favourable than the per diem rates of major consultancies and without the full-time employment costs of pensions, car, etc. The individual gets the advantage of guaranteed employment for a fixed time with the opportunity to supplement the balance at a different and possibly higher day-rate with other customers. This type of contract has been common in private management centres and is increasingly being adopted by commercial organizations, especially those with residential centres to operate.

Fixed-term employment   Another variation is to employ someone for a fixed period, on a full-time or part-time basis. This could be particularly attractive when the business plan indicates a resource need for a fixed period, say three years, after which it might be difficult to employ the individual. A fixed term contract would be particularly appropriate in a turn-round situation, especially if it incorporated a success bonus on termination. It might be necessary to attract senior managers who are prepared to work particularly hard on change for an agreed period and who enjoy the risks and benefits of a turn-round situation. Another advantage of the fixed term contract is that it could be renewable after, say, two or five years. This gives both parties the opportunity to terminate or extend the arrangement.

Self-employment   An individual may prefer to set up as self-employed and, in the early days, work on contract for a fixed number of days. As the business becomes established, the individual should then create a wider customer base.

Networking   The networking approach can be used to resource specific needs. One derivation is the establishment of a 'faculty'. Each associate or faculty member can be paid a retainer and guaranteed a minimum number of days work. The associate undertakes to get to know the organization by working in it and builds up a business knowledge which informs his professional contribution. The organization gains the benefit of breadth of experience without the lack of relevance so often found in external resources.

Work/job sharing   Can also be a useful way of meeting individual needs for independence while ensuring the organization's needs are met. Job sharing is very suitable both for professional staff and administrative and reception roles.

Consultants and educational institutions   The purchase of services from the wide range available needs to be taken into account when considering the desirable mix for setting up and operating the employee development function.

Agency staff   Short-term problems can be covered by agency staff, particularly in the clerical and administrative areas and for information technology tasks.

Taken overall, the best balance of staff resourcing and means of employment needs to be identified at a strategic level. It may be essential to adopt approaches such as networking or fixed-term contracts to employ certain staff. A commitment to excellence plus reward comparability considerations may lead a college or a consultancy to offer a middle-range salary plus, say, 50 days free for personal consultancy. The severe shortage of excellent professionals and the increasing recognition of the central contribution of employee development in achieving business results will require more and more imaginative approaches to remuneration including, no doubt, some forms of share options and equity participation.

Combining roles in practice

The frameworks outlined above may be used in the rather hierarchical way described or combined into more imaginative roles, reflecting the variety of responsibility combined with diagnosis through to delivery, which can offer a satisfying professional role. Some examples are:

1 *Consultant for a business area coupled with acting as programme director for a particular programme*   This combination was particularly useful in moving from a menu-driven course approach to a business-specific service, backed by core programmes designed for flexible application across a large corporation. Business areas were examined and internal employee development consultants were assigned on the basis of their background and experience. Thus, the newly established Group Pensions plc might be assigned a recently recruited consultant who was familiar with diagnosis and the development of resourcing plans for professional staff. The Property Services Company, because of its size and growth rate, was assigned a senior consultant with retail experience supported by a less experienced consultant from a retailer and a sales training manager from the insurance company. Each of these individuals would also have specific responsibility for corporate programmes. Thus, the consultant working in the investment company could be working on a programme for newly appointed junior managers, the majority of whom were from life administration. Equally, the consultant for pensions could be

responsible for the 'Younger Manager' two-week programme for high-potential managers. This matrix approach demands professional staff but considerably sharpens the business awareness of all development staff.

2 *Business skill delivery coupled with practical business experience* The combination of current business skills and employee development professional competence can be achieved by short-term secondments of successful practitioners. Taking sales training, the secondment needs to be short enough for the individual to remain sharp in the skill and up-to-date while developing sufficient competency in the development activity. Experience indicates that the shortest useful period might be 12 months for competent district managers to become good set advisers in an action learning programme and then to pay back their investment by running 6–10 sets. The typical time for sales trainers to train new sales representatives was 12–24 months, with 18 months being ideal. To develop higher levels of sales training skills would require longer. In more technical areas, such as CBT programming, a more realistic period is probably in the order of two years. Similar logic applies for other specialists from banking tutors through to craft instructors.

3 *Operational management and development* One of the perennial problems of R&D is the tendency to move away from the exigencies of practicalities towards the 'ivory tower'. One way of combating this is to include the development manager as an integral part of the employee development management team and to ensure that he or she has had previous operational experience. Assigning responsibility for specific implementation projects and rotating staff between development and operational training also helps to build a practically focused R&D unit while gaining the advantages of full-time application to research and development.

4 *Programme director and subject specialist* A further way of gaining breadth and variety is to create the role of programme director for individuals who are also recognized as subject specialists. Thus, in a management college, it can make a lot of sense for the finance specialist to be programme director for a senior management programme or for a sales specialist to direct a programme for young managers.

The use of the various options described in this chapter to construct an organization which is right for a particular business context will require imagination, experimentation and courage. The shifting nature of organizations and the rich variety of businesses and tasks which organizations undertake make the use of simplistic prescriptions very inadequate. Careful diagnosis and an awareness of the options, coupled with rigorous questioning of what exists and often what is proposed, are essential in today's complex organizations.

The next section of this chapter will examine what is involved in setting up an organization and how to go about changing an existing one, together with some thoughts on attracting, selecting and keeping good staff.

Setting up and developing an employee development organization

The most common situation found is the redevelopment of an existing organization for employee development. It is relatively unusual to start with a clean sheet though there are a number of situations where this could occur. Some examples are:

- The building of a green-field site such as the Toyota car plant near Derby.
- The creation of a new organization such as the Prudential Holborn organization that was set up to serve individuals of higher net worth.
- The acquisition and creation of a new business organization.
- Diversification such as the move by accounting groups into mainstream consultancy.
- A smaller company growing to the point where it requires a dedicated employee development resource, which might be a training officer and an administrative assistant.

The steps are basically common and would follow this process:

1   Decide that a full-time or part-time resource for employee development is required. Commit the resources and decide how to specify the size and shape of the task.

2   Identify needs and specify resources. This process could be carried out by an independent consultant or by the senior management of the new organization.

3   Give careful consideration to the job and personnel specifications to identify the type of individuals required. The smaller company might, for example, need someone with broad experience spanning management training through to employment training trainees. The financial services company might need someone to engender a sales culture. Discussion with an executive search organization or recruitment agency could be of considerable help.

4   Once the initial resourcing and diagnosis has been carried out, set priorities which reflect the business priorities, and develop proposals for implementation. The content of Chapters 7, 8 and 9 would be particularly relevant here.

If the organization is to be of reasonable size, the senior individuals, once they are in-post, need to work through with senior line management many of the issues covered in this section. Decisions on the degree of centralization, the competence in employee development required in decentralized units, the possibility of using seconded staff in the setting-up phase, and the numbers and types of individuals to be recruited will have to be made. In particular, specification of the role, the need for internal consultancy skills and the timing will be crucial as well as the input from the parent company, in some cases.

The approach should follow a logical cycle and be geared closely to the business vision and mission. This might be achieved more effectively in the early stages in the smaller organization where the delivery can be much more closely linked to the chief executive. In any situation, decisions at this stage will influence the culture and professionalism of the employee development effort significantly.

Changing an existing employee development organization

Many businesses are experiencing rapid change and this is reflected directly in the employee development function, which is effectively one of the barometers of change. A turbulent, fast-changing business situation will read directly across into the employee development function. Some examples of why the need to change is generated are:

- Business changes demand new skills that the existing employee development management cannot deliver.
- The whole strategy of employee development needs to be changed from, say, a menu-driven course approach to an internal customer-centred consultancy service.
- Decentralization creates new roles as individual businesses seek to focus on their specific employee development needs.
- A major shift, such as privatization of a hospital or a college requires new and different strategic approaches to be implemented.
- A new chief executive or personnel director brings different values to a situation, e.g. the need to cut costs.
- A new employee development executive with commitment to specific strategic options, such as open learning or action learning, might prompt change.

There are many similarities between the steps in changing an organization and setting one up. The process for changing is basically:

1 Review current practice and senior individuals' views of the appropriateness of what has been done. This might actually be quite demanding in terms of finding out and quantifying precisely what has been done and who, among the political barons, has real power and should be given particular attention. This review should identify the main aspects of current plans, the volumes and costs proposed, the delivery and organizational strategies and the availability of competent staff. Any serious disquiet about the employee development contribution should be identified.

2 Identify the business issues, both from this process and by discussion with a wide range of senior individuals. Then identify needs in broad

terms and the resource requirements. At this stage priorities should be firmed up and agreed with interested parties. For example, sales training might be seen as a higher priority than improving the already acceptable actuarial development. It might be decided to delay the upgrading of head office training for two years until regional training is put on a sounder footing.

3 Then work out the change strategy and identify the type of skills required for the new organization. This phase will require working through the employee development plan for the next two to three years in detail and identifying which skills will be needed and how they can be acquired, and what skills will be redundant.

4 The next, and sometimes painful, decision is to identify which staff will form the core of the organization, who will need to be redeployed within employee development and who will need to leave the function. The typical options here are a transfer to another task, sometimes movement into a more suitable role, secondment to a task outside the organization, redundancy or, as a last resort, dismissal.

The configuration of the organization, role specification and reporting lines are all key components in building success. The senior posts for managerial and consultancy staff are key. In this, getting the balance between continuity and knowledge of the organization and the incorporation of new and different skills is probably the key issue. Too much change and new blood can lead to rejection by the organization. Too little can leave the employee development function on the sidelines as change steamrollers past it.

5 A clear statement of direction coupled with milestones and feedback is an important step and one that is often not well done. The phases of the change should be highlighted and shared and repeated measurements taken on progress. The temperature of the organization and its progress varies over time and feedback loops need to be built into the process of changing the employee development organization.

6 Leadership and basic humanity will sometimes be an issue. Many of those key to achieving success will have been integral parts of the pre-change regime. It is very unusual and effectively impractical to start with a clean sheet of paper. In making changes, as in battle, many of those who observe the process will take careful note of how the casualties are treated. It is a point worth bearing in mind.

Overall, changing an existing organization may require more patience, more courage and more opportunism than establishing one from scratch. The latter situation does not involve comparison with what went before, vested interests, or the need to establish credibility against previously delivered development. It may require careful judgement on timing and, almost certainly, as long as this is possible within the organizational content, the attraction and selection of good staff.

Attracting and selecting competent professional staff

As a general rule, an organization can never have too much talent dedicated to the development of others. In practice, the talent available is usually nowhere near sufficient to achieve the demands and rate of change of most organizations. The basic steps in defining what is required of professional staff are similar to any selection process:

- Identify clearly the organization configuration and roles to be carried out. In particular, take into account probable changes in degree of centralization/decentralization, the acceptability of the internal consultancy role and the phasing of major change projects.
- Specify the experience and skill mix required.
- Put together a reward package that appeals to the motivational drives of the target market.
- Make sure that the attraction channels used reach the target market, i.e. decide what mix of advertising, word of mouth and search is necessary.

Once the basic attraction process has been defined, care needs to be given to defining the culture within which employee development will function and to the employee development culture itself. It is sensible in a professional organization to use a high degree of participation in the selection process. Exchange on professional standards and vision and a mutual exploration of fit between the applicants and the existing team is essential.

The way the employee development function is managed should be a key factor in whether individuals join and whether they give their full contribution. Some of the values and indicators to look for are:

- Commitment to the development of individuals, possibly with some sort of learning contract.
- A management approach that encourages individual initiative and growth.
- Excellence as a clear part of the employee development mission.
- Fit between the values of employee development and those of the organization.
- Evidence of what delivery mechanisms are actually in use. Espousal of, say, CBT is much more credible where learning resource centres fitted with CBT are in operation.
- Career opportunities through a credible structure that permits progression through to internal consultancy or management roles.
- The experience mix and achievements of the senior staff in the employee development function will often be a good indicator of what the organization has the capacity to do.

- The nature of the experience and change offered in terms of its fit in the career pattern of the applicant is also worth exploring.

Taken overall, competence and experience in much of what has been described earlier in this book, and fit with the organization, coupled with an attractive and achievable vision of the employee development contribution, are key in attracting and matching competent staff with particular roles.

Summary

This chapter has described some of the main considerations involved in designing an organization to deliver the training plan. It has reviewed how to set up a new organization and how to change an existing one. The main areas covered are:

- The scope of employee development and where it usually fits in an organization. Consideration of the benefits of locating employee development within personnel, sales and marketing, information technology or the line function.
- Wherever the function is located, the various roles that need to be covered range across reception and administration, technical support, direct training, training advisory work, internal consultancy, specialist tasks such as CBT programmer and employee development management. The coverage and relationship between the roles and the various combinations were described.
- The coverage of employee development can range across training policy, training delivery, residential college delivery, career management and management development, performance appraisal, performance management systems, recruitment, research and development and personnel operations. The various options and combinations were described with consideration of what is most appropriate in various situations.
- Key strategic organizational issues were explored. The impact of decentralization and the advantages and disadvantages of both centralization and decentralization were illustrated. The role and importance of research and development in employee development, together with the benefits that can be achieved, were described. The increasing importance of project management and impermanent organizations was considered. The input of cost reduction programmes and how they impact on organizational strategy and the contribution of employee development in these circumstances was covered.
- Profit centres, cost centres and the mechanics and advantages of operating employee development as an internal profit centre were highlighted.
- Issues concerning how best to employ staff in terms of conditions offered and the pros and cons of using full-time staff, term contract staff, part-time staff, networking and job sharing were focused on

with consideration of how roles can be combined with different employment conditions.

● The processes of setting up and changing existing employee development organization structures were examined. The importance of identifying fit with the organization's overall mission, how to phase changes and the crucial importance of defining current and future roles highlighted the dynamic nature of organization change. The impact of other factors discussed in the chapter, such as decentralization, were described together with triggers such as the appointment of a new chief executive.

● Finally, some of the broad considerations involved in attracting and selecting professional staff were identified and guidelines and key values described.

What you can do

1 Draw up an employee development organization chart for your organization and identify what roles it should have in 12 months' and 24 months' time.

2 Review your organization against the roles and scope described in this chapter. Rate on a scale 1 to 5, with 5 high, how well each unit of your organization meets the organization's current needs.

3 Using the roles described, assess which areas of your organization are strong and which are weak.

4 Draw a chart of the employee development organization in your organization:　(a) two years ago
　(b) now
　(c) two years ahead

What main trends are evident?

5 What is the main organization feature that inhibits your success and causes you most problems? What will you have to do to overcome this obstacle?

PART THREE

The individual perspective

11 Learning, motivation and the brain

The importance of learning styles, motivation patterns and brain hemisphere preferences

It is at best paradoxical and at worst grotesque that the process of learning itself has been so little studied, researched and acted upon in institutions which proclaim themselves as being concerned with the development of managers.

Alan Mumford

Just as organizations need to invest in training and development to survive, so do individuals. This chapter will look at development from the individual's perspective. It will consider why individuals need, in practice, to develop continuously and how you can do so either within an organization or on your own. The needs that any organization will have for you to improve and adapt your skills will be explored from your perspective. It is a simple though sometimes overlooked fact that your skills belong to you. Their development and maintenance are your responsibility.

The process of individual learning will then be considered. This will be done from the perspective of helping you to develop yourself, rather than from a theoretical or academic perspective. Alan Mumford and Peter Honey's adaptation of David Kolb's learning process will be used for this. It is, of course, of only limited use to understand your own learning style if you are not motivated to use your abilities. Thus, some time will be taken to consider what it is that motivates people to learn and grow. A longer-term perspective on development throughout life will then be introduced. This will parallel for you, the individual, the types of processes often described as career management or management development. Finally, consideration will be given specifically to how you use knowledge about learning to improve your own work and learning performance.

The importance of focusing individual development

As described earlier, it is a basic fact of life that all organisms, including individual learners, have to adapt and change to survive. At the extremes, organizations have to change to survive. Individuals in the 1990s have needed to focus and change the skills they have simply to obtain and retain employment. The need for focus is considered here:

- **Survival**　In a period of intensive competition, restructuring of organizations and threat from overseas competition, the cost effective development, training and continuous self-development by individuals has increasingly been recognized as necessary for organizational success and ultimate survival.
- **Competitive edge**　Development and learning are more frequently recognized as the means of gaining competitive edge. The individual who can offer some distinctive or particularly relevant skill will gain advantage. For example, the Chairman of Barclays Bank identified two skill areas as essential for future directors, i.e. information technology skills and language skills.
- **Strategic learning**　Many organizations now have vision statements and fairly detailed strategic plans. Individuals need to ensure that they possess the sorts of skills that these plans will demand. As more emphasis is given to selling financial services by building societies, for example, individuals will need to acquire knowledge and skills in related areas such as insurance and banking. It may well be a good personal investment to acquire a qualification outside the traditional field but in the right strategic direction.
- **Self-selection**　Individuals have always had the opportunity to put themselves forward for attendance at training courses. A recent development has been the transfer of choice from the employer to the employee for certain, admittedly limited, aspects of development. The EDAP scheme at Ford and the LEAP scheme at Midland Bank/ Hong Kong and Shanghai Banking Group are examples. Individuals need to take this further and regard themselves essentially as purchasers of training and development for themselves. As a customer, you can work out which product you want at what price and quality and whether it meets your need.

One consequence of recent trends will be to shift control of learning more to the individual as a customer. The shift in thinking about training and learning from being deliverer- or supplier-centred to being customer- or learner-centred has been quite profound in recent years. Ideas and concepts about training and learning have shifted in the direction shown here. The move has been away from an approach where:

- The learner took a largely passive role, for example, listening to and taking notes on a lecture.
- The ability of the lecturer/teacher was regarded as paramount.
- The learning was often difficult to apply back at the workplace.

A lecture on leadership or a game involving throwing eggs or building Lego towers may or may not lead to improved leadership, but the trainer would probably enjoy it.

- Off the job training can be controlled and free from interruptions. It may be economic in time and provides a relatively safe way of learning.
- The responsibility for learning is sometimes far from clear. The learner can opt out almost completely if he/she chooses.

Current thinking is much more focused on the individual's learning. The learner is situated more at the centre of the process. A learner-centred approach might be characterized by:

- Active involvement of the learner in real work and in skill areas of his or her choice.
- Much greater focus in terms of the relevance of the learning to the learner's world.
- Learning may be disjointed and sometimes time-consuming, as real life demands interact with the learning process.
- The learner will need to take real responsibility and risk may be involved.
- The individual's boss may be actively involved as mentor/coach.
- The individual learners can build up their personal skills and experience whilst taking real responsibility.

The essential point is that the individual is the only person who can achieve learning for himself or herself. Thus rather than the 'trainer' setting out to 'train' the 'trainee', we have at last begun to focus on the 'learner' needing to 'learn'.

Learning Learning is the process of acquiring new knowledge, skills and abilities. The result of learning is that an individual knows or does something he/she did not know or was not able to do before. It is possible to learn and remember new things without actually using this knowledge. In practice, our brain observes and records far more information than we actually use in any physical way. Learning has interested thinkers since time began. Plato's *Republic*, for example, was a lifelong development strategy for the development of the 'Guardians' or leaders of a Greek city-state. In view of the tremendous importance of the need for learning since the Industrial Revolution, it is indeed surprising that the process of learning has itself been so little studied, as Alan Mumford pointed out in a paper as recently as 1989/90. There have been a number of studies and approaches to the learning process ranging from Pavlov's conditional response, through stimulus–response (S–R) learning theories such as that described by B.F. Skinner through to the cognitive theories of F.C. Tolman and the classical Gestalt psychologists. The key difference is that S–R theorists believe learning is about responses or habitual actions whereas the cognitive view encompasses the use of facts, frameworks and concepts. Thus the stimulus–response view would argue that new problems are solved by using past habits or trial and error. The cognitive theorist would argue that perception provides conceptual insight into relationships and variables involved. These differing views have similarities with Reg Revans's P (Programmed) and Q (Questioning) notions referred to later and to the left brain–right brain dichotomy described later in this chapter.

The essential point about learning is that there is no *one* right description of how an individual learns, since individuals learn differently. The work of David Kolb presented in his book *Experiential Learning* published in 1984 and the subsequent development by Peter Honey and Alan Mumford offer what is probably the most valuable, if not the only, comprehensive theory about learning in use currently for employee development.

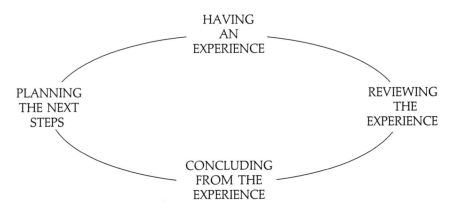

Figure 11.1   *The learning cycle*

The learning cycle

Thinking and understanding about learning was considerably enhanced by the work of David Kolb and his theory of the learning cycle. This approach was adapted and developed by Honey and Mumford into the 'four stages' cycle (see Figure 11.1):

Thus learning involves having a concrete experience, reviewing that experience by observation and reflecting, concluding from the experience often by developing abstract concepts and then planning the next steps by testing the concepts. Thinking about the learning cycle in this way integrates the approaches of Kolb, and Honey and Mumford. The learning process can be regarded as a complete cycle though learning can occur at each stage. It is essential that the learner should be aware of each stage if optimum learning is to be achieved. An example might help to clarify the process. If you consider that the learning objective is to be able to ride a bike the following process could be observed:

1 Having an experience.   The new, inexperienced rider sets off and quickly overbalances. He/she learns that falling on concrete hurts and coordination of balance and turning the pedals is difficult.
2 Reviewing the experience.   The learner can observe that it is necessary to both propel the bicycle and keep it in balance. At this stage doing both is too difficult.
3 Concluding from the experience.   Thinking about the experience, the learner decides on reflection that it might be better for a helper to steady the bike whilst pedalling is mastered. Alternatively, a pair of stabilizers might be fitted.
4 Planning the next steps.   The learner then tests the concept by asking a helper to hold the saddle and steady the bike whilst the pedalling is mastered.

The other alternative would have been to continue just having the experience and gradually balance may have been mastered. This would have been a frustrating and painful experience.

A key point about the learning cycle is that individuals may show a preference for one or more aspects of the cycle. Thus a tourist may set out to visit a city on a more or less random basis (activist), visit the obvious sites and trust to luck for refreshments (pragmatist). Alternatively, our tourist may use a guide book to review other people's experience (reflective) and, concluding from that experience, plan all the steps of the visit (theorist). Either tourist would probably have different learning experiences. Of course, both would need to be to some extent activist to be a tourist at all.

Honey and Mumford developed a questionnaire using 80 behavioural statements which can establish an individual's preference for each component of the learning cycle. A learning style profile can then be produced which identifies individual preferences. Each component of the cycle is labelled as described in Figure 11.2:

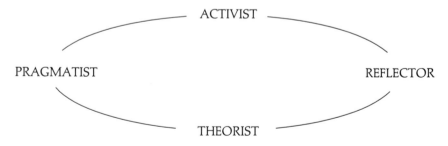

Figure 11.2   *Learning styles*

Each of the four basic styles are described and it is possible to generate a description of an individual's style of learning. It is essential to understand that although one style may be preferred, most people use all four styles to some degree. Thus an individual may prefer mainly to learn in an activist–pragmatist mode or a reflector–theorist mode. The activist–pragmatist is the 'can–do' learner. The reflector–theorist will 'sleep on' the learning or say–'I will think about it'.

In very broad terms the learning styles can be described as follows:

- *Activists* live in the here and now, enjoy immediate experiences and are gregarious. Expect the activist to want to get on with learning.
- *Reflectors* are the quiet learners who listen and put things together. Thorough analysis and synthesis will lead to integrated thoughtful learning with a broad context.
- *Theorists* will explore assumptions and develop or use theories or models that 'explain' what they see. They prefer 'logic' and certainty and dislike subjectivity and intuition.
- *Pragmatists* try out ideas to see if they work in practice. The pragmatist is down to earth and practical and is about making practical decisions.

Honey and Mumford have produced some excellent descriptive material which provides well-presented help for those who wish to identify, understand and enhance their learning styles. Their database has allowed them to produce 'norms' or examples of typical profiles for a range of occupations and their *Manual of Learning Styles* contains very helpful material on how the learner can use learning styles for self-development and how the boss can use learning styles to improve managerial effectiveness. An example might be a high activist boss who wants results 'now' struggling with a high reflector subordinate who wants to think about the problem, consider all the angles and leave no stone unturned in producing an answer next week.

Knowledge of learning styles provides an excellent basis for discussion between such a high activist manager and high reflector subordinate. Indeed it is correct to regard learning styles as a basis for discussion and improvement rather than some sort of test. What you achieve from knowing your learning style is a better understanding of how you have preferred to learn, how others learn and how you might develop and expand your ability to learn by expanding your preferences for ways of learning. If you are serious about self-development you need to know and be developing your own learning style.

The brain

The most important element of how you develop yourself will be how you habitually use your brain. The last fifteen years have seen an explosion in the amount and relevance of knowledge about how the brain functions. It has been clearly established that speech is controlled from the left side of the brain. The two hemispheres of the brain (the left and right looking towards the front of the head) have unique and complementary functions. Their specialization, and our habit of using preferred modes of thinking in much the same way as we use preferred learning styles, means that each of us is a unique but describable human being in terms of how we think and how we learn. The conventional description of the brain describes the brain in terms of left and right hemispheres. Ned Herrmann, an American brain 'guru', has developed a metaphor which divides each hemisphere into upper and lower segments. An overall description of current thinking might depict the specialization of functions as is indicated in Figure 11.3.

Left brain, right brain preferences

Left	*Right*
Controls right side of body	Controls left side of body
Controls speech	Concerns people and concepts
Concerns words and numbers	
Works in logical sequence	Visualizes, pictorial
Uses analytical evaluative approach	Integrates and is holistic
Uses fact-based data	Intuitive
Essentially quantitative	
Concerns detail	Spontaneous
Processes data sequentially	Concerns feelings
Uses planned approach	Concerns senses, e.g. touch
	About people

Figure 11.3 *Left brain, right brain preferences*

Thus it can be seen that those who habitually prefer left-brain hemisphere thinking and learning will focus more on logic, analysis and detailed approaches whilst those who habitually prefer a right-brain hemisphere approach will be more about concepts, intuition and feelings. Thus a left-brained accountant (this is a profession which often attracts those who prefer the left-brain approach) will be concerned about facts, analysis and planning. A right-brained partner who is more concerned about feelings and spontaneity may find it very difficult to understand that the couple cannot go out for a delightful surprise dinner to celebrate their first wedding anniversary as the accountant has to obtain more facts that evening to complete the planned audit report by the middle of next week.

Knowledge of your brain preference can be obtained at a general level by considering Figure 11.3 and assessing where your preferences lie. At a gross level and through discussion with some honest friends or colleagues you will probably be able to assess whether you are more 'left-' than 'right-brain-hemisphere-inclined' in how you think and act. Your habitual approach may be deeply ingrained. However, you would be able to modify your behaviour to at least some degree by concentration on any changes you wish to achieve.

It is highly likely that your brain hemisphere preferences and learning styles impact on how you develop yourself. They will also have a major impact on how you are seen by others. At the extremes, very spontaneous, abstract approaches might be quite incompatible for planned, detached individuals. A creative, abstract artist will almost certainly need a mentor who can at least relate to that mode of thinking if the two are seeking to develop the artist's style.

Motivation to learn

An essential element of any individual's learning and development is that individual's motivation to learn. A key question to answer is what motivates you to learn?

There is no generalized theory of motivation which applies to all people at all times. The classic theories of motivation, i.e. what driving force leads a particular individual to attempt to achieve some aim to meet some personal need, concentrated essentially on content or process. Thus Maslow's hierarchy of needs or Herzberg's 'motivation' and 'hygiene' factors sought to explain motivation in terms of what motivates individuals.

In contrast the 'process' theories are more concerned with the actual process of motivation or how behaviour is generated and sustained. Vroom's expectancy theory is an example of this. In essence, the individual learner will find it helpful if not essential to understand his/ her personal motivations. Thus the reader is recommended to study in more detail the theories described. If possible any associated 'instruments' should be completed to build up a map of how you are motivated.

One particular approach which the author has found particularly helpful is the System for Identifying Motivated Abilities (SIMA) which is an assessment methodology developed by People Management Inc. It was referred to in Chapters 1 and 7.

By reflecting on your own experience—if reflection is a style that you are comfortable with—it is possible to identify patterns. A combination of awareness of your preferred learning style, your preferred brain hemisphere style and careful consideration of events in your life may give you insight into how you learn best. Thus one or more of the following may be indicative of how you learn best:

- I like to read in detail about a subject and then buy the latest equipment in the field that I can afford.
- I enjoy watching how people behave on training courses and then working out how effective their behaviour is.
- Taking an engine apart using the manual and then reassembling it myself was the best way for me to learn mechanics.

- Reading about concepts in political history books really helped me to work out how best to deal with office politics.
- I like to study on my own and thus to achieve the passmark set by an expert.
- I chose to study pottery by discussing what was on offer at the local college with the tutors. I felt comfortable with the pottery teacher.

A useful exercise is to write down in detail occasions or events where you have achieved really meaningful learning. Try to be as specific as possible. Does experimenting or reflecting suit you best. Do you prefer broad concepts or detail. Do you like spontaneity or do you prefer things to be well planned. Do you like to test ideas, perhaps to destruction, or are you more comfortable building theories.

The importance of *how* you learn and *what* you learn best is that if the learning experience suits you, you will learn better. The wrong content, circumstances and motivation can be very uncomfortable. A caring, holistic, intuitive interpersonal care assistant might find a structured, detached lecture on caring for the elderly anything from boring to theoretical. But such lectures happen. They may be just what is wanted by a left-hemisphere dominant, reflective administrator who needs to make detached budget recommendations in this area.

The longer term view

In this chapter, the realities of how individuals learn have been described and discussed. An individual's learning is unique to that individual. The way he/she learns will depend on brain hemisphere preference, preferred learning styles, the circumstances in life, the individual encounters, specific motivations to learn, individual capabilities and, of course, the available opportunities.

Wherever possible the effectiveness, speed and relevance of learning needs to be enhanced. One approach to achieving this is a careful, reflective review of your learning strategy for the future. Just as organizations can plan their futures, so can individuals. Some useful steps in this regard are as follows:

1 Where am I now? Review your learning to date and produce an inventory of your current situation. A portfolio of competences might be helpful. Consider:
  (a) What skills do I have?
  (b) What learning methods have I experienced?
  (c) What approaches to learning suit me best?
  (d) Which areas of learning have I been successful in? e.g. language, car driving.
  (e) Which areas of learning have I been least successful in? e.g. managing staff.
  (f) What is my learning style?

(g) Which areas of success in my life have given me the greatest satisfaction?
(h) What activities do I least enjoy?
(i) What opportunities am I following now to achieve learning and growth?
(j) Am I growing in terms of learning or am I just marking time?
This snap-shot of the present can be as detailed as you wish.

2 Where do I want to get to? Review your hopes, ambitions and dreams for your future personal, business, family, professional and leisure activity growth:
(a) Are you satisfied with things as they are?
(b) What changes would you choose to achieve?
(c) What changes might you be forced to achieve? e.g. if you lost your job.
(d) What new skills do you want? e.g. to play the guitar or to learn word-processing.
(e) What ambitions do you want to achieve? Will these involve learning?
(f) What skills do you have but feel are underdeveloped? e.g. the basic ability to draw or play the piano.
(g) Do you have a plan for your career? What learning and experience will this require?
(h) Are there any personal skill weaknesses you want to eliminate? e.g. learn to swim if afraid of water.
(i) Are any other people involved in your hopes? e.g. would you learn Spanish with your partner prior to buying a property in Spain?
(j) Do you plan to continue to grow and if so, how?

3 How do I get where I want to go? The basic steps, whatever stage you are at in life, will be:
(a) To focus on a clear picture of what you want to learn and why.
(b) To create the circumstances so you can learn in a way that suits you, e.g. change jobs, enrol for an Open University course, start a business using a hobby.
(c) To choose your learning methods and styles just as an organization would for you, if it were developing you.
(d) Review and evaluate progress, the relevance, cost and appropriateness of your learning.
(e) Continuously adapt and refocus your personal and professional development *to keep learning and growing.*

The process described, which is the same in principle to that described earlier for organization development, can be used to produce an outline direction for personal development. This would indicate broad areas and opportunities which point in your desired future direction. It might cover a one-year period, a three-year period or some other convenient time span. The approach can be used to review the pattern of your learning throughout life to date. Some broad judgements can then be made about future direction over long time periods.

In order to make the most of learning opportunities either after a training event or a review of learning opportunities it can be helpful to draw up an action plan. This is considered next.

Learning and action planning

It is sometimes useful to prepare a written personal development plan. This might particularly appeal to the more left-brain dominant reader or those who prefer a reflector–theorist style of learning. Any personal development plan will require the following basic steps:

1 A list of those areas and abilities which you wish to develop. These may include for example, your ability to listen, speed read or use a personal computer. Ideally, the areas should be as specific as possible.
2 A plan of action for how you will achieve your learning and development. Ideally you should develop learning objectives which will clearly state the outcomes you are aiming for and a time-scale. Learning objectives should be measurable where possible. They should enable you to decide if you have achieved your aims.
3 An indication of methods. This should indicate how you will learn. A survey by the author on individual methods showed that approximately 40 per cent of managers interviewed planned no action, 10–15 per cent used technical or professional development through colleges or the Open University, 10 per cent were studying languages through colleges, 20 per cent followed the activities of their professional institute and 10–15 per cent undertook self-study, e.g. reading, CBT etc., correspondence courses.
4 Facilities. The personal development plan needs to identify what facilities will be used. Some options are the use of universities, the Open University, correspondence courses, local colleges, in-company learning programmes and learning centres, libraries, colleagues, work experience, etc. It is particularly helpful to have access to at least one or two individuals who can provide support and help with motivation when the going gets tough. The support of partners is absolutely key.
5 Planning and monitoring. Monitoring should be based on a project plan of some sort, however much in outline. The first step is often the most difficult. Try to specify milestones and finish point and include continuous monitoring. Monitoring should be based on learning objectives and include measures for success. For example, by the end of three months I will be able to use all the basic functions classified in Section 1–5 of the handbook for the XYZ Personal Computer. After one month, I will be able to set up, manipulate data as described in Section 2, 'save' and print to a standard that I find professionally acceptable. My partner will provide assistance on a request-only basis during phase 1.

6 Review next steps. Learning needs to be continuous in today's fast-moving competitive environment. Personal development planning should always be up-dated as new areas unfold. Continuous professional development keeps individuals up to date. It ensures that the rate of learning will exceed the rate of change. When this is achieved, personal growth that keeps ahead of change is assured.

Summary

This chapter has focused specifically on the individual. It has compared and contrasted the organizational perspective with the way in which an individual needs to consider learning and motivation. It has covered the following main points:

- The importance of bringing sharp focus to the question of personal development. It described how learning and development are central to competition, organizational survival, the way in which individuals select and achieve personal growth and the impact of the shift towards more learner-centred approaches.
- The importance of the learning process and how to use the learning cycle. In particular, the way in which every individual is unique and learns differently was outlined. Ways of thinking about learning and the practical application of Honey and Mumford's work were shown to be particularly relevant to learning and self-development.
- Brain dominance. Recent thinking on the way in which the use of the brain affects how individuals think and behave was described and reviewed. The importance of understanding that individuals have a preference for using some combination of the right hemisphere and left hemisphere of the brain was emphasized. Current knowledge of left-brain and right-brain preferences was outlined and the way in which our brain preferences might directly affect how we learn were considered.
- The issue of motivation was then considered. Various theories were described in outline. The work of Art Miller on using biographical data to identify individuals' main motivated drives was highlighted specifically.
- A means of reviewing individual learning strategy was then described together with some guidelines on how to draw up a personal development plan.
- The material outlined, whilst valuable in its own right, also provides a basis for Chapter 12 which goes on to describe how an individual can approach self-development.

What you can do

1 Identify in writing three examples from your experience in which you felt you learned most effectively. The examples should be very specific to enable you to specify *how, what, where, when* and *why* you learned and why you felt the experience was successful. Select examples where you enjoyed the experience.

2 Complete a Honey and Mumford learning style questionnaire to identify your learning preferences. Discuss the outcome with your boss, a colleague or your partner.

3 Compare your learning style preference with the examples you identified in point 1. Identify which elements of your learning experiences relate to which elements of the learning styles.

4 Consider the descriptions of behaviour attributed to left- and right-hemisphere brain preferences in the section on the brain. Identify your habitual preferences and any areas where you wish to achieve changes.

5 Identify your main motivation(s) to learn, your preferred methods of learning and use this information to review the suitability for you of the next learning programme you undertake.

Recommended reading

Honey, P. and Mumford, A., 1992 *The Manual of Learning Styles,* 3rd edition, Peter Honey Publications.

Miller, Art and Mattson, T., 1989 *The Truth about You,* Ten Speed Press.

Herrman, Ned, 1990 *The Creative Brain,* Brain Books.

12 Achieving self-development

God helps those who train themselves.

Lord Young of Graffham

Chapter 11 described approaches to learning, outlined how brain hemisphere dominance might affect learning preferences, described the importance of motivated drives, and considered the principles of personal action planning. This chapter will focus on various approaches to self-development from the point of view of the individual. Just as the organization needs to consider strategic options for development, so also you as an individual need to decide how you will achieve your development goals.

Chapter 4 addressed how an organization moves from strategic plans to action. It identified a range of options for development. In this chapter we will consider what options are available to the individual and develop some of these in detail. Broadly, the options are:

- Set up opportunities for regular feedback. Assess the feedback and decide if you wish to modify your behaviour.
- Do your own development through reading, discussion and planned experience.
- Attend a training programme at a college or organizational facility.
- Work with a counsellor or consultant on personal development.
- Develop a learning contract with your manager or peer(s).
- Use an organization's learning centre or resources (such as the Midland LEAP Programme mentioned earlier).
- Use computer-managed learning resources on your own PC or at a convenient centre.
- Use distance or open learning through correspondence courses, the Open University or similar provider.
- Produce an NVQ portfolio and identify personal development needs.
- Use company or government funded programmes or loans to buy training facilities.
- Participate in action learning or self-managed learning.
- Use an appraisal or performance management scheme to identify and promote your own development needs or wishes.
- Use instruments such as the learning style questionnaire or Belbin's team roles to identify personal profiles.
- Practise continuous personal/professional development (CPD) as an approach to keeping up to date managerially and professionally.

- Undertake a learning experience through coaching.
- Identify a mentor and build a relationship to enable personal career development.
- Use project experience or job secondments to build new skills.
- Undertake non-employee activities such as school governor.
- Extend your experience into new sectors, functions or roles.

As indicated earlier, much of any individual's adult development will take place either at work or in other aspects of an individual's life. On average an individual might spend 5–10 days on a formal training course in any one year. The balance of each year is available for personal development.

Just as an individual may learn something or nothing from a training course, that same individual may learn a great deal or very little from the opportunities life provides. It is probable that most people experience the great majority of their development at work or through life. Before considering the rich variety of possibilities provided on-the-job and in life, it may be helpful to consider first maximization of what training courses have to offer.

Making the most of training courses

The first thing to be clear about is where responsibility for development lies. This chapter argues that the responsibility is primarily with the individual for his/her own development.

The organization will broadly be seeking the following from formal training programmes:

- The meeting of learning objectives which it has determined as necessary to meet its organizational objectives.
- An economic provision of learning and skill development for an optimum number of participants for its own needs. For example, you may not be trained for an occupation simply because you want to follow it.
- Cost effectiveness for the organization in terms of unit cost for trainees.
- A return on its investment in terms of contribution to competitiveness and profitability or whatever organizational goals it is pursuing.

The individual, on the other hand, may have different and competing objectives. For example:

- To acquire skills to become more attractive in the market-place.
- To develop skills and to gain certification to further the individual's career independently of the organization's current needs.
- To fit the learning programme to the individual's learning style, brain dominance and personal motivations.
- To impress the organization through high performance on the

programme. This will possibly be at the expense of the other individuals' learning.

There is almost certain to be some conflict between the 'scatter-gun' aim of the organization's programme and the 'rifle' aim of a well-motivated and prepared individual. Some of the steps an individual can take to get the most from a training programme are:

1 Be clear about what you want from the programme. If possible, discuss your needs with your boss and what the programme provided with previous participants.
2 Use the programme as an opportunity to practise in a safe environment if at all possible. Decide what skills, roles or behaviours might be useful for you to develop and use every opportunity to do so.
3 Exploit your learning preferences. If you prefer to learn through activities, be positive in taking opportunities. If you are a reflector or a theorist, use your style to enhance your rate of learning.
4 Use networking if this suits you. A significant amount of personal growth can be achieved by your interaction with other participants.
5 Conscientiously undertake action planning. One of the main limitations with formal programmes is the issue of transference of learning back onto the job. Planned actions to improve specific personal skills can help to bridge the gap between the course and reality.
6 Take personal responsibility for your learning. Try to clarify your learning contract with the programme leader. Specify your expectations at the start of the programme. Ask for additional material or specific sessions or specific perspectives if these would help you. The learner is essentially the customer in a training programme. As such he/she has a right and a responsibility to give feedback on the suitability on the training product delivered.
7 Evaluate the contribution of any formal development programme to your actual performance and behaviour after a suitable period. Compare your behaviour with your original objectives. Identify any additional action, such as practice at work to improve proficiency, which could be used to maximize your personal development.

It is sometimes seen as fashionable to criticize formal training programmes. However, used positively they can provide significant development in a focused and cost-effective way. It is always important to be clear about who is in fact accountable for the individual's success. Particularly in today's modern organizations,with rapid and unpredictable rates of change, the skill of developing oneself is becoming more and more important. Decentralized and more modern approaches to work will increasingly put pressure on individuals to take responsibility for their own development. A positive, challenging approach to formal training programmes can greatly help to ensure participants gain the maximum for themselves from any general training programme.

Getting and using feedback

In the context of the learning organization, as described in Chapter 14, it was shown that feedback and adaptation to the demands from the external environment are essential for organizational survival. In a similar way, individuals need feedback to function effectively. Feedback is an essential component of learning and self-development, especially in the area of changing behaviour. Individuals vary in their natural ability to recognize and use feedback. Some examples of the ways in which feedback can be obtained are as follows:

- By observing expressions and non-verbal behaviour, e.g. a yawn can convey boredom.
- Through discussion with a colleague, family member or partner, e.g. when you are late yet again.
- From a professional counsellor or consultant who may act as a sounding-board.
- By the results you achieve in an examination, e.g. passing a driving test.
- At a performance review or appraisal meeting where results are discussed.
- Through the use of psychometric or other tests e.g. Myers–Briggs or PAPI.
- By undertaking a task and establishing what you can and cannot do.
- Using video to record an interaction or period of behaviour and then to analyse what was happening.

As described in the preceding chapter on learning, feedback and adaptation of behaviour are essential components in the learning cycle (see Figure 12.1).

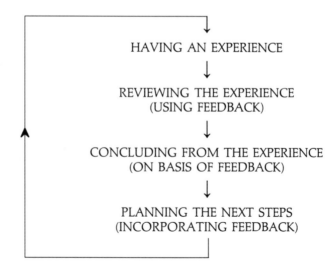

Figure 12.1 *The importance of feedback in the learning cycle*

Feedback can be a difficult process to incorporate into self-development. Many individuals are reluctant to give accurate or even any feedback. It is not always easy to accept and use it. However, feedback must be a key element in the process of comparing what you aspire to become as an individual with how both you and the outside environment perceive your behaviour.

Performance appraisal and performance management

From the individual's viewpoint, any formal review process to appraise performance can be a privileged occasion to obtain feedback. It can also provide the ideal platform for discussing and agreeing developmental opportunities. Some of the issues which an individual may usefully explore are as follows:

- How does performance compare with agreed performance objectives?
- What are specific examples of where the individual has met or failed to meet expectations?
- What behaviours are seen as disfunctional by the boss, peers or subordinates?
- What specific development opportunities are available to build on strengths or to reduce or eliminate weaknesses e.g. projects, assignments, training programmes?
- What, in the view of the appraiser, are the key behaviours or attitudes which might be a factor in preventing promotion from or threaten retention of the individual's role?
- How can the boss help the individual to develop?
- How might the individual help the boss to their mutual advantage, e.g. by the individual representing the boss at important meetings to free the latter's time and improve the former's networking and visibility?
- How do both appraiser and appraisee see the future career path or personal development of the appraisee? Specific feedback on current performance and views about future potential can provide a useful strategic reflection on possible avenues for self-development. For example, a successful junior manager might as a result of such a discussion, decide to enrol for an MBA.

Performance management systems, with their specific focus on how results are achieved and specific, focused measurement by using performance standards can be particularly useful. Future performance demands and future skills requirements should be identified as specifically as possible. Any performance gaps give an immediate agenda for improvement action and provide a platform for some form of 'learning contract'. This idea will be described next.

The two essential components of self-development described thus far have been the need to identify specific performance standards for individuals and to use formal and informal methods of obtaining and giving feedback to enable appropriate development action to be identified.

Drawing up a learning contract

A 'learning contract' may be explicit or implicit. Its purpose is to clarify the commitments and responsibilities of the partners to learning where more than one person is involved in the learning process. Thus, when agreeing on development action, it can be useful to discuss and agree:

- Who is taking accountability for what.
- What learning is involved. If at all possible, the development of learning objectives will help the process. Thus boss and learner may agree to improve the level of service offered to customers, or the objective may be for the student to complete successfully an educational or vocational programme and, by satisfying the examination requirements, to achieve a certificate.
- Who will pay for specific elements of learning.
- What effort will both partners put in. This may involve a commitment of the use of personal time by the learner.
- Agreement on the learning methods to be used.
- Identification of how feedback will be handled.
- Agreement to a series of formal review points or milestones where appropriate.
- What each party will get out of the contract. Thus a learner may seek to improve his/her ability at contributing to meetings and in return agree to represent the boss at specific meetings once he/she has achieved an agreed level of proficiency.
- What values, rights and responsibilities are involved. For example, that the learner will take responsibility for his/her own learning, and that the boss will give honest feedback when asked for it.

Overall, the purpose of the learning contract will be to clarify the relationship and to enable a clear and honest relationship. The 'contract' will sometimes be written and may be in the form of an action plan. A training programme may include a form of 'learning contract' by identifying participants' expectations at the start and then by reviewing and evaluating the degree to which they are met through process reviews. The idea of a 'learning contract' is implicit in an action learning set, a coaching situation, a mentoring relationship and many other forms of learning activity. The 'contract' provides a ready means of evaluation by comparing the outcomes to the terms of the learning contract.

Getting the best from a mentor

Mentoring has received a significant amount of attention in the UK in the 1990s. 'Mentoring' is the activity carried out by an experienced contributor to enable the development of peers, younger, junior or less experienced colleagues or subordinates. It is said to take its name from Greek mythology. Odysseus appointed a wise and trusted friend, Mentor, to oversee the education and development of his young son Telemachus whilst Odysseus was away on his epic voyages. Thus the mentor acts as a counsellor, adviser, friend, sounding-board and role model for the individual's development.

From the point of view of the self-developer, some of the characteristics to look for in a potential mentor are as follows:

- Firstly, the wish and the ability to undertake the role on the part of the mentor. Providing help and guidance of the sort necessary is a fairly rare skill. Look for evidence of prior success in terms of others who have received mentoring and gone on to success.
- The mentor must have the time to provide guidance and preferably the organizational influence to open doors of opportunity for the individual.
- Mentoring skills include the ability to listen, to help with the focusing of problems, appropriate experience to provide perceptive and practical advice, the confidence to challenge and support proposals and the preparedness to get satisfaction and joy from helping to create progress for others. Early discussions should give clues as to whether these attributes exist.
- A track record as a mentor would clearly be very relevant. If the mentoring relationship is part of an organization's employee development strategy it may be possible to get reliable views on how the mentor goes about the task. It is of crucial importance to establish the right supportive relationship. Mentors who have high needs for power and control should be treated with caution.
- The ability to influence or bring about career opportunities can be invaluable. As the recipient of mentoring, the individual will be looking for help in developing personal skills and experience. The ability to tap into networks and influence job appointments is clearly vital. One creative example of this might be the middle manager who attended an organization's course for high-flyers. Attendees were required to identify and negotiate their relationship with a senior manager to act as their mentor. This middle manager rang the Employee Development Director and arranged a meeting to discuss the latter acting as his mentor. The Employee Development Director was responsible for nominating all appointments to middle and senior management roles. He agreed to act as mentor, though clearly the role would have to be strictly impartial as regards career development.

Mentoring is essentially a long-term strategic process. The person with a mentor will have access to counselling, discussion, support, guidance and coaching. Feedback can be impartial and relatively objective and the individual will gain access to significant managerial experience. It can be rather like having your own personal board of directors for your career. Both strategic and tactical decisions can be informed and hopefully improved.

Creating coaching opportunities

As mentioned at the start of this chapter, a significant amount of personal self-development takes place at work. Coaching is one of the key approaches in this area. Coaching is the conscious use of work experience to improve or create specific skills or behaviours. It uses what is done to achieve business objectives to also extend and develop personal skills. Coaching can be regarded as tactical in most cases, in contrast to mentoring which involves a more strategic long-term approach.

An individual may be coached by a boss, peers, a colleague, subordinates, a consultant or in reality anybody with whom he/she comes into regular contact. It is essential to be clear what the coaching is seeking to achieve. Thus some discussion on aims and methods is important. Thus, a person being coached may be seeking to improve his/her ability in making presentations. This requires identifying precisely what aspects need improvement, practice in ways of achieving the desired behaviours, feedback during practice and possibly in the actual presentation and a review of how things went. The person who seeks to use coaching for self-development could usefully ask whether the potential coach has all or most of the following skills and abilities:

- The ability to listen sympathetically to what the individual needs.
- Experience of reviewing performance and identifying gaps in behaviour which prevent success.
- Either the ability to explain and demonstrate the skills or performance that needs to be improved by coaching or sufficient experience of the coaching process to enable the learner to work through the problem. For example, a coach to a world-class sports person might have only limited technical ability in the sport but needs to understand coaching techniques, motivational patterns and how to improve specific performance.
- The commitment, time and resources to enable the self-developer to grow.
- The ability to identify learning goals with the person being coached, to be able to spot opportunities to develop the skills and the ability to round off the coaching. This most difficult step of letting go, and encouraging the developer as an independent adult can be very demanding. It is an attitude which those seeking to be coached well should seek out.
- The integration of coaching as an integral part of the coach's managerial or operational style. The approach to coaching can be seen in the way a parent coaches a child to speak or walk, right

through to the way in which some chairpersons take evident pleasure in developing senior executives.

Since learning and personal growth are key determinants in achieving organizational success, the choice of a 'boss' who is a committed and competent coach is clearly central. It may often not be possible to select your boss. However, part of many managers' career success can be attributed to the fortunate or conscious association with a coach or mentor.

Making your development continuous

The increasing rate of change in organizations has led to radical revisions of how we think about development, particularly in the professional areas. There was a time when an individual could graduate either through a degree course or a professional qualification and then the knowledge and skills gained would basically serve him/her for the rest of their professional life. There has been an explosion in the amount of knowledge and skill demands since about the 1970s. In some areas now, half of what is learned as a graduate will be out of date within five years. The study of the brain is a classic example, where a significant proportion of what is now known has been discovered in the last five years.

This change in the rate of growth of professional knowledge has led to the concept of Continuous Professional Development (CPD). This is sometimes described as Continuing Professional Development. The idea is that all professionals should continuously update themselves and demonstrate that they have done so through a learning diary. Thus an individual who is undertaking CPD as part of self-development might usefully undertake some of the following:

- Join a professional institution, e.g. the Institute of Mechanical Engineers. For some institutions, you may need to demonstrate a minimum number of days of CPD per year with the associated verification of activities.
- Regularly read the institute's professional literature.
- Attend selected branch meetings to participate in discussions of current developments.
- Attend workshops and conferences to keep up to date and to extend one's personal competence.
- If appropriate, prepare papers for publication or present papers at conferences or workshops.
- Participate in the activities of an institution, e.g. as student adviser or programme arranger.
- Act as a coach or mentor for more junior professional colleagues. Contact with current issues at a junior level can help to keep you up to date.

CPD can be a useful way of generating a portfolio to demonstrate learning which might otherwise not be recorded. Those areas of rapid and significant growth such as projects/experience of assignments to solve key problems can be captured for your portfolio. Similarly, much of the activity described elsewhere in this book, such as attendance at training courses, academic courses pursued and use of CBT, might form an integral part of your CPD folio. If possible, it is suggested that the active self-developer should not only aim to keep up to date professionally but should also have a vision of his/her future. The aim, then, would be to focus professional development on this vision or aim and to create opportunities which contribute to achieving that vision. For example, if your aim is to be a European manager, a spell of working in Europe at the early stages of your career could considerably enhance the learning of say French or German that you feel is necessary to be an international lawyer or company legal adviser in the European Union in thirty years' time. This way of thinking might more accurately be described as Continuous Personal Development.

Using action learning

It can be argued that there can be no learning without action. In some senses, all action can lead to learning. Our understanding of the deliberate use of action to learn in a systematic way is barely fifty years old. Action learning was pioneered by Reg Revans at the National Coal Board after the Second World War. It set out to use the experience, growth and prior learning of comrades-in-adversity in an active way to solve problems. In the process, by sharing their hopes, aspirations, successes and trials, each participant learned. This learning was made explicit at the 'set' or group meetings. Action learning or one of its derivatives such as self-managed learning has been fairly widely used over the last 10–15 years. As a self-developer, individuals can use this structured method of learning by and through action in a number of ways as described below:

1 Find out if action learning is being used in your organization. If so, talk with the organizer and see if you can join a set.
2 Explore the possibilities of joining an external action learning set. Some organizations belong to consortia which use forms of action learning to develop their managers.
3 Try to set up a group using the basic principles described. Support groups as part of a formal education programme or self-managed action learning sets are examples.
4 The basic principles of identifying a real problem, setting out actions and reviewing what has been learned can be used in many situations not normally regarded as formal action learning. For example, a coach or mentor could, and often does, create an action learning environment. Learning contracts are clearly a derivative from the original thinking.
5 Undertake an academic programme which uses the principles of action learning.

The issue of learning from experience, either by personal reflection, actively working with others or by the use of concepts, is central to the learning theories of Kolb and Honey and Mumford mentioned earlier. Revans's system beta shares the same conceptual perspective. The use of action learning concepts together with the formal visioning idea described in the organizational context earlier in the book give a sound basis for personal self-development. Some of the tactical or implementation options are summarized next.

Self-development options

There are many means of achieving self-development. Some of the more common are described briefly below:

1 *Reading* a programme of selected readings of books and articles can make a useful contribution. Once you have a picture of which areas you wish to develop, selective use of bibliographies, magazines or computer-based information systems, such as the National Lending System, can provide focused reading lists. Ideally this could be combined with discussion with your coach or manager.

2 *Correspondence courses* can provide a well structured programme in specific areas. Materials are often produced to a very high standard and incorporate tutor support and possibly weekend programmes for other students.

3 *Open learning* Once you have a clear idea of your personal development needs, a wide variety of methods and media is available. The Open University provides an excellent combination of television programmes and text, many organizations have access to open learning resources, schemes such as the LEAP programme at Midland Bank provide substantial access to texts, audio and video tapes and computer based material. Open learning resource centres both in organizations and colleges provide access via personal computers, interactive video and multi-media packages to a wide range of material. It is almost certainly true to say that opportunities for self-development have never been so readily available.

4 *Project-based experience* The rapid rate of change has created extensive opportunities to gain new experience through project work. Projects have become a common way of providing the opportunity to tackle real problems, often at the leading edge such as introducing telephone banking or cross-channel multi-skilled train operators. A positive commitment to seek out opportunities and use approaches such as learning diaries and discussion groups on learning achieved can provide substantial benefits.

5 *Training programmes* These might be in-company or at an educational establishment. They can range from one-day seminars to postgraduate degrees. The essential point is to commit your time only to activities which will help you to achieve the right self-development for you.

6 *Planned experience*   This may take the form of a planned career move initiated by the organization or of a move that you yourself generate. In essence, it is providing the work-based opportunity for you to develop specific areas of skill and experience.

Whichever approach you adopt, the process of self-development involves the following simple steps:

1 Know what you want to learn.
2 Pursue the most appropriate methods to achieve your learning and development objectives.
3 Get whatever help you need, e.g. the right boss, environment or coach.
4 Obtain and use feedback.
5 Develop continuously.

Achieving your optimum self-development is one of the most worthwhile investments you are ever likely to make.

Summary

This chapter has looked at the issue of employee development from the perspective of the individual. It has sought to draw some parallels with organizations and to demonstrate how individuals and organizations need to go through similar processes to develop and cope with their changing environments.

The main issues covered were:

- The range of development options available for the individual committed to self-development.
- How to use formal training programmes to meet personal goals. Dealing with the conflict between the organization's needs and the individual's needs.
- The essential role that feedback plays. How to obtain feedback and use it to improve the quality of self-development plans.
- Using performance appraisal and performance management systems to clarify personal development needs. Identifying self-development programmes and gaining the commitment and resources necessary for success.
- How to enter into a meaningful learning contract. What the contract should contain and how it can contribute to improved self-development.
- The role of mentor, what to look for in a potential mentor and how the mentor can contribute to strategic self-development.
- What is involved in coaching. How the person being coached needs to identify personal development opportunities. Matching the needs of the individual with the abilities of the coach.
- Continuous professional development and some of the ways in which it (CPD) can be achieved. The increasingly pressing demand to

keep up with changes especially for those in the professions.

- Action learning and how it can be used in everyday life to focus and magnify opportunities for learning. The strategy and tactics of thinking through a personal action learning programme.
- How the various approaches described can be implemented using the wide range of self-development options now available.

Overall, this chapter and the preceding chapter on individual development, motivation and learning give pointers on how to succeed in personal self-development.

What you can do

1 Identify your career or job goals. Discuss these with selected colleagues or friends to sharpen realism and focus.
2 Identify areas where you would wish to improve your performance. Try to be specific and to identify measurable learning objectives.
3 Consider methods of achieving the improvement you seek. Review the methods and approaches identified in this chapter. Identify any which you are not using that could help you to meet your goals.
4 Discuss your self-development aspirations with your boss and appropriate colleagues, e.g. a training officer. Identify outline plans for the next year or two.
5 Identify the first step you need to take, with whom and when.
6 Do it.

Recommended reading

Clutterbuck, D., 1992 *Everyone needs a Mentor*, 2nd edition, IPM.
Fletcher, C., 1993 *Appraisal Routes to Improved Performance*, IPM.
Honey, P. and Mumford, A., 1992 *The Manual of Learning Styles*, 3rd edition, Peter Honey Publications.
Moorby, E., 1994 Mentoring and Coaching, in J. Prior (Ed.) *Gower Handbook of Training & Development*, 2nd edition, Gower.
Revans, Prof. R., 1983 *ABC of Action Learning*, Chartwell-Bratt.
Stewart, J., 1991 *Managing Change through Training and Development*, Kogan Page.

PART FOUR

Completing the cycle

13 Is it all worthwhile? Evaluation

This book is about how to succeed in employee development and is built mainly on a range of assumptions. Most of these assumptions can be readily justified in everyday life. Some are at such a basic level of common sense that they are not even questioned. It would be suicidal to let an unqualified individual take off in a Boeing 747 Jumbo from Heathrow as the pilot. There would be some risk even if the potential pilot had flown every type of aircraft in existence except the Boeing 747, and the plane would certainly not be allowed to take off. The need for training is evident because 300 lives might be at stake. Let us consider some of the implicit assumptions behind the belief that it is worthwhile to develop employees.

- Skills can be created more cost effectively than if the individual acquires them randomly or by trial and error.
- Off-the-job development allows skills to be learned and practised safely, whether this is in a flight simulator or using a case study.
- Best practice can be conveyed to large numbers of people cost effectively.
- Developing your own staff can be cheaper than recruiting and the organization can establish the culture it desires.
- Skill is a competitive weapon and a lack of skill can effectively preclude an organization from competing in or even entering a market. For example, the enormous lack of free-market or entrepreneurial skills in Eastern Europe is a major constraint to survival.
- The basic knowledge of a civilization or an organization has to be passed from generation to generation and planned training and development, particularly of young new entrants, provides this continuity of human capital.
- Industrial, commercial and public undertakings are now so complex that the high-level skills required have to be developed positively. The use of technology, even at a basic level such as word processing, is an illustration of this.
- Individuals start with fairly primitive skills and one means of

achieving their ambitions and motivational needs is to develop new and valuable skills.

Despite the obvious common-sense basis of much of the commitment to development, an integral part of any learning process is feedback and reflection. This is essentially the use of knowledge of results to affirm or alter the development experience provided. Thus to achieve meaningful success it is necessary to ask continually: Is it all worthwhile? It is worth also expanding the question to illustrate what kind of questions lie behind it. Some examples are:

● Is development cost-effective?
● Am I getting value for money as an individual or an organization?
● Could the same development be provided more cost effectively?
● What will the organization get out of sponsoring five staff to study for MBAs?
● Should I invest in new technology for delivering training?
● If I release my staff to attend a training programme how will I get a return? How long will it take in improving performance?
● Does the fact that other economies invest twice as much as this country in vocational training mean that they are right and we are wrong?
● Who should pay for basic skills, the state or the individual organization?

How the question is asked and, in particular, how scientifically or rigorously it is approached is one of the areas in employee development which has attracted considerable attention. The approaches have ranged from attempts to identify the return on investment for specific initiatives to evaluation sheets or 'happiness' sheets which are completed at the end of sessions on a course. It will be helpful to review some of the more conventional or academic approaches and then to consider more pragmatic views.

Conventional approaches

This chapter can do little more than outline the issue of evaluation. For readers who wish to take their knowledge further, the book by Mark Easterby-Smith titled *Evaluation of Management Education, Training and Development*, and *Evaluation: Relating Training to Business Performance* by Terence Jackson are recommended.

The issue of evaluation can be considered in the following components:

● Validation
● Evaluation
● Performance standards
● Performance measurement

All these components are made up of the process of comparing outcomes with what was proposed or aimed at. The big problem is the ability to isolate cause and effect and thus demonstrate for example that a particular effect, say the sale of £100 000 of service, was the direct and sole result of a training and development intervention. The Department of Employment's *Glossary of Training Terms*, published in 1971, gave useful definitions of validation and evaluation which are worth repeating.

Internal validation   a series of tests and assessments designed to ascertain whether a training programme has achieved the behavioural objectives specified.

External validation   a series of tests and assessments designed to ascertain whether the behavioural objectives of an internally valid training programme were realistically based on an accurate initial identification of training needs in relation to the criteria of effectiveness adopted by the organization.

Evaluation   the assessment of the total value of a training system, training course or programme in social as well as financial terms.

The approach, implicit in both validation and evaluation, is essentially the scientific method. It seeks to capture whether the purposes or objectives of programmes have been achieved and, in the case of evaluation, it is also evaluative in the sense of deciding if the value of the activity is acceptable in financial and social terms. The latter would be very difficult to determine and would be greatly influenced by the political standpoint taken. The basically subjective nature of forming values, covered in Chapter 3 on politics and power, is also an important issue in deciding whether an investment in employee development has been worthwhile.

Attempts to determine the return on investment or some form of cost: benefit analysis have also been part of the conventional approach. It is possible to do this, as these examples show:

- Sales achieved with actual customers by section managers attending a course on sales coaching. Each manager accompanied a local agent and by coaching achieved significant sales volumes. The resulting surplus was something like ten times the cost of the training.
- Managers on an action learning programme were able to shift their districts up a progress list or league table during the six-month programme. The modest cost of the programme was covered many times over by the increased profit resulting from the improved business results.
- Indirect evaluation can be inferred from the contribution of programmes such as 'Putting People First' in a turn-round situation. The British Airways turn-round illustrates perfectly the limitation of cause-effect thinking. The airline has clearly had a considerable improvement in its return on investment over an eight-year period. In that time, however, it had a new chairman and new chief

executive, the UK economy boomed, the airline made thousands of staff redundant and experienced countless other changes including the takeover of British Caledonian. It would be quite impossible to identify objectively the direct result of employee development in a dynamic, flexible situation such as this. However, managers are paid to make decisions and judgements on the basis of the best information available and this is what has to be done most of the time.

A further way of looking at evaluation is to consider employee development in terms of outcomes, the process and the context or situation in which the events take place.

Outcomes evaluation

- Can be specified at the planning stage. Standards can be agreed.
- Can be measured or counted at the end of the process.
- Judgement can be made after the event as to whether the outcome was achieved.
- This evaluation approach cannot be used to improve learning or change course during the event or process leading up to the outcome.
- It may not be possible to isolate cause and effect but if, for example, better managers or more knowledgeable salespeople are produced this can be a powerful measure. An example might be that all salespeople achieved a 90 per cent pass mark for product knowledge. This would probably lead to more sales and would certainly be recognized by their peers and supervisors.

Process evaluation

- Is carried out during the process.
- Usually involves some form of feedback either during a process or at the end of a senior exercise or meeting.
- Widely used in process consultation where the consultant employs some format for observing the process and intervenes where appropriate. Classic approaches to team building are often based on measuring, say using 16PF, and displaying the team working process being used. For example, the chairman might be dominating the proceedings and cutting off constructive debate. Process evaluation asks the group to consider and evaluate how it is working while it is working.
- Highly specialized forms of process measurement such as behavioural analysis use frameworks to observe what is happening and then display the result of observations back to the participants during the process.
- There may be no measurement of outcomes as such. The approach is essentially about *how* things are done rather than *what* is done.

Context evaluation

- Looks at evaluation of the context in which the event takes place.
- More liable to be affected by political viewpoints.
- Can be more affected by *why* the event is run. For example, whether it focuses on change and is designed to modify or create new approaches.

Taking a view

Evaluation really ranges in scope from a research-based approach, using statistical sampling and control groups, through to a marketing approach based on identifying the unique selling point that the manager with the power will buy and looking for data in that form. Those interested in fully understanding the research approach could usefully explore the 'new paradigm' concepts written up by John Rowan. At this end of the spectrum it is necessary to have a strong grasp of scientific method and research methods. The academic approach to evaluation has had fairly limited application in most organizations.

The other end of the range, i.e. the marketing view, is most powerful when closely allied to a drive to improve results. This almost inevitably moves the employee development practitioner towards the financial disciplines. Put very simply, the budgeting and monitoring process is based on estimating probable expenditure and then controlling expenditure so that a profit is created from the excess of income over expenditure.

It is this financial perspective which is of most use to the employee development function in organizations. The employee development initiatives need to identify what they seek to deliver, e.g. competent staff in branches, or salespeople who can demonstrate they understand the requirements of the Financial Services Act, and to be as specific as possible on how the delivery can be measured. By then controlling expenditure the essential dynamic is created of minimizing the cost while maximizing the benefit.

In my experience, the sort of questions raised in many textbooks (such as identifying return on assets) have just never been relevant, and my experience has included one of the most financially aware organizations in the world and two major financial institutions. The following are examples of actual questions encountered.

1 The most rigorous was a requirement to complete a capital requisition pro-forma for a welding training school. This form had, as its final line: Confirm that the projected return will equal or exceed 15 per cent net return per annum. The pro-forma explored all the cost items and probed what benefit or income the investment would deliver. This approach was mandatory for any capital investment above a certain level for any purpose. The overall purpose of the

scheme and the aim of enabling semi-skilled operators to undertake production welding was explained to the finance function and the requirement to complete the form was waived. In that particular Detroit-based organization such a waiver was quite exceptional.

2 Civil Service procedures required the submission of detailed cases for all specific programmes, which had to identify programme aims, costs and staff requirements—in effect, the desired outcome and the cost of achieving it. These cases were debated thoroughly at a dialogue meeting and contained an element of evaluation of the previous year's outcomes as well as a conceptual base for assessing and evaluating the 'worthwhileness' of the project. The process itself worked within 'ceilings' for programmes and was therefore slightly mechanical but quite effective.

3 A comparison of the expenditure with competitors' expenditure and a discussion of the comparative merits of the organization's programmes with highly respected competitors was another question encountered. This evaluation effectively tested the judgements in the plan rather than the absolute individual amounts. It then applied an overall perspective to the aggregate. Thus, if the individual components were accepted as valid in the context of the business, an evaluation was made of the size of the investment that was acceptable. This was compared with the investment requested for marketing and for information technology.

4 A different approach, used by an organization to cut costs, was to employ consultants to examine proposed organizations and investments line by line. All proposals were then subjected to a 'challenge' meeting which applied arbitrary standards and required justification for every item. An example of standards might be: Recruit half the graduate intake proposed. The overall aim was to cut some 25–30 per cent out of the budget. This form of challenge is a perfectly legitimate approach to evaluating the investment if done professionally.

Performance management and profit contribution

One way of defining whether development is worthwhile is to measure the levels of management performance during the year. Specific initiatives such as customer-care training can then be reviewed against the performance measured. When a performance management system is in place or job objectives are linked to profit or performance pay, it is possible to carry out some interesting evaluations. One performance management system, for example, included the following skills areas:

- Managing and motivating staff
- Marketing and business development
- Serving customers
- Judgement and decision making
- Self-development

Each area can be rated annually or quarterly and is rated by both boss and 'grandfather'. Evaluation of achievement of targets such as fee and commission income are included.

It is now quite possible to run, say, decision-making courses or use a CBT programme or open learning on decision making in June–December and to measure individual and aggregate rating for any selected population as at June in the following year. Then, although a direct cause and effect relationship cannot be established, it would be possible to say that the aggregate rating for branch managers on judgement and decision making had moved from 60 per cent to 75 per cent or 60 per cent to 55 per cent in the period immediately following the provision of a training programme on this area. Since the performance management system is processed by computer, it would be relatively easy to examine the rating or actual achievement in identified competencies, e.g. decision making and selling insurance, for individuals or groups of managers. Thus, if all the managers in the bottom half of the Midlands Region progress list received development in managing the selling of insurance products, the actual results achieved could subsequently be identified and compared with the base-line before the training was initiated. Again, no cause and effect relationship can be identified. Just being asked to attend the training might have scared them sufficiently to improve.

The power of performance management systems lies in the wide range of numerical techniques used to achieve maximum objectivity. This begins to allow evaluation to be integrated into the management process and offers great potential for the future.

Where it is possible, the actual contribution to profit of jobs and components of jobs can be identified and used to question whether development is worthwhile. For example, the profit contribution of a general branch insurance policy such as motor insurance can be estimated. If training can increase the volume sold, a form of evaluation comparing the cost of development with the profit contribution generated can be established. This approach is a little theoretical but worth pursuing. Asking what, if anything, specific actions contribute to profit is probably more important than asking whether employee development is worthwhile.

Political aspects of evaluation

The 'worthwhileness' of the investment in employee development can be and usually is a very political issue. In the absence of hard measures the view formed about the contribution will be influenced by where the viewer stands. Some senior managers have what is effectively an ideological support for the training of young people. Many organizations have specific institutions and experiences which many senior managers will have shared, e.g. the Ford Trade School, the

Henley Middle Manager Programme. Their disposition will usually be to see the continuance of the investment as worthwhile, particularly if their experience of it was good.

Another political consideration is what view the evaluators take on substance and form. An action learning group held in the local pub in a Welsh valley could make a significant contribution to improving results. However, some individuals would be much more concerned with holding the event in a four-star hotel. Significant sums would be invested in producing glossy literature and the audiovisual aids used would be expensive and computer-generated. The worth of the content would be judged by the cost of the wrapping. It is a political reality that, for some, form is much more important than substance and the evaluation process then takes on a different complexion. Cost is no object and the results had better look right, at least in the short term.

Some common political aspects are:

- Who gets the credit?
- Does recognizing the contribution of employee development strengthen or weaken the position of any key player?
- Is there any reason to downgrade the contribution of development? For example, if the sales director or marketing director wants to take over sales training from personnel, there is little point in their seeing any good in what is done.
- Does one of the senior executives wish to create a strong external image about employee development, perhaps to create a reputation for the development of young people? If so, strong support for the function would be forthcoming.

There is usually nothing sinister in the political standpoints adopted about evaluation but, clearly, whether a thing is worthwhile depends very much on what the person evaluating it expects.

One way of creating an informed debate about the contribution of employee development is to identify clear performance standards and ensure a wide discussion of these within the personnel function and the employee development organization and with executive directors and line managers.

Standards of performance

Standards of performance set out to identify what should exist when the employee development function is operating successfully. In the current environment of integrating development with business strategy and performance, increasing attention is being paid to identifying standards. This is particularly true where profit-related pay is being used. Some examples of standards of performance for employee development are:

- To ensure all district managers:
  —are regarded as competent for the task;
  —shift from an overall rating on aggregate of 55 to 60 on the performance management system.
- To introduce a 'fast-track' approach for senior succession so that:
  —the top 50 key jobs are identified, and 80 per cent have one successor identified or ready to succeed within two years;
  —for the 200 next level management jobs, all career management action is taken in line with the agreed policy guidelines in identifying potential and releasing staff on promotion;
  —objective criteria are identified to establish how many graduates from which mix of disciplines should be recruited over the next two years.
- To improve the cost effectiveness of training and development by:
  —reducing the cost per day of training at the residential training centre by 10 per cent by the end of the current year;
  —identifying the overall cost per day for all training undertaken by the organization and reducing the figure by at least 10 per cent by the year-end.
- To create a professional employee development organization within two years by:
  —ensuring that the head count and budget approved by the review team are adequate for the task;
  —recruiting to fill all jobs where current incumbents are not able to meet standards required;
  —introducing development programmes to improve the level of competence of existing staff to the defined standard of competence required.
- To ensure that the training and development of staff has a high profile within the organization and is the subject of informed debate in the context of meeting business needs by:
  —developing a communication programme to ensure the various options for employee development are understood;
  —targeting key players and establishing a regular dialogue on employee development issues.
- To ensure the organization has the skill and design capability to achieve the maximum cost-effective contribution from new information technology-based approaches by:
  —identifying the strategic contribution required with individual companies;
  —generating debate and identifying the policy issues associated with computer-based training and open learning.

In the context of evaluation, establishing standards of performance automatically provides a means of measuring whether what was proposed was delivered. The process of developing and agreeing the standards is where the question of whether the proposed contribution is worthwhile should be asked. This focus moves the logic from a process where objectives for development were identified, the development was carried out and then the contribution was evaluated. By bringing the requirement for justifying aims and objectives into the planning process it is possible to decide in advance what to do in order to ensure that what is done is worthwhile.

The 1990s have seen the movement of employee development very much into the mainstream of business and the economy. Education and training have been described as the most important issues in the socialist manifesto. This has put pressure on applying business thinking to how it is managed. Particularly in the areas of performance standards, budgeting and financial control, this has led to a much more commercial approach. This in turn has highlighted the need to address the question of whether it is worthwhile even before the funds are allocated.

Summary

The main points covered in this chapter are:

- Conventional evaluation and validation approaches have been over-scientific in trying to establish objective measurement of the benefits created by employee development.
- Evaluation can be aimed either at the outcomes of activities or the process being carried out. Judgements need to be made about the context within which the evaluation takes place.
- The use of performance measures and performance management systems may provide a basis for making better judgements about the outcomes of activities.
- Evaluation has a political dimension. The view of whether employee development makes a contribution depends on the values and motivations of the evaluator.
- Standards of performance can be used to identify and debate the potential contribution of employee development and measure whether the benefits are worthwhile.
- Considerably more development work will need to be done to improve the quality of evaluation approaches.

What you can do

1 Identify what benefits the employee development function has achieved in your organization.
2 Prepare a one-sheet summary against each main section of the development strategy showing what the investment was and what benefits have been achieved.
3 Prepare for six to eight key aspects of your role a statement of standards of performance. Agree with your boss how best to measure the outcomes.

Recommended reading

Bramley, Peter, 1995 *Evaluating Training Effectiveness*, 2nd edition, McGraw-Hill.

Easterby-Smith, Mark, 1986 *Evaluation of Management Education, Training and Development*, Gower.

Jackson, Terence, 1989 *Evaluation: Relating Training to Business Performance*, Kogan Page.

Rowan, John, 'New Paradigm Research', *Training Research Bulletin*, ATTITB, Spring 1981.

14 What next? A view of the future

Debates about visions and strategy invariably explore some future state. This chapter will seek to put some of today's trends in context and to look at how employee development might evolve. It will unashamedly take an evolutionary standpoint. Most of the changes that will be experienced by the year 2000, will already exist at least in embryo form. In the much more speculative twenty-year frame there may be some really spectacular advances in technology but these can only be guessed at.

The major themes of my vision of the successful future of employee development are these:

1 There will be increasing focus on business results with improved means of measuring contribution.
2 Commercial approaches to the provision of employee development will increase. Providers will have to supply more business-related products.
3 Much better debate about employee development will be generated as it becomes more politically and economically important to get it right.
4 The traditional view of locating employee development in the personnel function will break down. The responsibility will be more diffused into line operations and by using external suppliers.
5 There will be a severe shortage of competent professionals which will trigger national initiatives to grow development skills.
6 Organizing employee development will require a more organic and responsive approach.
7 Pressures on costs and demands from individuals will cause a significant growth in distance learning and open learning approaches.
8 Technology will be increasingly used. The inherent cost advantage of CBT coupled with decreasing technology unit costs will encourage much wider use of computer-managed learning.
9 The various competencies initiatives will generate significant

opposition but will form the basis for the UK's vocational training and education to the end of the century.

10   The power and influence of the individual will increase. Moves towards action learning and self-managed learning will grow, though not dramatically.

11   The learning organization concept will gain in acceptance. Strong examination of the contribution of management and organization development will continue.

12   Feedback and means of keying employee development into reality and actual results will become increasingly important.

13   Increased attention will be paid to making the most of strengths. This will encourage efforts to find out what motivates individuals. Strategic employee development will increasingly address the identification and development of commercially valuable gifts that individuals possess.

To complete the picture, a very gross view of trends will probably include a growth of about 20–25 per cent of approaches such as CBT matched with a decrease of, say, 10–20 per cent of conventional course programmes. Since the total demand has never been anything like satisfied, the four threads of course programme training delivery, computer-managed training, strategic employee development consultancy and research and development into training and development will see shifts in emphasis. However, the gross development product or total amount of employee development generated in the economy each year is unlikely to decrease but will not increase dramatically. To focus within these overall trends, each of the main areas will be considered.

Business relevance

One of the key shifts in the 1990s has been the increased integration of employee development into the mainstream of the business. This trend will continue. The demand for new and higher-level skills, coupled with a relative failure in the supply of skills, will make it increasingly difficult for organizations to obtain the skills they need. The threat to the business will cause much greater attention to be paid to making the most of skills attracted into the organization and to making greater efforts to improve the skills already in the organization. The two main areas will be entrants to the workforce who deal with customers, mainly school leavers and older or semi-retired workers, and the line managers closest to the point of manufacture or service delivery.

The ability to identify what skills are required to achieve the business plans, to assess what the organization already has and to generate the programmes to remove the obstacles will be crucial. Senior management will need to keep as much grip on skill flows as cash flows. The strategic planning process and the human resourcing process will come closer together. The almost certainly smaller number of more highly skilled people will need to be managed more skilfully. The merging of business skills and development skills will become more crucial. One probable application of this will be growth in the importance of coaching and mentoring. Performance management systems will act to promote this, and self-development and success at coaching are two features that are already rewarded in some profit-related pay systems.

This trend will put demands on the employee development specialist who will need to understand business strategically. As skill becomes more central to business competitiveness, the ability to develop skill will become more of a requirement in managers. The development of commercially aware professionals, at home equally with finance or psychometric testing, can be expected.

The heightened integration of development with the business will have a knock-on effect, particularly on delivery systems. Approaches that deal with reality will become more attractive. It makes more sense to use action learning as a vehicle to help managers cope with the massive change programme they are in the middle of, than to spend time working on a case study that happened ten years ago on another continent.

Thus the position and role of employee development, the skills required and the way development is delivered are all likely to shift centre stage as a result of increased business relevance.

The informed debate

Picture the scene. The managing director, with a glazed look, is sitting in the office discussing the training strategy with the employee development director who enthuses about the newly introduced learning centre and the interactive video programme the organization has just produced. The meeting concludes with an agreement on the budget allocation. The managing director provides a signature to go under the preface of the college prospectus. But is there a meeting of minds?

The need to bridge the gap in understanding between executives who have risen through specialist channels such as marketing or surgery and those who have spent an equal time becoming professional in the employee development area is one of the key challenges. To the finance professional and some general managers, the debate about current-cost accounting would be crucial in terms of the presentation of business results. Managers work to understand cash flow and balance sheets. The question of learning styles and how people learn could be just as important fundamentally to achieving results. However, the debate is very unlikely to occur with many general managers.

What is needed is to convey the basic notions of employee

development in a form that is palatable to line and functional managers, who already have enough information to cope with. An informed debate is necessary mainly to make the right decisions. A few books such as *In Search of Excellence* and *The One-Minute Manager* and earlier contributions such as *Management and Machiavelli* have sold strongly to general audiences. More written contributions of this type that reach a general audience will be forthcoming. The excellent columns such as that by Michael Dixon in the *Financial Times* will continue to inform and challenge. The real crunch will come as skill shortages bite. The need will be to debate policy issues ranging from the school curriculum to what, if anything, should be done to prepare the increasing number of older members of the population for a retirement of potentially 20 years—retirement at about 55 with a life expectancy of 75 plus. In organizations the options broadly are:

- to leave development to the line managers;
- to appoint successful line managers to be responsible for employee development;
- to leave it to the personnel director;
- to hire or grow people who have themselves acquired a professional standing in employee development;
- to use outside consultants or colleges from the private or public sector.

Unhappily, employee development is a topic, much like education, where everyone knows how to do it but few succeed. It is intriguing that we would not think of allowing someone to drive a bus without a licence in case people might be injured. Yet we entrust the growth of individuals to managers in ways that are sometimes bizarre. Increased knowledge through informed debate offers one of the most cost-effective ways of achieving significant improvements in the success of employee development.

Commercial perspective

Another trend that will accelerate and become significant through the next decade will be the perception of development as a commercial activity. Until relatively recently, education and training have been regarded more as social contributions than commercial issues. The great outcry about making education more vocational reflects this view, whereby education is seen as something much more abstract than making money or creating wealth. In-company development is increasingly seen as an investment that is made in competition with other demands for the money. Over the next decade, more organizations will regard their employee development as profit centres. The employee development organization may effectively be spun off and sell its services to the parent organization. It may also sell its products on the open market. Organizations will market the experience they have gained. Some balance will need to be struck so that employees who gain commercially valuable employee development experience continue to contribute to the organization—perhaps as retained consultants.

The commercial pressure will encourage the growth of internal marketing skills for employee development and the growth of 'branding' and packaging will occur.

The use of training centres by outside organizations, particularly at weekends, will increase. No commercial hotel would operate on a five-day week and residential centres will shift to seven-day operation.

The push to more commercial operations will also encourage the use of lower-cost delivery systems such as CBT and low-cost training approaches such as distance learning and action learning.

The focus on commercial operation within organizations will put pressure on providers to deliver value for money. The growth of partnerships whereby organizations can have more say in what the provider delivers and consortia where organizations associate to direct a provider on what they collectively want delivered may be significant. The general economic effect of these commercial and competitive forces should be to push down the cost of development and to encourage high-quality niche-market responses. Providers who operate to less commercial values may well find it difficult to survive.

The shape of employee development

The shape of employee development organizations, whether they are within organizations or are private independent providers, will shift away from off-the-job delivery towards consultancy. The basic functions will be:

- Delivery through courses, open learning and distance learning centres, CBT and new technological means.
- Consultancy based primarily on employee development skills but increasingly integrated with business consultancy.
- Research and development to identify new methods and to develop the software for CBT and the content for distance learning packages.
- Focus on specific sectors of activity such as health services, local government or finance.
- Some form of linkage with other human resource management functions. The areas of performance management systems and even recruitment and compensation and benefits might be incorporated. As a minimum the motivational aspects of performance and the assessment and development approaches will be routinely part of the organization.

The prime focus will be to create relevance to particular businesses. Basic skills such as training needs analysis and programme design will be the starting point. The main driving force will lie with the ability to consult either on business issues or individual development needs. Organizations will be more transient as change creates shifting patterns and reconfigurations. The employee development specialist will need to deal with this by being responsive to changing demands. There may be a shift towards contract employment as the notion of continuous permanent employment becomes obsolete.

New roles may emerge. For example, a broker on training delivery methods could save the less-informed buyer considerable sums, just as the good insurance broker can for a client.

Open learning and distance learning

Open and distance learning will increase in their scope and quality. The main advantage of these approaches is their greater flexibility. Some of the key advantages are:

- The learners can decide what they want to learn.
- Control over when the learning takes place is with the learner.
- High-quality resources can be produced as wider audiences can be accessed.
- Learning can be carried out at a distance.
- Large numbers of learners can be covered by relatively few tutors.

The scope of applications will expand to include wide-scale delivery of development through self-study texts. The open programmes will be increasingly able to link via satellite with programmes from other countries. The EU will encourage the use of distance learning with television as the medium. The use of video tapes as a means of distance learning will expand.

Open learning will be extended to cover higher education and the Open University could become, together with centres such as Henley, a major supplier of MBA programmes. This could expand dramatically the output of the higher education sector in this area.

Methods of integrating distance learning with conventional programmes will increase under the pressure of cost effectiveness. Initiatives based on open access to distance learning and CBT materials will increase. The pattern pioneered by Midland Bank through its 'LEAP' programme will be widely taken up. Initiatives such as the Ford Employee Development and Assistance Programme (EDAP) will be widely adopted and will probably become part of the negotiation process as an employee benefit. This change would encourage the internal provision of resource centres and distance learning. There will be a need to rethink employee development strategy and the interrelationship between open and distance methods and conventional training.

New approaches will be much easier to bring to the market through the use of desktop publishing. This will make smaller production runs feasible at good standards of quality reproduction. It will be necessary to overcome political barriers within companies, as open learning in particular can be seen as threatening managerial control and the right to decide what development is provided. The strong need to create responsive organizations will overcome this constraint and move the choice of what employee development shall be carried out much more towards the customer. This need to be more open will generate an increase in the contribution of open learning and distance learning, though it will not seriously threaten conventional methods in the decade up to the year 2000.

Computer-managed development

This area is likely to be one of the most exciting and cost-effective sources of change over the next five years. To date, there has been a significant growth in the provision of generic CBT programmes, widespread interest in the use of tailor-made programmes, substantial investment in hardware and increasing use of interactive video. Some of the key developments are likely to be:

- The creation of more interesting and motivating programmes to a much higher standard. The benchmark will be the standard achieved in the best commercial applications, for in-company work.
- A reduction in cost and then wider use of greatly improved generic programmes. Some collaboration within sectors will continue to produce programmes for specific application, e.g. financial services.
- Mainframe approaches will be used more so that developmental programmes will be delivered and be easily accessible on terminals used for commercial applications.
- Interactive programmes, touch-sensitive screens and professional quality video will become the accepted standard. Interactive disks will be available on the domestic market—initially for games but then for development purposes.
- The use of computer power to manage learning will be developed much more widely. The audience for development will become increasingly computer-literate as the effect of the use of computers in schools in the 1980s works through the system. Individual learning plans coordinated by a central computer facility will become increasingly possible. Local learning centres will flourish and individuals will be able to use a personal disk to obtain guidance on suitable CBT programmes and feedback on progress, to take tests and even to gain certification.
- Learning centres or knowledge shops will be opened in the high street. They will be similar to early learning centres but their product will be computer-based software. Effectively, electronic libraries-cum-study centres will be available both in-company and for public access. The development of the delivery system will lead to cost

reductions in the products as usage increases, and this will accelerate the process. The computer-managed system could achieve the sort of step-change that Caxton's printing press brought about.

● The development of domestic applications such as the miniaturized video recorder and player and wider applications of CD principles will also accelerate the process and make less expensive management of learning possible.

Known technology alone will make a significant impact on the future of employee development. The contribution of what is yet to come will doubtless have even more effect by the year 2010 than we can imagine.

Competencies

The late 1980s and early 1990s witnessed the widespread adoption in the UK of the competency model developed in the early 1980s in the USA. In essence, this approach was the latest in a line starting with Sune Carlson's study of managers in the early 1950s. It seeks to establish what competencies are possessed by those who are successful at jobs and how to test whether others can demonstrate them. The following initiatives are based on the concepts written up by Boyatzis and described as the Competency Model.

The Management Charter Initiative (MCI)   This initiative sets out to improve the quality of management education and thence management in the UK. It has identified the competence standards to be required of managers and introduced a national framework of certification covering different levels of management. The identification of competencies was based on consultation with some 3000 people in various sectors of the economy, professional and academic institutions, and the Training Agency and National Council for Vocational Qualifications. One feature of the initiative is its attempt to recognize existing experience and the ability to demonstrate competencies not gained through an academic input.

The effect of the initiative will probably be to cause some increase in the volume of management training. It will fill the place occupied by the Diploma in Management Studies that since the mid 1960s, has been effectively the only management qualification other than the MBA. The MCI is well placed to take advantage of distance learning and the use of mentors through the Institute of Management or its own organization. The American Management Association initiative, which is in many respects its model, was rigorously thought through but has not had any dramatic impact on the worldwide employee development stage.

National Council for Vocational Qualifications (NCVQ)   This institution was set up in the late 1980s. It is seeking to reorient the vocational training and eduction in the UK. Essentially, it is concerned with encouraging education and training that results in the achievement of measurable competencies which can be certified in sensible groupings or units.

The NCVQ is likely to make a significant impact. It will shift the input of knowledge and skill away from loosely structured or ill-defined syllabuses and qualification courses and move it towards outputs and the ability to demonstrate competence. It will move the focus away from the education and development process used for most of this century towards an output or achievement focus. This in turn opens the door for much more certification of development to be done in-company and for the recognition of previous experience that might not be academically based and yet contributes to the acquisition of competence.

Lead bodies   These are an integral part of the competency jigsaw. They were set up by the Training Agency and numbered about 150. Their task is to identify competencies and qualification frameworks for segments of industry and for functions. Thus, the MCI is the lead or standard setting body for management and supervision. There was also a lead body for training and development that defined the scope of training and development and the competencies required together with the Personnel Standards Lead Body. Both have now been incorporated into an Occupational Council.

The outcomes of all these competency initiatives will be to focus employee development more on business outcomes, to increase the visibility of development and thence the investment in it. Overall, the initiatives will make more of a touch-on-the-tiller contribution than a sea-change contribution. The big unanswered question, once this great mass of work has been done on the 'science' of development, will be: What of the 'art' component? The most likely outcome is a swing away from the scientific model.

Self-managed learning

One way of avoiding all the analysis implicit in much employee development is to shift the focus away from describing and prescribing, as much academic work does, towards individuals making their own decisions. There will be increasing development in this direction. The approach used at Thomson International in which groups of high-potential executives were allocated a substantial sum of money and, in effect, an academic broker to arrange what they wanted by way of development experiences will become more common. There will be increasing influence from the customer as skill becomes more and more key in career progression, and individuals will want to take more control of their development. The Ford approach of allocating grants to promote skill development will grow. As much as 25 per cent of the employee development budget could be allocated to funding development activities based on self-managed learning.

There will be tensions between the need of organizations to focus the development investment on business requirements and the desire of individuals to manage their own destiny. The self-managed MBA approach will become more widespread and the recognition of these and action learning-based degrees and MBAs will become more institutionalized. The development of self-management skills will mushroom and the notion of employee development specialists will come under pressure. The need to diffuse the skills of coaching, development, identifying development needs and learning design may move the focus away from content concerned with managerial and technical skills, e.g. budgeting and financial control, towards development activities, e.g. how to develop skills in comparing actual results with plans. In many ways there will be an application of the advice: Give a person bread and you feed them for a day, teach a person to grow wheat and you feed them for life.

The trend towards self-managed learning will be greatly accelerated by the use and development of technology and open learning and distance learning approaches. Being able to choose from a very wide range of subjects and mixes of media will greatly open up choice and enable the individual to manage learning. The days of reading a book, writing an essay and seeing a tutor once a fortnight have been replaced by a choice of books, distance learning package, video, audio tape, CBT, interactive video, teleconferencing, summer school, weekend seminar, satellite-relayed lectures and many more. The ability of individuals to manage what they want to learn, when, where and how, will grow. The issue of who pays for development, and how, will move more towards the control of the individual or customer as the acquisition of skill comes to be seen more as part of the remuneration and benefits package.

The learning organization

Research in the late 1980s, particularly the work of Peter Senge, Mike Pedlar and Richard Pascale, introduced the notion of the *learning organization*. This concept involves regarding the organization as a living organism existing in its environment. As such, the organization needs to have good feedback mechanisms and the ability to adapt to changes by taking timely action. To survive in a changing business world it needs to learn to cope with what its sensors tell it about its environment. In essence, a much more biological than mechanical model of organizations is being developed.

One of the key developments in the next ten years will be the development of feedback mechanisms, as change and competition become more intense and the sheer volume demands of change increase. The pace and scale of change will force organizations, and institutions, countries and even continents, to adapt or effectively become extinct. Means of measuring the environment and shifts away from the usual preoccupation with internal politics to the outside environment will push organizations into the need to be learning organizations. Many will endure considerable internal stress as they strive to move from the predictable, controlled environment they imagine towards the 'chaos' that Tom Peters describes.

The introduction of performance management systems will become widespread. Notions about profit-related pay, however, will need to be refined. One of the essential points about any learning, and thus about the learning organization, is that there has to be a reason for the learning. This might range from survival to the pursuit of excellence or from aggression to self-actualization. The crude notions of money or profit-share equalling motivation will come under increasing pressure.

One further possible implication of the learning organization is a shift away from the bureaucracy and control of many planning and budgeting systems. A wider debate about the budget and mechanisms for achieving this will be developed. Some form of credits to spend on identified elements of the employee development strategy could easily be made available to line managers.

A much closer link between employee development and marketing, technology and strategic planning will need to be created. There is a strong argument for splitting employee development from personnel. The strategic development question is: What will the organization have to do to change and prosper in the environment of the future, i.e. what will it have to learn? There is no obvious reason why a central contributor to this debate, i.e. the employee development function, should be located within personnel.

The employee development function can be regarded as part of the 'brains' of the organization organism. The organism itself picks up messages about its environment from all its sensors. One such sensor is the manager in the local branch who feels the heat when the organization hits some problem with the market or the customers. Considerable advances will need to be made in ways of identifying what the environment is doing. Efforts like that by SAS Airlines to invert its organization and hold to such values as: If you are not serving the customer, you had better be serving someone who does, will become increasingly accepted. One of the more encouraging developments should be increased attention paid to what the line manager and the customer are saying. Their views will relay, into a learning organization that wants to know, how it should adapt to succeed or at least survive in its environment.

One of the most powerful equations about learning was devised by Reg Revans: $L = P + Q$, or Learning = Programmed Knowledge + Questioning Insight. Adapting this to the concepts of the learning organization, the appropriate equation would be: $L \geqslant C$, i.e. learning must be equal to or greater than change or (without confusing things by going into the use of differential calculus) the rate of learning must at least equal the rate of change.

If an organization does not fulfil this basic requirement, it must eventually fail by bankruptcy, abolition, takeover or extinction.

The need to learn is that serious.

The importance of motivation

Much of employee development thinking in the past has been based on a remedial model. The concept of analysing jobs and then appraising the suitability of applicants or the standard of performance against requirements has been widely used. An alternative approach is to assume that everyone has talents or gifts and that the task is to match these gifts with opportunities to express them. The work of Art Miller of People Management Inc. and Don Clifton of Scientific Research Inc. are based on this viewpoint. As the demands for skill increase there will be more and more pressure on squeezing the maximum out of the pool of talent. This will lead to a shift towards identifying individuals' talents and helping them to achieve what they have the gifts to do.

Approaches to identifying motivational abilities and drives will become much more widely used. Career choice and career counselling and the identification of those with potential for progressing to more senior management jobs will become more central. Career management and the ability to match what individuals are likely to strive to do with what future jobs will demand will become increasingly sophisticated.

The drive to make the most of the gifts an individual is born with is the essence of successful employee development.

To succeed in employee development you have to enable yourself or others to discover their talents and to use them.

Summary

This chapter has put forward a view of the future, with the following basic components of the contribution that will be made by employee development.

- Business relevance
- More informed discussion of development
- Commercial approach
- Responsive organization
- More open learning
- Wide use of distance learning and computer-managed learning
- Identification of competencies
- More flexible approach to qualifications
- The rise of self-managed learning
- The decline of conventional course-based approaches

- The evolution of the learning organization
- Greater influence of the customer
- Diffusion of responsibilities for employee development among the organization's employees
- Greater use of coaching and mentoring
- More attention to what motivates people to learn and to do things

What you can do　Write down your *vision* for employee development, identify your *gifts* and decide what you will *do* to achieve success.

Recommended reading　Pascale, R. and Athos, A., 1982 *The Art of Japanese Management*, Penguin.
Peters, T.J. and Waterman, R.H., 1982 *In Search of Excellence*, Harper & Row.

Bibliography

Albrecht, K. and Zemke, R., 1985 *Service America*, Dow Jones-Irwin.

Bentley, Trevor, 1990 *The Business of Training*, McGraw-Hill.

Boyatzis, Richard E., 1982 *The Competent Manager*, Wiley.

Bramley, Peter, 1995 *Evaluating Training Effectiveness*, 2nd edition, McGraw-Hill.

Clutterbuck, D., 1992 *Everyone needs a Mentor*, 2nd edition, IPM.

Easterby-Smith, Mark, 1986 *Evaluation of Management Education, Training and Development*, Gower.

Fletcher, C., 1993 *Appraisal Routes to Improved Performance*, IPM.

Garfield, C., 1986 *Peak Performers*, Hutchinson Business.

Gery, Gloria, 1988 *Making CBT Happen*, Weingarten.

Handy, Charles B., 1985 *Understanding Organisations*, Penguin.

Haynes, M.E., 1990 *Project Management*, Kogan Page.

Herrman, Ned, 1990 *The Creative Brain*, Brain Books.

Honey, Peter and Mumford, Alan, 1983 *Using Your Learning Styles*, Peter Honey.

Honey, Peter and Mumford, Alan 1992 *The Manual of Learning Styles*, 3rd edition, Peter Honey Publications.

Jackson, Terence, 1989 *Evaluation: Relating Training to Business Performance*, Kogan Page.

Jay, Antony, 1967 *Management and Machiavelli*, Hodder and Stoughton; 1987, Hutchinson Business.

Kakabadse, A., 1983 *The Politics of Management*, Gower.

Kanter, Rosabeth Moss, 1985 *The Change Masters*, Unwin Paperbacks.

Kolb, D., 1984 *Experiential Learning*, Prentice-Hall.

Kolb, D. and Fry, R., 1975 'Towards an Applied Theory of Experiential Learning' in *Theories of Group Process*, Cooper C.L. (ed.) Wiley.

Lewis, A. and Marsh, W., 'The Development of Field Managers in the Prudential Assurance Company', *The Journal of Management Development*, Action Learning Special Issue Volume 6, No. 2, 1987, MCB University Press.

Machiavelli, Niccolo, 1961 *The Prince*, Penguin.

Margerison, Charles J., 1991 *Making Management Development Work*, McGraw-Hill.

McCormack, Mark, 1984 *What They Don't Teach You at Harvard Business School*, Fontana/Collins.

Miller, Art. and Mattson, R.T., 1989 *The Truth about You*, Ten Speed Press.

Moorby, E.T., 1994 'Mentoring and Coaching' in *The Gower Handbook of Training and Development*, 2nd edition, Gower.

Moorby, E.T. 'Influencing the Decade', *Training and Development Journal*, Volume 5, No. 6, October 1986.

Morgan, G., 1986 *Images of Organisation*, Sage Publications Inc.

Mumford, Alan, 1980 *Making Experience Pay*, McGraw-Hill.

Mumford, Alan, 1993 *Management Development Strategies for Action*, 2nd edition, IPM.

Pascale, R. and Athos, A., 1982 *The Art of Japanese Management*, Penguin.

Pedler, M., Burgoyne, J. and Boydell, T., 1994 *A Managers Guide to Self-Development*, 3rd edition, McGraw-Hill.

Peters, Tom, 1988 *Thriving on Chaos*, Macmillan.

Peters, T.J. and Waterman, R.H., 1982 *In Search of Excellence*, Harper & Row.

Rae, Leslie, 1983 *The Skills of Training*, Gower.

Rajan, Amin with Fryatt, Julie, 1988 *Create or Abdicate*, Witherby & Co Ltd.

Revans, Professor R., 1982 *The Origins & Growth of Action Learning*, Chartwell-Bratt.

Revans, Professor R., 1983 *ABC of Action Learning*, Chartwell-Bratt.

Rowan, John, 'New Paradigm Research' *Training Research Bulletin*, ATTITB, Spring 1981.

Stewart, J., 1991 *Managing Change through Training and Development*, Kogan Page.

Stewart, Valerie and Andrew, 1978 *Practical Performance Appraisal*, Gower.

Thompson-McCausland, Ben, with Biddle, Derek, 1985 *Change, Business Performance and Values*, Gresham College.

Training Agency (now TEED), Qualifications in Training and Development—A Consultation Document 1990, Training & Development Lead Body.

Index

Further titles in the McGraw-Hill Training Series

All books are published by:

McGraw-Hill Book Publishing Company
Shoppenhangers Road, Maidenhead, Berkshire SL6 2QL, England
Tel: (01628) 23432   Fax: (01628) 770224